RESEARCH-BASED PROGRAMMING FOR INTERIOR DESIGN

RESEARCH-BASED PROGRAMMING FOR INTERIOR DESIGN

LILY B. ROBINSON

Design Institute of San Diego

FAIRCHILD BOOKS

NEW YORK · LONDON · OXFORD · NEW DELHI · SYDNEY

FAIRCHILD BOOKS
Bloomsbury Publishing Inc
1385 Broadway, New York, NY 10018, USA
50 Bedford Square, London, WC1B 3DP, UK

BLOOMSBURY, FAIRCHILD BOOKS and the Fairchild Books
logo are trademarks of Bloomsbury Publishing Plc

First published in the United States of America 2020

Cover design by Toby Way | Cover image: Theatre Designers Studio, London,
UK, Bere Architects © View Pictures / UIG via Getty Images

Library of Congress Cataloging-in-Publication Data
Names: Robinson, Lily B., author.
Title: Research-based programming for interior design /
Lily B. Robinson, Design Institute of San Diego.
Description: New York : Fairchild Books, [2020] | Includes index.
Identifiers: LCCN 2019027288 | ISBN 9781501327742 (paperback) | ISBN 9781501327759 (pdf)
Subjects: LCSH: Interior decorating—Practice. | Interior decorating—Research.
Classification: LCC NK2116 .R63 2020 | DDC 747—dc23
LC record available at https://lccn.loc.gov/2019027288

ISBN: PB: 978-1-5013-2774-2

Typeset by Lachina Creative, Inc.
Printed and bound in the United States of America

To find out more about our authors and books visit
www.fairchildbooks.com and sign up for our newsletter.

CONTENTS

EXTENDED CONTENTS

PREFACE

Great interior design doesn't just happen. Operating within a creative paradigm informed by the scientific community, interior designers must be able to evaluate information sources, conduct literature reviews, use case studies, and understand how scientific evidence is garnered and communicated. In addition, interior designers should be able to collect and analyze their own project-specific data using time-tested methods as well as marshal innovative techniques when the need arises.

This book represents an evolution of *Research-Inspired Design: A Step-by-Step Guide for Interior Designers* (co-authored with Alexandra Parman Pitts in 2009). The story behind *Research-Based Programming for Interior Design* began in 2015 when Alexandra and I responded to a team of peer reviewers who loved the book but suggested we split the large volume into two, more focused, texts: one for undergraduate and the other for graduate students. We divided the chapters almost evenly down the middle. This textbook represents previous Chapters 6 to 14 (condensed and updated), with some important introductory elements from Chapters 1 and 4. Since Alexandra had moved to Oregon and was expecting her second child, the task of writing the new editions fell to me as a solo project, with her support and continued guidance. As with any design project (and writing is no different!), the book grew so much new content that we decided to give it a more user-friendly name, one that accurately describes what this book is to be used for in a classroom setting, as the former title was a bit vague. Text from that book has been seamlessly interwoven with new text, without in-text citations to distract from the flow of the narrative. We hope that this will replace or become a companion to that textbook.

Users of *Research-Based Programming* will see a continued sequential approach established in *Research-Inspired Design*, connecting applied research to the design process, from pre-design through design development and beyond. We believe it to be a more refined execution of the same ideas. A revised table of contents better aligns with the design programming model, and a more succinct writing style overall. Descriptions of information-gathering techniques have been streamlined and updated, adding more resources for students to explore on their own.

This textbook retains many of the excellent student process work examples, along with some new project examples, and clear graphic explanations of complex concepts. Activities that help students brainstorm research topics, formulate research questions, conduct field studies, seek out experts, and create design concepts also reappear, with minor revisions. New activities help students identify programmatic concepts from an interview transcript, test their project program through peer review, integrate theory, and develop assessment checklists. Many of the activities are more open-ended to apply to a wider range of studio projects. The final chapter covers ways for students to share their projects with a broader audience through publishing and connecting with professional organizations. Finally, an Appendix provides a project program template and student example to help students visualize their own project program.

COVERAGE AND ORGANIZATION

Geared toward the two-year to four-year interior design and related degree programs, this book helps students achieve a basic understanding of research-based programming and begin their research-based design process. This textbook supports Crosbie's (2007) claim that the studio model for becoming a professional designer is the "crown jewel of design education" (p. 1). The text complements a variety of problem-based interior design studio curricula and approaches, helps students with design research, methodology, human factors theories, code compliance, building systems, site analysis, and ultimately how to frame and describe a problem clearly. The methods and strategies presented in this book seek to build on this problem-based, experiential learning model by suggesting a change of focus from one based on *problem solving* (through the manipulation of forms, material, and space) to *problem identification* derived from student-driven data collection. This adaptation calls for a bottom-up approach to the traditional studio classroom, encouraging students to write programs for spaces in response to their own exploration of the environment, culture, and context and to gain an increased awareness of human needs. Students using methods described in this textbook will gain confidence in fundamental pre-design skills, such as interviewing, surveying, observing techniques to gather their own data, as well as documenting and successfully incorporating the resulting data into their design solutions. Cary and Martin (2012) advocate incorporating *careful listening* into the design process as an important part of human-centered design, a movement toward dignifying the spaces for human interaction. This book is a starting point to consider the wide variety of resources that inform your interior design project, and the many ways to gain empathy for your clients and end-users, beginning with the everyday experience of talking to and observing people. It offers a way of looking at programming for interior design as a creative endeavor that is clearly distinct from design yet an integral part of the process.

Chapter 1, The Research-Based Design Process, begins by connecting research with the human-centered design process and listing valuable resources. *Chapter 2, Information Gathering Tools and Techniques*, helps students develop a balanced research plan that includes literature reviews, case studies, observation, surveying, and the art of interviewing, both traditional and image-based methods, including the patented ZMET (Zaltman Metaphor Elicitation *Technique*). Chapter 2 also includes *Building and Context Analysis*, which explores the influencing factors to consider in site selection and program development.

Chapter 3, Information Analysis and Programmatic Concepts, introduces the power of abstract thinking and problem synthesis as a means of bridging the gap between design research and design requirements. *Chapter 4, The Project Program*, is a step by step guide for creating a programming document for an interior design project. This chapter follows the structure of a sample program and template found in the Appendix A and B. *Chapter 5, Research-Based Schematics*, focuses on diagrams for ideation, and generation of multiple design solutions, based on a strong research-based design concept. *Chapter 6, Research-Based Design Development*, offers a glimpse into the many areas that further enhance a project program, including human factors theories, code compliance, building systems, and FF&E selection. *Chapter 7, Research-Based Presentations*, focuses on successfully representing and communicating research in the design presentation, and time management tips. *Chapter 8, Design as a Circular Process*, offers insight into the usefulness of assessments and how to incorporate feedback, evaluate design solutions, and further contribute to the body of knowledge of the interior design profession.

APPROACH AND FEATURES

Research-Based Programming for Interior Design takes a unique, student-centered approach to information gathering and design process in a workbook format. The format ties together information about research, programming, ideation, and design while placing the student at the center of the process by integrating activities, reflections, templates, and other tools to facilitate the act of data collection, analysis, and synthesis. The activities are designed to complement strategies found in the typical studio class without adding more work to the curriculum. The text provides templates of various types that students can adapt to their individual projects.

Through examples, activities, and a program template this book seeks to fill a gap in the interior design studio class, between data gathering and design program, to demystify the programming process and make it accessible to all designers; to empower both novice and seasoned designers to use many types of information, to always know the reason why behind each decision, and to be able to communicate it clearly, for the good of the built environment.

It is my hope that students reading this book will exhibit a fundamental shift in their identity as interior designers, from a personal perspective to viewing it as a team-based profession, linked to neuroscience, behavior, education theories, and natural sciences, with a clear need for further inquiry and continued dialogue among disciplines.

INSTRUCTOR RESOURCES

- Instructor's Guide provides suggestions for planning the course and using the text in the classroom, supplemental assignments, and lecture notes.
- PowerPoint- presentations include images from the book and provide a framework for lecture and discussion.

Instructor's Resources may be accessed at www.FairchildBooks.com.

ACKNOWLEDGMENTS

Greatest thanks to my mentors at Cornell University, Parsons School of Design, and University of California, San Diego, and to my fellow colleagues and treasured students, too numerous to mention here. Special thanks to the staff, faculty, students, and alumni of Design Institute of San Diego, and to my family and friends, Sandra and Sherman Robinson, Binnie Robinson, JC Harkins, Tatiana Berger, Elizabeth Spinello, Ellen Zimmerman, Casey Green, and Aly Pitts. With sincere gratitude to my husband, Chris Iandolo, who once said, "the true purpose of this book, as with any endeavor in life, is to become happy." To all students of interior design, I hope this book helps you to discover the greatest abilities in yourself which will yield the greatest joy.

The Publisher wishes to gratefully acknowledge and thank the editorial team involved in the publication of this book:

Acquisitions Editor: Emily Samulski
Senior Development Editor: Corey Kahn
Editorial Assistant: Jenna Lefkowitz
Art Development Editor: Edie Weinberg
In-House Designer: Lachina Creative
Production Manager: Ken Bruce
Project Manager: Rebecca Marshall, Lachina Creative

THE RESEARCH-BASED DESIGN PROCESS 1

Among twenty snowy mountains, the only moving thing was the eye of the blackbird.

— WALLACE STEVENS, Thirteen Ways of Looking at a Blackbird (Stanza I)

CHAPTER OBJECTIVES

When you complete this chapter you will be able to:

- Describe the five phases of the interior design process.
- Explain how research informs the design process.
- Understand basic research terminology, components, and concepts.
- Explore your design-related interests to develop a research topic and research questions.
- Identify and seek out research-based design concepts.

Since the early 1960s, with the advent of the term *architectural programming* by Caudill and Peña, data collection and analysis, and other aspects of the programming process have become integrated into the practice of **interior design**. More recently, the **Council for Interior Design Accreditation (CIDA)** and the **Council for Interior Design Qualification (CIDQ)** have put a greater emphasis on the role of the interior designer in the programming process—CIDA in interior design education, and CIDQ in the profession. Now considered integral to professional services, conducting research and gathering information throughout the design process, especially in the programming phase, can be creative and exciting endeavors—with the active participation of client, end-users, as well as other points of view.

The design process used by architects, interior designers, and other design professionals is based on a sequence of the *five phases of design*. Each phase can be identified in a contract with a set number of billable hours. Each phase includes various tasks and ends with an identified deliverable that should

KEY TERMS

Academy of Neuroscience for Architecture (ANFA)

American Institute of Architects (AIA)

American Society for Interior Designers (ASID)

Applied research

Art-based design concept

Basic research

Brainstorming

Building Resource Information Knowledgebase (BRIK)

Certificate of Research Excellence (CORE)

Concept mapping

Contract administration

Contract documents

Council for Interior Design Accreditation (CIDA)

Council for Interior Design Qualification (CIDQ)

Design concept

Design development

Environmental Design Research Association (EDRA)

Evidence-based design (EBD)

Five phases of design

Google Scholar

Human-centered design (HCD)

Interior design

Interpretivist

Pre-design/ programming

Positivist

Qualitative

Quantitative

Research

Research-based design concept

Research-based programming

Research questions

Schematic design

Theory

be signed off by the client before moving to the next phase. A designer may not take on every task, but choose from the menu of options in each phase. For interior design to be distinguished from decoration, an interior designer must consider taking the project through each phase of design, which builds upon each other, as follows: The **Five Phases of Design** Process (NAAB, CIDQ & CIDA, 2013)

I. **Pre-Design/Programming**: establish goals, collect information, uncover concepts, determine needs, define problems to solve.
Conclusion of this phase: Written *project program* or *design brief*; client and designer agree on the problems to solve.

II. **Schematic Design**: generate multiple solutions.
Conclusion of this phase: Selection of single scheme.

III. **Design Development**: fully articulate one scheme.
Conclusion of this phase: Design Development package which may include presentation boards.

IV. **Contract Documents**: communicate design solution to builders, suppliers, and codes officials.
Conclusion of this phase: Construction documents, including dimensioned drawings, details and specifications.

V. **Contract Administration**: perform tasks throughout construction and move-in.
Conclusion of this phase: Built project; evaluation of project effectiveness; addition to designer's portfolio of built work.

Looking at the preceding list it is easy to get the impression that design is a linear process—similar to a checklist or a mathematical equation—and that when one step is completed the next one begins in sequential fashion until the correct answer is found. There is some truth to this. For example, a space cannot be built during the contract administration phase unless there are contract documents to refer to in the building process. But since a built work, completed at the end of the contract administration phase, can be evaluated and used for further study, the process can be viewed as more *circular* than linear.

As an interior designer, you have choices about how you approach your own design process. When your practice has a strong foundation of information, it yields designs that seek to solve problems without taking away from your creativity. We are living in an "information age," where clients demand to know the "why" behind the design decisions

that shape their space (Guerin & Dohr, 2007). Approaching a client with evidence to support your claims greatly enhances your credibility and ability to sell your design ideas.

RESEARCH AS AN EVERYDAY EXPERIENCE

Research, or systematic inquiry, is not necessarily a new task or skill to be learned, but rather a deliberate and thoughtful practice that you can further cultivate. In fact, it's a process that is part of your daily life. Every day we seek out information, document or save it, sort it, and analyze it in order to make informed decisions about our life and the world around us. That familiar process is the foundation for how students go about developing an information-gathering strategy for a research-based interior design project.

As it is applied in this book, *research* can be broadly defined as the gathering of information that includes both previously published statistics, findings, and opinions coupled with your own experience in order to advance your knowledge about a design problem, the context surrounding it, or topics related to it. Research can be divided into four steps: (1) defining a problem, (2) gathering information about it, (3) analyzing and evaluating that information, and (4) presenting the information and citing your sources (Library at UOIT, 2008).

You could look at the experience of moving to a new home as an example of this process. You first identify a problem: your current living conditions are not suitable. You begin gathering information by reviewing lists of available places, neighborhood reviews, looking at maps, and photos (previously published data). You would use parameters to help you narrow your search, such as a price limit or amenities you hope to have, such as a parking space or a dishwasher. You could then talk to people who are familiar with the neighborhood (conduct a survey) and visit the place to see the exterior and interior conditions (site visit). You might spend some time in the neighborhood taking in the sights, sounds, and smells (observation).

In this very common process of finding a new home, your research plan has employed four of the information-gathering techniques that we will be discussing in Chapter 2 of this book; reading, interviewing, conducting site visits, and personal observation. Taking the time to do some research, and knowing what to look for, helps you avoid making poor choices. You may not want to rush in to signing a lease just because you were attracted to the way a place looked, only to discover that the bedroom window faced an alley filled with dumpsters, or that your new home was located in the airport's flight path.

HUMAN-CENTERED DESIGN TERMINOLOGY AND RESOURCES

Research-based design is built on the premise that humans and their well-being are at the core of every design problem and solution. This human-centered approach draws on research methods from a variety of social and scientific disciplines.

Evidence-Based Design

In 1984, Roger Ulrich conducted a landmark study "View through a Window May Influence Recovery from Surgery" (Marberry, 2010) published in the journal *Science* that influenced the role that information plays in the design of medical facilities. He set up a simple experiment that compared the length of stay and amount of pain medication taken between two groups of patients: those staying in rooms that looked out to a park and those in rooms facing a brick wall. He found that patients facing a park view took less pain medication and had shorter hospital stays than patients facing a brick wall. Since then, using measurable outcomes to support design decisions has become a standard practice in the design of healthcare facilities. There is a growing trend that **evidence-based design (EBD)** practices are now used for a variety of other project types, counteracting the notion that design of the built environment is a purely artistic endeavor, and that the nature of design is both mysterious and inscrutable.

Hamilton and Watkins (2009) call evidence-based design "a process for the conscientious, explicit, and judicious use of current best evidence from research and practice in making critical decisions, together with an informed client, about the design of each individual and unique project" (p. 9). Designers have always had input into their designs based on knowledge, but this method emphasizes the collaborative efforts of both expert and novice, designer, client, and end-user, as well as information from a variety of other sources and disciplines

such as human-environment behavioral studies, neuroscience and human biology, education studies, and medical science. **Human-centered design (HCD)** is an overall approach to problem solving that starts with a concern for the well-being of people. As research-based designers, we always have a choice in where our focus lies. Are we interested in research that promotes mechanical efficiency, visual interest, technological advances, or novelty in materiality or form as a primary goal? Or do we have an interest in how the design is ultimately perceived, used, and maintained over time by people? IDEO.org states that "human-centered design sits at the intersection of empathy and creativity." We can harness our creativity for the benefit of others, in a socially responsible manner.

According to researchers at Cornell, evidence-based design bridges the gap between research and real life, but has a very specific meaning: it is a process that incorporates the use of the scientific method, which at some point involved conducting an experimental or quasi-experimental research design with findings that have been replicated in more than one study (Powers, Hall, & Pillemer, 2018). In **research-based programming**, therefore, we use evidence produced by scientists in this manner, supplemented with our own experience, and can conduct data collection that is project specific. Evidence-based design is an underlying philosophy of research-based programming. Therefore, research-based interior designers keep up-to-date on currently published studies, seek to employ design to test out research findings, share information with others, and allow their work to be critically evaluated by peers. If this seems overwhelming, take heed! There are many resources available to help you.

One place to start looking for published studies is online. In keeping with their mission to make the world's information universally accessible, Google teamed up with libraries and research databases to link you to peer-reviewed papers, abstracts, and technical reports in a search engine called **Google Scholar.** Here you can sort by date, name of author, or subject matter. Many articles are in pdf format and available for download.

Produced and maintained by the University of Minnesota and sponsored by **American Society for Interior Designers (ASID)**, InformeDesign (InformeDesign.org) is specifically designed for use by interior designers seeking evidence-based design content and resources. Dedicated to improving design through an interactive and flexible web resource, InformeDesign is one of the first places interior design students will want to go to explore summaries of previously published studies related to human-centered interior design. Here you can search by three main categories: *space, occupant,* and *issue.* Subcategories of the occupant category include age ranges, abilities, genders, and type, which includes further groups such as parent, student, visitor, and so on. The issue category includes social needs such as identity, proxemics, and behavior and other important design issues such as codes, aesthetics, and research on building materials. You can also interface with design educators and practitioners, and be a voice in the ongoing conversation, contributing to the body of research that informs interior design. Of particular interest to novice researchers would be their three-part research tutorial, *Research 101,* which offers a condensed, yet in-depth, snapshot of the research-based interior design process.

Founded in the late 1960s by one of the leaders in research-based design, Henry Sanoff, the **Environmental Design Research Association (EDRA)** (http://www.edra. org/) promotes social awareness and inclusiveness in the built environment. According to their website, "EDRA's purpose is to advance and disseminate research, teaching, and practice toward improving an understanding of the relationships among people, their built environments, and natural eco-systems . . . and advocate for environments that are responsive to diverse human needs." The website includes many student resources. The EDRA's **Certificate of Research Excellence (CORE)** program showcases prominent projects that can serve as examples for students to learn from, as well as links to the winning design teams' websites, downloadable project briefs, papers, and studies.

Academy of Neuroscience for Architecture (ANFA) (anfarch.org) brings together designers, educators, and scientists in a unique forum that promotes an interdisciplinary approach to design of the built environment. The website includes conference proceedings, lectures, videos by prominent neuroscientists and architects, talking about the implications of architecture on the brain, nervous system, perception, vision, and memory. It also includes a link to a very comprehensive searchable database, **Building Resource Information Knowledgebase (BRIK)** at www.brikbase.org, sponsored by the **American Institute of Architects (AIA)** and the National Institute of Building Sciences.

Finally, at humancentereddesign.org, healthcare interior designer Vickery (2014) built "a library of empirical data

that serves . . . to guide our design decisions for future projects. Our research primarily focuses on design choices and operational processes that impact the patient experience and staff efficiency." As we will explore in Chapter 2, this website, as with the others mentioned, provides access to examples of previously built projects and findings we can use to begin research for our own projects.

USING RESEARCH TO DEVELOP YOUR DESIGN PROJECT

Hospital architect Don McKahan stated, "the expectation of designers is that they understand and use research-based decisions to create built environments with reliable outcomes in four main areas: functional, operational, sociological and experiential" (personal communication, 2018). In order to do this, designers draw on research that comes from a wide variety of disciplines from biological/neurological, physiological, behavioral, psychological, sociological, anthropological, geographic, cultural perspectives to studies in technological advances, materials testing, chemistry, physics, geology, and climate. Interior designers must understand that different research practices operate with regard to different theories. Research is typically divided into categories of *basic* and *applied* (Merriam, 2009, p. 3). While **basic research** tries to understand a phenomenon for general knowledge, **applied research** seeks to improve the quality of a particular practice, such as interior design.

All research studies are conducted using a theory. A **theory** is an *attempt to describe* or a *lens* through which one looks at a phenomenon. A theory also belongs to a particular world view or perspective, which is the underlying philosophy. Whether you are aware or not, your actions stem from a particular perspective and are guided by a theory. For example, do you believe that there is a single external reality or that individuals create their own reality? If you believe that there is one objective reality, then you would subscribe to a **positivist** perspective, and you would operate under the assumption that you could predict, control, and measure outcomes. If you believe there are multiple realities, then you would take on an **interpretivist** perspective, which seeks instead to describe, understand, and interpret occurrences within their contexts (Merriam, 2009, p. 11). Generally speaking, scientists studying the physical and natural sciences differ in their approach from social scientists (those studying human behavior, thoughts, and interaction), but not always. When approaching research, examine your own assumptions about the world, and be aware of the perspectives and theories other researchers use. You can use **quantitative** data, which includes numbers, sizes, and other measurements such as statistics to prove, support, or compare. Many clients will respond positively to your proposed solution if, for example, you tell them that 90 percent of the people surveyed preferred this color, or that using this material will reduce sound transmission by one half. In addition, you can use **qualitative** data which are descriptions or entities that cannot always be measured such as character, behavior, beliefs, history, preferences, feelings, aesthetics, and cultural traits. How a particular family was observed preparing a meal can be used as evidence to inform the layout of their new kitchen. How members of that family described the feeling they desired in their home may inspire and support the material and lighting choices.

DEVELOPING A RESEARCH QUESTION

The first step is to come up with a research topic to explore. In some situations, a topic, issue, or project type will be assigned. Other times, you will have an opportunity to choose your own topic. Even if you are given a topic, embarking on a research-based design journey will begin with you defining your own question to guide you.

Brainstorming is a process that can be used individually or in groups to come up with a "quantity of alternatives by spontaneously generating ideas and by deferring judgment on them" (Sanoff, 1991, p. 8). Brainstorming is a nonjudgmental free flow of ideas, and it is your most valuable tool at the beginning of the research process. Do you know what excites you about interior design? Take a few moments to jot down some thoughts about this question. As you answer it, think not only about your personal interests but also about how you want your designs to reach beyond yourself to impact others. Think about the types of places and people that inspire you, concern you, or draw an emotional response from you. Where do you find meaning in this field?

To guide you in creating a list of potential topics for your research is a tool called **concept mapping**. This tool is inspired by Burkhardt, MacDonald, and Rathemacher's book *Teaching Information Literacy* (2003). In simple terms, concept maps are a sort of "family tree" for your thoughts and ideas. Creating this family tree for your ideas allows you to track and organize your thoughts throughout the research and design process.

Concept mapping is being introduced here to help you begin exploring (by both expanding and then narrowing) the field of potential research available to you as you begin the programming process. The goal of the concept map is to brainstorm ideas and then mark the meaningful relationships among them. Figure 1.1 is an example of a concept map created by a group of students in a studio class. Because "travel" is something we are all familiar with, you might assume that it is too simple to be a research topic. But this unpretentious word could lead you to ask questions about more exotic or intriguing topics such as different travel destinations, types of travelers, environmental concerns, or psychological issues associated with travel such as anxiety or boredom.

You can see that some ideas or concepts—such as "reasons" and "destinations"—were directly related, while other ideas—such as "environmental issues" and "food"—were more remotely connected. When you see these concepts on paper, the ideas that once seemed only remotely related might hold more meaning for you than those ideas that are directly adjacent on the concept map.

Concept mapping translates easily from academics to the interior design profession. It can help you sort out challenging and complex concepts and ideas. For now, use it to help find connections between ideas that might eventually lead to your asking questions that could become the foundation for your project.

There are other ways to develop a research topic. Some of them (adapted from Groat & Wang, 2002) are listed here to help you begin developing your own.

- Suggest improvements to an existing body of work or theory. For example, how can we further reduce stressors in healthcare environments?
- Compare multiple approaches to an existing body of work or theory. For example, how do different theories about education affect the design of classrooms?
- Examine another person's existing theory to test a related idea or theory of your own. Can Appleton's theory of prospect and refuge along with Feng Shui principles be applied to emergency housing to increase a sense of safety and well-being?
- Question, test, or expand on an existing project type or concept. Do grocery stores support healthy eating habits?

Figure 1.1 Sample concept map

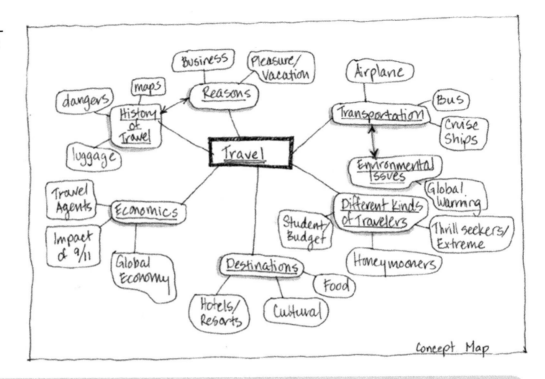

Concept Map

ACTIVITY 1.1
Creating a Concept Map

Purpose: To practice using a tool that helps you explore an area of interest; to form new connections or an innovative direction for your research topic. After reviewing the example in Figure 1.1, create your own concept map.

1. In the middle of a large piece of paper, write down a word or phrase that represents something you are interested in. It does not necessarily need to be related to design. Maybe you have an interest in a certain kind of activity, such as "sports" or "cooking," or cultural ritual such as "marriage." You can also start with a certain type of person you would like to explore, such as "artist," "military veteran," or "child." Or you can start with a more abstract concept, such as "health," "spirituality," or "death." You may put a box or bubble around your initial word.

2. Around the first word, write five or six words or phrases that immediately pop into your mind, or directly relate to your first word in some way. For example, if your topic is "death" you might think of "funeral," "fear of," "wearing black," "mourners," and "graves."

3. At the next level, think of words or phrases that relate to each of these words and write them around those words. For example, next to mourners you might write "stages of grief and grieving" or next to funeral you might write "different customs." Next to graves, you might write "cremation versus burial" and "design of ancient gravestones."

4. Continue expanding on your concept map until you feel you have exhausted all the possibilities of that topic—this may take a large piece of paper!

5. At the end of the process, review and highlight (or create a bold line among) the branching thoughts to trace a connection that provides an interesting direction for your research. Write down a full sentence that summarizes what you have discovered. For our example, you might find that an interesting direction for your research is to look at the "customs associated with funerals that are meant to help with the grieving process" or "current sustainable practices surrounding death and dying."

6. Complete this sentence: An interesting direction for my research is to look at: _____
   _____
   _____

- Offer solutions to a problem that has not yet been solved. Can shelters be designed that make pets more adoptable to eliminate the need for euthanizing healthy animals?
- Relate two previously unrelated ideas or functions to create a new one. Can an intergenerational day care be designed to bridge generation gaps and help reduce loneliness in elders in the United States?

From this list, can you see how a previously explored *theory* (a belief, policy, or procedure followed by practitioners in the interior design field) can inspire you by giving you a place to start your research? You can then use your imagination or concept mapping to build upon an existing idea to create new connections. You will need to whittle your broad research topic down to a narrowed topic that will bring you closer to your project goals and help you to manage your research process. There are three layers to consider to help you focus:

1. The first layer is your *broad topic*. The broad topic is often the area of interest you begin with. It could be a key word, a subject, an author's name, or a title, which you enter into a search engine or database—the idea that tends to be found at the center of your concept map. Examples of broad topics include art, education, healthcare, hospitality, travel, homelessness, marriage, meditation, recreation, etc.
2. After you begin researching your broad topic, your *restricted topic* is a layer that chooses a direction along one of the branches of the concept map. For example, your broad topic might be "healthcare." Your restricted topic might be "mental illness" or "assisted living."
3. It's likely that you will need to focus down even further, to a *narrowed topic* that allows you to identify information specific to a place (project type or geographic location), type of person, and an aspect or component of the restricted topic. For example, you could look at how residences for patients with *Alzheimer's* have integrated *art or music programs* for therapy purposes.

At this point you should have a pile of ideas on your hands, as concept mapping likely has helped you to create some meaningful connections that you explored further through restricting and narrowing. The questions you begin to naturally develop as you focus your research topic are called your **research questions**. Your research question (or questions, as is often the case) will be open-ended, leaving room for many answers to surface. Be careful, as they should not be a yes/no question! These emerging questions inspire and motivate the research process as you seek all the possible answers to these questions. Eventually this will lead to the identification of a problem and, later, a proposal in the form of a written program, which will be discussed in Chapter 4.

Elements of a good research question for interior design:

- It is a valuable idea worth pursuing. Confirm this with your colleagues and professor.
- It has a connection to the built environment.
- Information on the topic is readily available.
- It is current and relevant.
- It is open-ended and could generate many answers.
- It poses a question that can be solved through interior design and evolves accordingly.

Table 1.1 shows a few examples of how students have taken a broad topic, narrowed it, and then developed a thoughtful and provocative research question.

The following is a list of student research questions to inspire you to come up with one of your own:

- How do the needs of hearing-impaired children differ from hearing children in a school setting?
- How can we make playgrounds more accessible to children on the Autism spectrum?
- How can we help waiting areas in urgent care be designed to reduce spread of illness?
- What can enhance the quality of life in nursing homes?
- How can we reduce waste and increase sustainability and efficiency in retail spaces?
- How can I revitalize the cultural identity of a community through design?
- How can I empower people with limited mobility through the application of Universal Design?
- What factors contribute to stress in a work environment, and how can we reduce them?
- How can I make a gym more welcoming to women?
- What factors contribute to a feeling of connection in places of worship?
- What is the best environment to heal a wounded veteran? Even more narrowed: What are the design preferences of young men in the military with PTSD?
- What creates a sense of privacy in a public restroom?
- What affects adoption rates for animals in shelters?
- How quiet should a library be? Is the traditional model of silent behavior within libraries still appropriate for today?

TABLE 1.1

FROM BROAD TOPICS TO RESEARCH QUESTIONS

Broad Topic	Transportation	Universal Design	Healthcare	Travel	Privacy
Restricted Topic	Airline Travel	Accessibility	Obesity	Hotels	Prospect and Refuge
Narrowed Topic	Environmental stressors in airport waiting	Outdoor cultural events	Childhood obesity and poor eating habits in the U.S.	Reducing use of natural resource	Balance of privacy and supervision in group homes
Focus of Inquiry or End-User Category	Airline travelers and local businesses	Music enthusiasts who use mobility devices	Overweight children and their families	Visitors and staff	Teens and staff in group homes
Research Question	*How can airport design and amenities contribute to positive use of wait times?*	*How can temporary music festivals be more accessible?*	*How can fitness centers be designed for children and families to increase wellness?*	*How can we encourage more sustainable behaviors through hotel design?*	*How can group homes be designed to balance supervision with sense of privacy for teens?*

As you begin writing ideas for your own research question, you might spend more time rejecting young ideas than you spend exploring and nurturing them. As James Adams says in his book *Conceptual Blockbusting* (2001), "If you analyze or judge too early in the problem-solving process, you will reject many ideas" (p. 49). This is detrimental for two reasons. First, newly formed ideas are fragile and imperfect; they need time to mature and acquire the detail needed to make them believable. Second, ideas often lead to other ideas, laying out a path that can lead to something truly innovative.

Metaphorically, you could say that ideas are a lot like delicate seedlings, needing the chance to grow naturally and develop to their full potential. If you plant a tree, you have to wait for it to grow. If you judge it as a tiny seedling for not looking like the grand tree you had envisioned, you might prematurely squash it, never giving it a chance to evolve into what it could be.

Figures 1.2, 1.3, and 1.4 illustrate student presentations of research questions they developed for a broad topic that was assigned to them: adaptive reuse of a building located in community park called North Park. One student presentation asked the question, "Who is the community and are they concerned about the environment?" The second student presentation posited, "What are the roles of open spaces and parks in urban communities?" And

the third student presentation focused on "What is the history of the park and how does the community currently use it?" You can see how a broad assigned topic became individual research questions which led each student group to formulate a different research approach, led to diverse findings, and, ultimately, to different interior design project programs, concepts, and design solutions for the space.

DEFINING A PROBLEM TO SOLVE

As you look at your newly minted research question(s), think about *where* you could make a change for the better. It is okay if you don't yet know how you will make a change for the better. What matters is that you can identify a problem connected to your question and feel motivated to use your talent and professional skills to solve it.

In *Conceptual Blockbusting* Adams says, "Motivation is essential to creativity" (2001, p. 69). The reality is that no matter how talented you are, problem solving and the design process involve tedium, frustration, and challenges. Adams goes on to say that "unless you truly want to solve a problem you will probably not do a very good job" (p. 69). That means that unless you are convinced that a change needs to happen in a certain area within the realm of interior design, you are not likely to question or

ACTIVITY 1.2
Crafting Your Research Question(s)

Purpose: To create comprehensive research questions for a research-based interior design project.

Using the table, write a broad topic in the first column. Write a more restricted topic in the second column, then narrow to a place or project type. Finally, write down who your potential end-users will be in the fourth column. Do this exercise for at least three different broad topics.

Broad Topic	Restricted Topic "What, specifically?"	Narrowed Topic "Where?"	Who Does This Serve or Involve?

Put your three research questions here. Show these questions to a classmate, instructor, or colleague to get feedback. Can they help you decide which one seems most promising? Can they offer improvements on the words you have used? Is it clear? Is it compelling?

1.
2.
3.

Figure 1.2 Student presentation of data collection for the research question: "Who is the community and are they concerned about the environment?"

Figure 1.3 Student research question "What are the roles of open spaces and parks in urban communities?" led to research-based concept "flock," based on the idea that birds form an efficient v-formation to reduce fatigue and fly longer distances, a metaphor for how public spaces can allow community to come together and help each other.

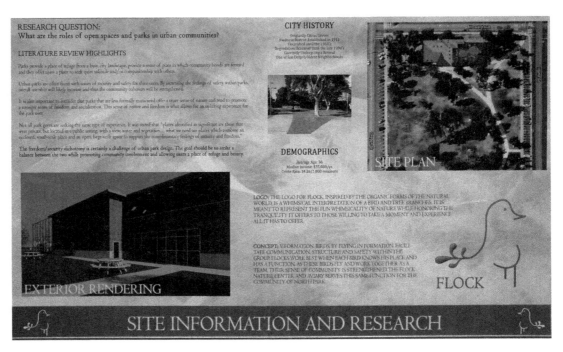

Figure 1.4 This student presentation examined the history of the site, represented in a timeline, pie charts illustrating the current uses, and a flyer from a nearby recreation center showing services offered to the community.

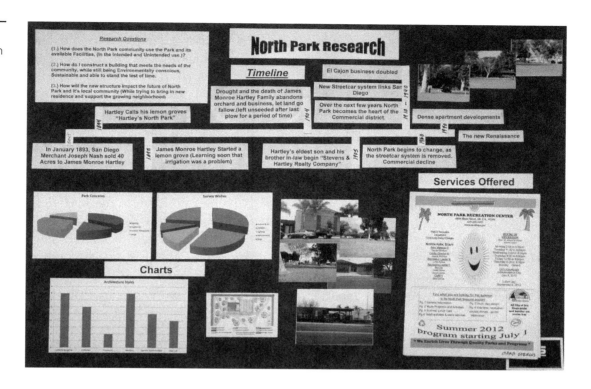

hypothesize and propose a solution for how that change can and will happen (Adams, 2001).

The goal of your research-based project is to "make a novel contribution" (Weisberg, 2006, p. 62). Focus on innovation and adding to the body of knowledge within your field: interior design. Because each professional field and its body of available knowledge are always moving, a novel contribution to the field "can change the direction of the field, or propel the field in any number of directions" (Weisberg, 2006, pp. 70–71). Your ideas might support the direction in which interior design is already headed, or they might propel it in a direction that is entirely different.

Innovation can happen at any level in your interior design project. It could happen in your selection of research topic, or perhaps in how you program the spaces in your building, or in how your project explores some specific subcategory of design with a new approach. If innovation is there in the beginning, in the end it will infuse your design solutions. Innovation could even be how your project combines and cross-pollinates issues from different disciplines, such as anthropology, psychology, or neuroscience.

If your research question was "how do the needs of hearing-impaired children differ from hearing children in a school setting?" and you have successfully answered this question through gathering information, it will be easy for you to translate the question to a problem to solve: "How can school design empower deaf and hearing-impaired students?" Some research questions are easier to translate than others. The key is to operationalize abstract concepts into a project type, sponsored by a client agency that serves an identified end-user population, into a specific site or location.

Strategies for describing the problems to solve will be discussed in Chapter 3. The strategy for solving efficiency in an intensive care unit may come from a *type of circulation*, which is an example of a programmatic concept. For example, a research study may find that a *centralized* nurse's station works better than a series of *decentralized* nurse's stations. So you could propose this kind of layout for your facility's program. Incorporating ideas like this into a written program will be discussed in Chapter 4.

Art-Based versus Research-Based Design Concepts

In addition to descriptions of the problems to solve (without necessarily offering a physical design solution yet), you will also need a well-developed and inspiring **design concept**. A design concept is a poetic statement about how you plan to meet the requirements in the project program. It is a concise and often metaphorical expression of the aesthetic and operational goals, or underlying inspiration for the eventual design solution; the *"how"* behind the *"what."* Once a design concept has been proposed by the designer and accepted by the client, all ensuing design decisions should support the design concept. For example, the design of an office for a doctor of Eastern medicine could be based on the strong design concept of the "Five Elements Theory," which is a philosophy describing the balance of energetic properties of metal, wood, fire, water, and earth. The designer could use this concept by making all design decisions in consideration of the nature of these five elements and how they can be used to create balance within the built environment, and how they might impact the human experience in the space physiologically, emotionally, and spiritually. The "Five Elements" design concept would become the conceptual "glue" that serves to create cohesiveness between the flooring, furniture, lighting, walls, and artwork; decisions possibly made by multiple members of a design team.

There are multiple ways to approach forming a design concept. In fact, there are two main categories: *art-based* design concepts and *research-based* design concepts. In an **art-based design concept**, the designer would apply an outside theme or concept to the space. For example, a designer inspired by Picasso's *Man with Guitar* could use that painting to form an underlying concept for, say, a local coffee shop. In this example, the creative idea for the ultimate design solution of the coffee shop was inspired by a source outside of the coffee shop. Many schools use an art-based approach to design. A Bachelor of Fine Arts (BFA) in interior design is an example of a degree program of study that would emphasize an artistic basis for design solutions.

However, interior design is an area of study in which you can also get a Bachelor of Arts (BA) or a Bachelor of Science (BS) degree. These programs may expect that you derive your project solution from considering either a social or physical (biological or neuroscience) science perspective, or the methodologies associated with obtaining results using and applying the scientific method. In a **research-based design concept**, a design concept is *derived from* analyzing the information the designer has gathered about the project or the design problem to be solved. Say, for example, that while collecting information for the aforementioned coffee shop through interviews and observation, the designer determined that the artists in the area need a place to show their artwork. The designer could propose an "art gallery" design concept for the coffee shop, based on displaying local artists' work, to guide subsequent aesthetic and functional decisions.

Sometimes it is easier to defend a design concept that has been *derived from* research than it is to defend a design concept originating from a designer's own preference, which has been *imposed on* the project. However, regardless of whether the source of the design concept is derived from the project or is applied to it, the concept is to be the basis for all subsequent design decisions—from space planning to color selection. Thus, in your own work, the fundamental research needed to form your design concept is critical in the ultimate acceptance of your project solution, whether by professors, peers, or the client and/or end-user of the space.

EXAMPLES OF RESEARCH-BASED DESIGNS

This chapter concludes with a look at two examples of research-based interior design projects generated by first-semester seniors attending a four-year BFA in interior design program in southern California. Each student was given the same site, an 8,000-square-foot existing building at the north end of a community park in an area called North Park. Students generated their own research-based program, or project proposal, by first studying about an issue, an end-user type, and then the site itself. They derived research-based design concepts as well from information they collected about the site, client interviews, or from the nature of the facility itself.

Please review the projects to see how research informed the process work, the layout, and the material and color selection. In Figure 1.5, student Chad Sterud presents his research question, data collection methods, summary of findings, and how he translated this data into a creative and appropriate design solution. His audience is eclectic, consisting of a panel of community members who would potentially use the space, a representative of the city park acting as client, a local code official, and a professional interior designer who can comment on the viability of the solution. He addresses his audience using terminology that is appropriate and understandable for each of them, answering clarifying questions and supporting his design decisions with evidence.

Figure 1.6 shows Chad's final presentation boards. He describes his design concept as "pulling from the historical significance of the surrounding mix of architectural styles—Mission, Spanish, Bungalow, Ranch and Modern—as well as drawing on the whimsical pond motif of the popular playground added in 1990," this project seeks to create a distinctive, eclectic community hub to unify the neighborhood and last many generations.

The structure features large patios, exposed eaves, and sustainable materials that epitomize the indoor/outdoor California way of life. The color palette was influenced by the natural elements of the park: greens, blues, and calming neutrals.

Students who worked on the project shown in Figure 1.7 conducted an extensive survey. They asked people who regularly use the park what amenities would complement their current use of the park. Survey results showed a preference for art and a place for children. The students combined the two most popular "wants" into a single project they called the "Park Museum." "In addition to satisfying the desires of the current end-users, the project program also included interactive water features in an outdoor playground, which honored the history of the site (originally a reservoir) and in response to research that showed that safe and accessible water parks encourage movement in outdoor spaces for people of all ages and abilities.

Figure 1.5 Interior design student Chad Sterud presents his project to a design jury.

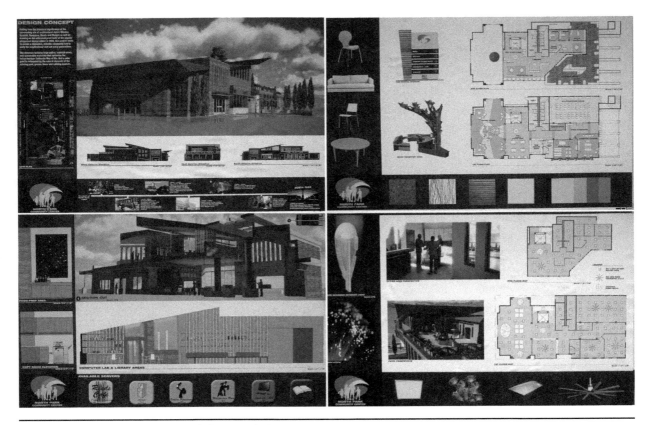

Figure 1.6 Chad's research-based design solution.

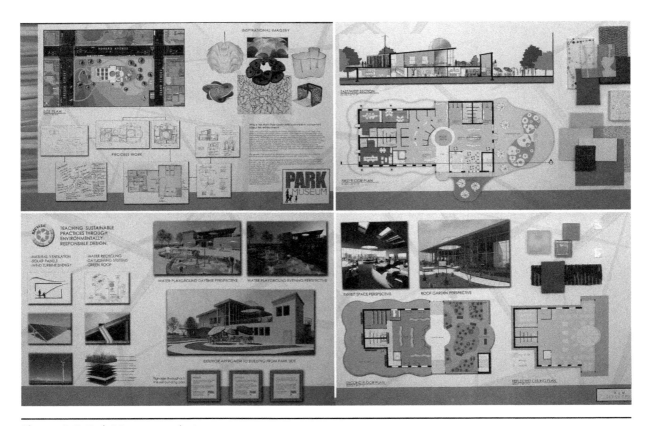

Figure 1.7 Park Museum project.

Conclusion

In school, every design project should begin with research. In your professional life, every design project should begin with research. Remember that doing research is not always about finding answers. It is often about helping you find the right questions to ask. "Research allows you to know enough to ask the right questions" (V. Bissonnette, personal communication, December 2007).

The research-based design process follows the five phases of the interior design process. Research can inform and enhance each phase. This chapter has helped you explore your design-related interests to develop a comprehensive and compelling question and understand the benefit of a research-based concept. The role of the design concept, how to develop a strong design concept, how to implement it, and how to communicate it during presentations will continue to be explored throughout the book.

No project exists without an end-user (or users) who will be visiting, living, or working in your future design solution. To help ensure that their experience will be what you envision for them, you must develop a deep understanding of your end-users. Their abilities, tendencies, preferences, behavior patterns, and rituals of how they will use the space, as well as their physical, mental, and emotional state must be considered in your design process.

As an interior designer—or any other type of designer, for that matter—you gather information as a continuous and conscientious process. This expansion of your knowledge becomes the foundation of expertise that allows you to program and design a new and unfamiliar project type, or to improve a familiar project type. The next chapter will help you develop a research plan and use data collection methods as part of your design process.

References

Adams, J. L. (2001). *Conceptual blockbusting: A guide to better ideas.* Cambridge, MA: Basic Books.

Burkhardt, J. M., MacDonald, M. C., and Rathemacher, A. J. (2003). *Teaching information literacy.* Chicago: American Library Association.

Groat, L. and Wang, D. (2002). *Architectural research methods.* New York: John Wiley.

Guerin, D. and Dohr, J. (2007). *Research 101: Part 1 research-based practice.* Retrieved May 15, 2018, from Informedesign.umn.edu.

Hamilton, D. K. and Watkins, D. (2009). *Evidence-based design for multiple building types.* Hoboken, NJ: Wiley & Sons.

IDEO.org. Retrieved August 2019.

Library at UOIT, https://guides.library.uoit.ca /researchprocess. Retrieved January 2008.

Marberry, S. (2010). A conversation with Roger Ulrich. *Healthcare Design*, 10(11), 40–49. Retrieved May 19, 2018, from https://www.healthcaredesignmagazine .com/architecture/conversation-roger-ulrich/.

Merriam, S. B. (2009). *Qualitative research: A guide to design and implementation.* San Francisco, CA: Jossey-Bass/John Wiley & Sons.

Powers, J., Hall, S., and Pillemer, K. (2018). *Evidence-based living: Bridging the gap between research and real life.* Retrieved May 15, 2018, from http:// evidencebasedliving.human.cornell.edu/.

Sanoff, H. (1991). *Visual research methods in design.* New York: Van Nostrand Reinhold.

Vickery, C. G. (October 22, 2014). *Research tools for healthcare design.* Retrieved April 14, 2018, from http://www.healthcaredesignmagazine.com/trends /perspectives/evaluating-right-healthcare-design -research-tools/.

Weisberg, R. (2006). *Creativity: Understanding innovation in problem solving, science, invention and the arts.* New York: John Wiley.

2 INFORMATION-GATHERING TOOLS AND TECHNIQUES

I was of three minds, like a tree in which there are three blackbirds.

— *WALLACE STEVENS, Thirteen Ways of Looking at a Blackbird* (Stanza II)

CHAPTER OBJECTIVES

When you complete this chapter you will be able to:

- Develop a balanced research plan.
- Evaluate and utilize high-quality sources of previously published information to conduct literature review.
- Understand the value, purpose, and types of case studies.
- Conduct interviews, surveys, observation, and explore other experiential techniques to collect original data.
- Collect information about the project site.
- Represent data graphically and in written form.

TRIANGULATING YOUR DATA

When approaching a new interior design project, what do you think comes first: Reading? Looking at the space? Asking questions? There is no right answer. Information gathering can begin at any one of these tasks (Figure 2.1). Once you have an idea of the many research methods available to you that are discussed in this chapter, you can begin to develop a research plan. You may want to first *observe* people waiting in an emergency room and notice their discomfort. You can then *read* about research studies that examined environmental stressors such as long wait times, poor lighting, awkward furniture configurations, noise, etc., in these environments. As a third step, you may prepare a list of questions to ask people who have experienced waiting in an emergency room, receptionists, doctors, nurses, maintenance staff, or design professionals who specialize in medical

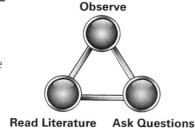

Figure 2.1 Triangulating your data means getting information from more than one source.

Observe

Read Literature   Ask Questions

In which order should you do this?

facilities. Asking a few individuals will yield their personal opinions, their experience, and may be biased or not truthful. So we often use the other two methods (reading and observing) to confirm what a person says is true, to offer a differing point of view, or to get information that cannot be conveyed through conversation.

As you begin to develop a research strategy for your design project, do not think of the research as something outside of yourself that must be completed for an assignment. Instead, make it a personal experience and think of yourself as an investigator seeking out questions and answers that will impact the greater good for those individuals who experience the spaces you design. The idea is to balance your plan using complementary methods (described in this chapter) that generate data along a continuum from generalizable to project-specific, as illustrated in Figure 2.2. After reviewing the graphic, choose at least three methods from this menu of options. For example, a good research design strategy may include (1) interviewing the client, (2) taking a tour of a similar facility, (3) attending a conference that relates to the project type.

USING PREVIOUSLY PUBLISHED INFORMATION

Before asking questions, some designers like to familiarize themselves with basic facts, statistics, and general information about a project topic or issue, end-user group, or organization. For example, before interviewing nursing staff in a Neo-Natal Intensive Care Unit (NICU), you may want to learn basic terminology about nursing or the area of specialty, caring for newborns. In fact, you may also want to know that nurses typically pronounce the acronym NICU as "nick-you." Similarly, if you were going to interview an elementary school teacher, it would be a good idea to familiarize yourself with acronyms such as ELL's or IEP's so that you can establish a level of credibility with your interviewee, and not interrupt to ask basic questions. A **literature review** is a great way to start learning about current knowledge in the professional and scientific fields surrounding your project, as well as controversial issues, and buzz words. You will want to start collecting information from previously published books, articles, studies, and websites to build a vocabulary for future interactions with potential clients and end-users of the space, and to use later when you present your design solution.

Evaluating Internet, Database, Peer-Reviewed Information Sources

In addition to the human-centered design resources listed in Chapter 1, there are other sources of information to get background, or foundational information, about your subject matter: databases, peer-reviewed journals,

RESEARCH METHODS & INFORMATION SOURCES					
Client and end-user interviews	Potential client and end-user surveys	Observation/ behavior mapping	Case studies	Quasi-experimental simulations	Controlled experiments
Site visit and analysis of building shell	Analysis of property and neighborhood	Tours of similar facilities	Professional and trade publications	Conference proceedings	Peer-reviewed journals
Project team consultations	AHJ/codes review	Shadowing an expert	TED talks and popular lectures	Academic lectures	Scientific studies
CONTEXT SPECIFIC			**GENERALIZABLE**		

BALANCED DESIGN RESEARCH PLAN

Figure 2.2 A balanced research plan considers data from the spectrum of context-specific to generalizable sources.

trade publications, and conference proceedings. Search for TED talks, lectures at universities, and other venues where architects, historians, and experts may talk about the impact of a project on its surrounding neighborhood, a technological breakthrough, a new building method, or offer insight into a social issue that has influenced previous architectural or interior design projects. Websites such as Architizer A+Awards (https://awards.architizer.com/) and Inhabitat (https://inhabitat.com/), tend to have high-quality articles that include reliable peer-reviewed information and are written by design professionals. Websites such as Houzz (https://www.houzz.com/) and Pinterest (https://www.pinterest.com/) tend to contain more trendy, consumer-driven information that is useful when creating image-based surveys but not as useful for establishing a baseline credibility with your subject matter.

What Is a Case Study?

The term *case study* is used in many fields. In the medical field, a case study would be a comprehensive look at a singular instance of a person who exhibited the classic symptoms of a certain affliction. The story of the "elephant man" was a case study in which a man was afflicted with an extreme form of the disease called neurofibromatosis. Documentation of the way his body was deformed, the way he lived, and the way he died served to inform medical science. Even after his death, his remains, and the detailed story of his life, still serve to inform science.

In the field of interior design, a **case study** is an in-depth examination of a previously completed, or proposed, project that has conditions related to your own project, so that it can serve as a prototype or an example

---

ACTIVITY 2.1
Beginning a Literature Review

Purpose: To begin compiling a list of sources (books, articles, videos, and other) that offer valuable information about, or related to, your research topic. List three items that you find from each of the following types of information sources. Include Author (date published) and *Title of Publication*.

- Articles or abstracts from *Google Scholar*
  1. _____
  2. _____
  3. _____
- Research summaries from *InformeDesign* (or similar source)
  1. _____
  2. _____
  3. _____
- Articles from a professional journal, database, or conference proceeding
  1. _____
  2. _____
  3. _____
- Books from the school's library or public library
  1. _____
  2. _____
  3. _____
- Video, popular lecture, or other Internet resource
  1. _____
  2. _____
  3. _____

Download the pdf file of the entire article or, at minimum, the abstract or link. Save each of these in a digital file or folder for future reference. Write one sentence about each item's possible value to your study.

of either a successful or an unsuccessful design solution. According to Research 101 Part III on InformeDesign this research activity "emphasizes the individuality and uniqueness of the participants and the setting." (Guerin & Dohr, 2007, p. 8). By studying the design elements of a comparable project type, user group, or program, you may be able to apply what you learn to your own project. Similarly, you can conduct a **comparative case study** in which you contrast two similar projects in an attempt to discern interesting differences. For example, you could try determine to why one was well-received by the public and the other was not as popular. As one researcher once explained, "If you know one thing, you don't know anything. You need to compare it with something else" (personal communication, P. Levin, January 8, 2016).

There are different kinds of case studies to explore. A **precedent study** usually refers to a project that exemplifies innovation in architecture or design, such as in its structural, technological, or formal (related to form) exploration. Another type of case study is the **historic precedent**, as we often go back in time to the first project of its kind. Or we examine a project that exemplifies a certain historic style or time period. We can also use recently constructed or cutting-edge projects as examples to illustrate technological breakthroughs and possibilities or trends in philosophy and design theory. Additionally, any project that solves a social problem or that benefits society, has an innovative program, or offers a unique solution can serve as a case study—for example, a museum for the visually impaired that relies on sense of touch, or a new idea for temporary housing in a disaster-stricken community.

When many designers point to a project as an icon, it operates as a reference point and may function as a focus for the founding of schools of thought. Such a project is often referred to as a **paradigmatic case**. A good example is Le Corbusier's Villa Savoye (1929–1931). This building illustrated the five points of modern architecture as stipulated in Le Corbusier's manifesto, published in 1926. Its construction ushered in a whole new understanding of modern architecture. Thus, a case study can serve as a singular example that says, "Here I am. Learn from me."

The terms *document* and *explore* are used over and over in this section. That is because the key to doing a case study is that it involves both representing and analyzing a previously built or proposed example. An underlying assumption in science is that if you dissect something, you can find out the inner workings of an organism or discover how it functions in its environment. Case studies are used in this manner, to be closely examined in order to compare what works and what does not. They can be used to compare the quality of designed environments, to track current design trends, or to provide an historical framework for your proposal. Or they can showcase the use of new technology, new materials or construction method, or a sustainable design feature.

To fully understand your project type, you may need to visit in person, or virtually explore, a few existing projects that are similar in scope, serve the same function, are located in a similar climate, or serve a similar community. When you find one that is innovative or has accomplished its goal successfully, you have found a subject for your case study. Next, you must document all the parameters of the project you found and dissect the project. What makes this project unique and a success? Or, on the flip side, what makes it a failure? We can also learn a great deal from another designer's mistakes, inappropriate use of color or materials, poor spatial configurations, or misguided assumptions about the way the users would use the space.

Where Do You Find a Case Study?

Case studies can be found anywhere you would find documentation of a previously designed, proposed, or built interior design project. Many professional organizations host competitions or showcase exemplary design projects. Periodicals that feature interior design projects typically are also a good source for case studies, although they may not have all of the information you would want to know. If the source lists the design team, you may reach out to the designers to get additional details about the project that may not be featured in the magazine article. Architecture and interior design firms often have their projects posted in a portfolio on their websites, or have articles written about the projects linked to their websites.

Organized and maintained by Institute for Human Centered Design (IHCD), an international non-profit organization located in Boston, Universal Design Case Studies (https://universaldesigncasestudies.org/) is a growing collection of projects that exemplify "best practices" in inclusive design, projects that empower individuals, and projects that celebrate variation of human abilities. Projects are sorted by category and region. Access to the information is free and does not currently require registration or membership. They have international examples of schools, health centers, and cultural facilities, and welcome input of all designers to add to their library if you would like to suggest or submit a project for their consideration.

Architectural Record (www.architecturalrecord.com/topics/306-building-type-studies) provides a wide variety of project types you can browse through, including adaptive reuse (focusing on preservation and renovation), civic buildings, colleges and universities, commercial/workplace, healthcare, hospitality, retail, K–12 schools, libraries, housing, performing arts, landscaping/parks, and other public spaces. For a free sign-up, you get access to current designs, complete with photos, floor plans, and commentary from the designer, as well as an opportunity to comment and share the project ideas with other students and colleagues.

The American Institute of Architects Committee on the Environment (COTE) (http://www.aiatopten.org/) showcases their annual top ten winning projects from across the United States. This site features the winners from 1997 to the present. Many of the projects include a floor plan and site plan, multiple photos of the exterior and interior, along with extensive text explanation of what makes the project cutting edge. The site also provides links to the architects and designers' websites so you can contact them for further information, or explore their other projects on their online portfolios.

The Health Design website (https://www.healthdesign.org/insights-solutions/open) promises, "the latest trends, tools and resources for improving healthcare environments." With a free log-in, you can access research reports, project briefs, and case studies that showcase design strategies and summaries of key points. You can also become a member and take advantage of webinars.

The Whole Building Design Guide (WBDG) maintains a database of exemplary residential, commercial, and institutional project types that subscribe to sustainable building practices. Many of these are winners of *Beyond Green High-Performance Building and Community Awards* sponsored by the National Institute of Building Sciences (https://www.wbdg.org/additional-resources/case-studies).

And the Academy of Architecture for Health (AAH) has a case study library that began in 2016 that features downloads in pdf format of fully documented, large-scale pilot projects from all over the United States (https://network.aia.org/viewdocument/case-study-library?CommunityKey=5ac54771-1122-4d1f-ac18-d2d12d6a94fb).

Learning from a Case Study

There are many things we can learn from reviewing a case study. We can learn, by example, how a design team used information to solve a problem. We can look at how they implemented a design concept, from circulation (how a visitor or staff member moves through the building) to way-finding techniques (how colors, materials, and signage informed visitors), and how they used daylight, natural ventilation, and views. If we study the floor plan or written program, we can learn how the size of each program area, the shapes, adjacencies, and sequences of spaces contributed to the success of the project. As one source summarizes, we can "learn about how a county directive to relocate different behavioral health programs into one location led to a unique design for serving low to high-risk populations in an integrated facility, and how collaboration among the architect, interior designer, landscape architect, owner, staff, and clients played an integral role in shaping the programming and design" (Project brief on www.healthdesign.org [February, 2018]).

The following student examples show how we can summarize the visuals and graphics to communicate what we learn to others in a poster format. Figure 2.3 shows how a student assembled information about an elementary school in the Netherlands that featured interior design components that encouraged students to move, a core element of the Montessori pedagogy. She sought to find key features she could apply to a school she was going to design: a school for the deaf and hard of hearing located in southern California. The similarities between the case study and her project were the emphasis on movement, tactility, visual access between upper and lower floors, and overall size of facility. Notice how she includes the building section along with the photo showing openings that connect the first and second floors, and a large floor plan with the spaces keyed to illustrate relative sizes and adjacencies.

In Figure 2.4 the plans of the case study are color coded to correspond to different program areas for greater clarity for comparison. This student poster also included quotes from various articles to supplement understanding of the built space.

Case studies are often grouped by project types by researchers. Can you identify which of the types the two

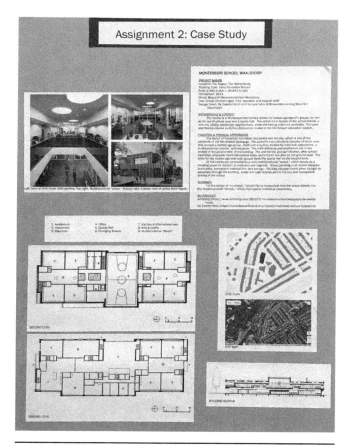

Figure 2.3 A student composed a poster featuring a case study of an elementary school located in the Netherlands.

Figure 2.4 A student poster featuring a case study of a school for wounded veterans.

student case studies fit into from the following common categories: commercial (retail, hospitality, office), institutional (educational, healthcare, museum), or residential (single family, multi-unit, temporary housing)? This convention makes it easy to reference case studies when you are searching for a project type in a database or on a website.

COLLECTING ORIGINAL DATA

After gaining some preliminary knowledge from previously published books, articles, and case studies, it is now time to start making a list of questions you still have about your topic. Take a moment to jot down some notes about what you want to know from interviewing people or from personal experience. Do you want to ask an expert about a particular method of treatment, or would you like to poll people who have been to places similar to the one you are studying? Would you like to experience the sights,

sounds, smells, and texture of a certain kind of event that you imagine to be going on in the type of facility you are going to design? Many of the methods discussed in this section can be used individually or be combined to create a customized journey of information gathering and can be adapted to suit your needs. In fact, you may stumble upon a research method that has not yet been used and be a pioneer in research methods. In order to do this, you should document what you do, the tools you use, and the way you record the data so that future researchers can attempt to follow your methods in their own study.

Collecting your own data can be a very rewarding and insightful experience. As mentioned in Chapter 1, typically, these methods can be divided into *quantitative* (which has to do with generating numbers, statistics, and comparisons utilizing a scientific positivist approach) and *qualitative* (which has to do with richly describing the complexity of social and cultural issues typically found in ethnographic and interpretive research). But this process is also about how information is *analyzed* (Harris et al.,

ACTIVITY 2.2
Documenting a Case Study

Purpose: To document and explore a previously proposed or built project that is similar in project type, function, end-user, or otherwise related to your area of interest. And to communicate what you have learned to your classmates and instructor. The following outline represents a good format for an interior design case study. Include as many of the following items as you can find and clearly display these items using both text and graphics in a poster presentation or PowerPoint slideshow format.

1. Project Basics
   - Project location—where is it located? What is the climate like in that location? How is it sited—on a mountain; in a valley; in an urban, suburban, or rural area?
   - Completion date—the date it was designed and/or the date it was built are very important to place the building in historical context and to compare with the past and present-day technology.
   - Building type—what kind of materials or building methods were involved in its construction? Is it a single story or multiple story?
   - Square footage—how large is this project? How does it compare to the size of the project that you are proposing?
   - Client—who sponsored or commissioned this project? Clients can be private, non-profit, or corporate.
   - End-users—who is the population served by this project? Who are the staff, the visitors, the community?
   - Design team—who designed this project? Were there multiple disciplines involved, such as engineers, architects, interior designers? Were there researchers involved who influenced the program?
2. Background and Context
   - Goals, mission, philosophy—what were the overarching goals of this project? Was there a particular theory or constraint that guided the design team?
   - Budget—is there any information about how much the project cost to build? To maintain (projected or estimated operating costs)?
   - Timeline of construction or relevant details—is there something innovative about how the project was constructed? Was it assembled very fast from prefabricated structures, or used recycled materials and slowly constructed over time by the local community members?
   - Historic or cultural milieu, design movement or time period—does this project represent a certain way of building in a culture (such as traditional Japanese tea house wood framing), or climate (adobe construction in the desert), to blend in with its surroundings (three-story brick in a Midwest residential area) or historic style (Victorian).
3. Function and Physical Appearance
   - Program—what are the overarching architectural and interior design concept(s)? What are the function(s) of the project?
   - Site plan or satellite view—how did the natural and man-made context influence the project's configuration on the site? Look at topography, views, adjacent buildings, and building orientation along compass directions. What is the relationship of the site amenities, parking, signage, landscape/hardscape?
   - Floor plans, circulation diagrams, and preliminary design sketches or models produced by design team—identify the various spaces, their approximate sizes, and their relationship to one another, adjacencies. Sometimes a case study will be color-coded to show the various uses, public versus private, visitor versus staff areas, sterile versus non-sterile, which is very helpful. Is there one main entrance or multiple points of entry? Is the circulation centralized or decentralized? (For discussion of circulation types, see Chapter 3 analysis diagrams.)
   - Sections, elevations and details—while all of these drawings are not always necessary, it would be beneficial to know information, such as ceiling heights and sustainable features involving the building shell, that generally shows up in sections and details.

- Photos of exterior and interior—these photos will highlight three-dimensionally what the finished space feels like based on use of interior finishes on floors, walls and ceilings, signage, lighting, furniture layouts, and artwork.
- Key design features and/or strategies to achieve design—perhaps there are design solutions that address "active waiting" incorporated into reception area seating design, or a new way to store strollers and backpacks in a daycare facility.

4. Implications for the Future
   - Performance studies—any POEs (Post-Occupancy Evaluations), end-user satisfaction surveys or interviews, or follow-up studies that verified the effectiveness or deficiencies of the built project, typically done one year after project completion.
   - Impact on surroundings, neighborhood, environment—were there any news articles that arose as a result of the project being built? Any legal issues? Are there any sources of architectural criticism subsequent to the design and build of the project?
   - Influence on other designers—is there any indication from news sources, conference proceedings, or personal communication with end-users that this project had an impact on the design community or serves as an example? Do they conduct tours to visiting professionals? Has the project been nominated or won any awards from professional organizations or design competitions?

5. Summary
   - Applicability to your project—what stood out to you about this project? What will be useful to you moving forward?
   - Anything else that you have learned—is there anything else you want us to know about this project?

6. References
   - Cite all sources. It is important to cite the source of any image that you did not produce yourself, as well as text such as statistics and direct quotes from the author of the original book, website, or article.

Refer to Figures 2.3 and 2.4 for examples of poster presentations by interior design students.

2008). For example, you can interview someone (which is typically considered a qualitative information-gathering technique) and then analyze their responses by counting how many times they have used a certain word, thereby turning the content of the interview transcript into a quantifiable statistic or number, as in "he used the phrase 'importance of nature' five times in 10 minutes." This can be further evidence to support your claim that the client understands the value of biophilic design.

Observing

We are constantly gathering information about our environment. When you take a dog for a walk, for example, he uses his senses of smell, touch, sight, and hearing to gather important information about his environment. This is also true of humans. Like a dog sniffing to see who has passed, we use our senses to obtain information about the current situation as well as events that may have happened in the past.

Observation is the use of one or more of the senses to obtain and record information on individuals, objects, or events, as a method of gathering information for interior design (Fraenkel, Wallen, & Sawin, 1999). In interior design, **environment-behavior research** is one way to study how people interact with their environment. Figure 2.5 shows the variety of techniques associated with this kind of research.

In his book *Inquiry by Design*, John Zeisel (2006), described the many ways we can observe people interacting in a setting. We can observe people casually to get a sense of how people generally use a space. Or we can *systematize* our observation, using a *place-centered*, **behavioral mapping** technique. We note the start time and end time. We can categorize people and count them. And we can document their movement and interaction

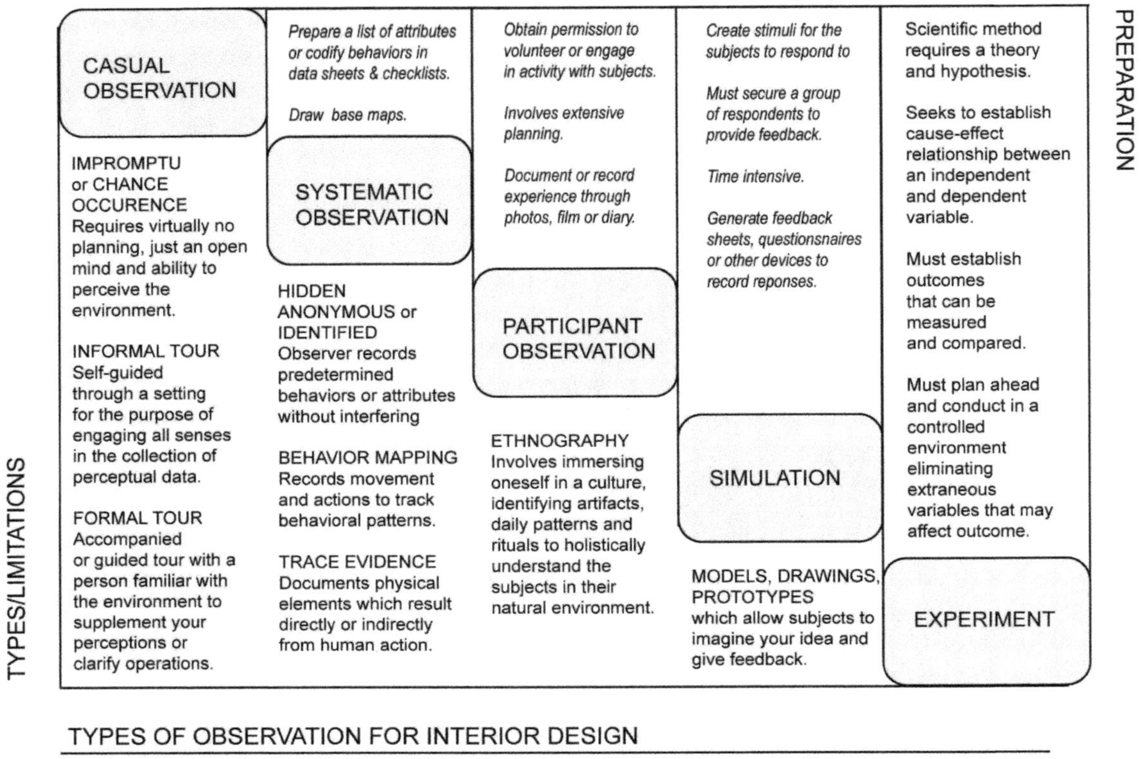

CASUAL OBSERVATION

Prepare a list of attributes or codify behaviors in data sheets & checklists.

Draw base maps.

SYSTEMATIC OBSERVATION

Obtain permission to volunteer or engage in activity with subjects.

Involves extensive planning.

Document or record experience through photos, film or diary.

PARTICIPANT OBSERVATION

Create stimuli for the subjects to respond to

Must secure a group of respondents to provide feedback.

Time intensive.

Generate feedback sheets, questionsnaires or other devices to record reponses.

SIMULATION

Scientific method requires a theory and hypothesis.

Seeks to establish cause-effect relationship between an independent and dependent variable.

Must establish outcomes that can be measured and compared.

Must plan ahead and conduct in a controlled environment eliminating extraneous variables that may affect outcome.

EXPERIMENT

PREPARATION

TYPES/LIMITATIONS

IMPROMPTU or CHANCE OCCURENCE Requires virtually no planning, just an open mind and ability to perceive the environment.

INFORMAL TOUR Self-guided through a setting for the purpose of engaging all senses in the collection of perceptual data.

FORMAL TOUR Accompanied or guided tour with a person familiar with the environment to supplement your perceptions or clarify operations.

HIDDEN ANONYMOUS or IDENTIFIED Observer records predetermined behaviors or attributes without interfering

BEHAVIOR MAPPING Records movement and actions to track behavioral patterns.

TRACE EVIDENCE Documents physical elements which result directly or indirectly from human action.

ETHNOGRAPHY Involves immersing oneself in a culture, identifying artifacts, daily patterns and rituals to holistically understand the subjects in their natural environment.

MODELS, DRAWINGS, PROTOTYPES which allow subjects to imagine your idea and give feedback.

TYPES OF OBSERVATION FOR INTERIOR DESIGN

Figure 2.5 Five basic categories of observation for interior design with preparation tasks involved for each method.

on sketched plans or maps. We can either be hidden from them, as is possible in a public setting. Or we can be an identified outsider when we take a tour of a facility or when people know they are being observed. We can engage with people we are studying in varying degrees of participant observation. We can participate peripherally, or we can fully engage with those we are observing. If our actions result in a benefit to those being studied, as a by-product or intentionally designed into our study, it is referred to as **action research**. We can construct models or prototypes that create simulations of reality and record how people respond to them. And, we can go further by setting up controlled environments to conduct experiments to observe how people act under given conditions.

Interior designers can also use other experiential techniques to document our sensory information by writing, taking photos, sketching, and audio or visual recordings. In this way we can capture more subjective impressions at a place or during an event.

Figure 2.6 shows a photo and field notes taken by an interior designer while she was observing a new feature installed in a Japanese garden. While observing for one hour, she noted how many people used the new stepping stones, rather than the wooden bridge, to cross a shallow water feature. She categorized them into three groups: men, women, and children (defined under the apparent age of 12). Her data showed that in 20 minutes, seven men, ten women, and 39 children had made their way over the stones. In addition to counting the number of people, she also made note of the snippets of conversation she heard. They seemed to indicate joy and encouraged each other verbally. Her sketched behavioral map helped her realize that the physical design of this feature—dimensions of the depth of the water and the size and placement of stones— contributed to the low risk and high reward.

Vickery (2014) recommends the following two techniques combinations for observing healthcare environments. **Photo journaling** combines photography and note-taking. Designers equip patients and staff with cameras and ask them to take photos of spaces, objects, or operational processes that enhance or detract from the patient experience. These photo journalists then provide notes describing the significance of each image. **Shadowing** allows designers to collect data in real-time situations

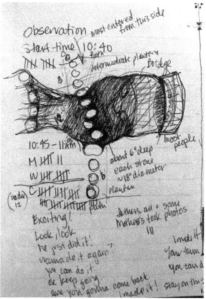

Figure 2.6 Observation field data taken to record behavior at stepping stones in a Japanese garden. Photo on left; field notes and sketched map on right.

Pictures taken during field research

by observing caregivers or patients while following them in their work activities. This *person-centered* data collection method allows you to look at workflow patterns, patient interaction, way-finding challenges, travel distances, inefficient practices, repetitive activities, or unsafe conditions. The observations are then captured and categorized. Shadowing and interviewing can be combined to produce *"a day in the life"* snapshot. A researcher shadows a patient and takes notes based on observations. Following the day-long experience, patients are interviewed to evaluate their healthcare experience.

Figure 2.7 shows a student's photo journal to record her observation of children in a playground. She decided to focus on the play equipment rather than take photos of the children, and caption each image with a summary of the behavior she observed.

Figure 2.7 A student's photo journal of observation in a playground.

Looking at Project Context

"The site is the one unique thing to every project. There are two places inspiration comes from: the site and the client. And there's the unique combination of the two" (J. Luce, personal communication, January 3, 2008).

When we start a new project, we must gather information about the site. The interior design of a space depends on the exterior. In fact, in most cases, the interior of a building is inextricably linked to the exterior. Your building is not hermetically sealed from the environment. It is organically and structurally connected to its surroundings. Figure 2.8 shows how the program must fit the site for the design solution to be successful.

Gathering information about a site can be very exciting and rewarding. All buildings are rooted in a context—whether it relates to natural features such as the sun, the ocean, or existing trees, as in a rural or country environment; or whether it has a relationship nestled between other houses in a suburban neighborhood; or whether it finds itself in the urban landscape surrounded by a "concrete jungle." Because no two objects can occupy the same place at the same time, each site is unique. Each site has particular zoning restrictions and building codes to follow, distinctive views, and so on. Buildings are like living creatures. They take in nutrients (deliveries, entrance of occupants, fresh air), they give off by-products (trash removal, plumbing waste, off-gassing), and they change over time (deterioration, future growth, and alteration). Viewing the building as an organic entity will help you to envision the type of information you need to collect before starting the project. For example, if you had the background plans for a building shell and did not gather information about the exterior environment as well as the interior, you might not know that the view of the ocean is to the west, the parking lot is on the north, and there is a very noisy school playground to the south. Without this information to inform your design of a corporate office, you might inadvertently locate the storage room to the west, the front entrance on the east, and the director's office to the south. Do you think the director would be happy with her office far from the view and adjacent to the noise? So you must look outside the building first to determine the constraints and possibilities of the site.

In the professional environment, many times it is the client who determines the site, because the client has already purchased or leased a property or wants to renovate a home that the family has lived in for years. But frequently, in both commercial and institutional design, a client will look to the designer to determine the best location for the project. The client may have a real estate agent assemble several choices for the designer's consideration. This kind of service is called a **feasibility study**.

A designer not only determines whether the building is physically suitable to accommodate the needs of the program but also may determine whether the local demographics (characteristics of the population living and working in the area) will support the new project, or whether the existing services (plumbing/sewer/electrical) will support the new function, as in converting a shoe store into a restaurant.

Where should you start? Figure 2.9 shows the concentric rings in which the project site is conceptually embedded to help you visualize the layers described next. Each layer has different key aspects to look at, listed here:

Region: What is the climate? Look at maps and travel websites to find out the natural features and weather patterns. What is the culture? Are there resources which highlight the history of the area? You may want to know what language is spoken here, or what are local community cultures? Visit www.census.gov.

Locale: What is life like in the neighborhood? Visit real estate websites that give vignettes: holistic, multifaceted neighborhood profiles that provide a snapshot of the life of the area, demographic information, crime statistics, and history. You may also look at local business districts or community plans and maps to note public transportation hubs, bus routes, and other traffic patterns. What is the walkability of the area? Identify local amenities such as parks, schools, coffee shops, etc. Also note potential sources of noise, unpleasant odors, or potential safety issues.

On the reality television show *Kitchen Nightmares*, chef and restaurateur Gordon Ramsay helps failing restaurants become successful. One of the first things Ramsay does is to look around for other restaurants in the neighborhood. He uses that information to determine what does NOT exist, so that the new restaurant will enjoy freedom from competition. It is notable that often what is NOT observed is just as important as what IS observed—if not more so.

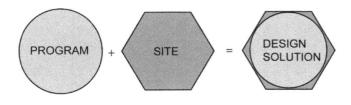

Figure 2.8 Conceptual diagram showing how the program fits the site for a successful design solution.

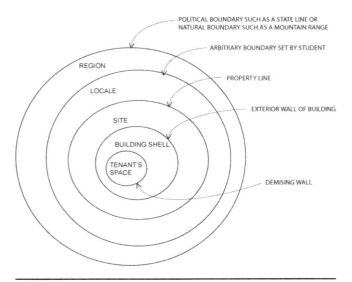

Figure 2.9 The concentric boundaries in which a project site is conceptually embedded.

Figure 2.10 Velcro wall in tile showroom allows designers to play, supporting the concept "an interactive playground for designers."

The author of this book was commissioned to design a tile showroom in Manhattan. She tells this story: "The first thing I did was visit all of the other tile showrooms in Manhattan. Each had a different way of displaying tile, and each had a different target audience. One used large full-scale vignettes of kitchens and bathrooms to illustrate how that store's tile could be used. With permission, I documented that showroom as a case study through floor plan sketches and photographs. Another tile showroom used small wood boards, approximately 12 inches wide x 18 inches high, to illustrate different tile patterns and materials. These boards were hung by cleats from continuous wood strips that ran the length of the room, allowing customers to view a variety of small amounts of tile. Seeing that these could be easily removed from the wall, I reached to take one down. Immediately, a salesperson came over and asked if she could help me. From this interaction, I realized that my gut instinct was to touch the tile and 'play' with it, which was not allowed in this store. Suddenly, I realized what was missing from the competition: a showroom that invited customers to 'play' with the tile." The design concept was born: "An interactive playground for designers" (see Figure 2.10).

Site: Where are the property boundaries? What is allowed? What is possible? What makes sense? Who owns the property? What are the activities and buildings directly adjacent? How will people arrive to the site? Websites such as scoutred.com give parcel information and overlay zones for applicable codes.

Property boundaries: Visit the site to note entrance(s) and exits, sun path, prevailing breezes, natural features such as lakes and foliage, other site amenities such as fountains or benches, lighting, sounds, scents, other sensory qualities of the site. What are the setbacks required by the zoning and other municipal codes. Are there other restrictions on the property such as easements? Chapter 6 will go into more detail about codes.

Building shell: Inquire at local municipal building department records, building owners, design firm, or real estate agents or property managers to get a background plan or CAD file. If possible, conduct a site visit and **field survey** to document the existing building conditions visually and with a tape measure. What is the condition of the existing structure? What are the constraints and possibilities of the structure? Is it wood, steel, concrete, or masonry? Locate the load-bearing walls and existing utility stacks and plumbing walls.

Tenant space: Look at entrance and exits at demising walls, ceiling heights, window heights, mechanical, electrical, plumbing, existing fixtures, and interior finishes.

Ideally, in terms of a base building plan, what you want is an editable CAD file that can be immediately opened and used. You may be able to obtain a native design document from its original source, the design firm that created it. With a little research, you may be able to locate the architect or designer and obtain the firm's written permission to use the file in your school project. Keep in mind that the design firm may not want to release the file to you due to cost and liability. These CAD files are protected by copyright law, which prohibits their use without the express written permission of the author of the original document. Be respectful when requesting this type of document. Emphasize that you are using the file only for a school project and not for profit. Even if you obtain this kind of file, however, you may want to verify the accuracy of the drawings by conducting a field survey and taking your own measurements of the building.

If you cannot obtain the editable CAD file, the next best thing would be the blueprints or copies of the construction documents. For most commercial sites, these documents would be part of the public record, kept by the local building or planning department in their records department. These documents can be located by their address or block/lot number and can be viewed via microfiche. Sometimes you can get printed copies. Again, the copyright laws protect the original designer, so in

ACTIVITY 2.3
Creating Field Survey of an Existing Building

Purpose: To practice an industry-specific, prescribed way to document existing conditions on a field survey. First, have a team of at least two people, if not three, each with a designated job.

- One person will be responsible for notations.
- The other two will do the measurements with a tape measure.
- One person will be responsible for holding the end of the tape measure and calling out what he is holding it next to ("to wall," "to door opening," "from sill to floor").
- The person at the other end of the tape measure will be responsible for calling out the numerical value in a consistent format. Decide, in advance, whether it will be in units of inches or feet-and-inches (centimeters or meters-and-centimeters), and try not to mix the two.

The person responsible for recording the measurements should decide which will be easier to interpret or which will be easier to enter into the computer when drafting. (Note: Inches tend to work better than feet-and-inches.) Many professional firms have replaced the traditional tape measure with laser measuring devices that give precise lengths.

Use a mechanical pencil with an eraser. A mechanical pencil needs no sharpening; just make sure you have enough lead. Use 8½ x 11-inch or 11 x 17-inch graph paper to sketch out each floor plan to fit on its own sheet of paper. For better results, put a sheet of graph paper underneath a sheet of vellum on a large clipboard and do your sketching on that. Pick one spot as the origin and use that spot to begin all of the measurements for that wall. In a multiple-story building, the spot should be structurally consistent on all floors. The following are standard abbreviations:

- M.O. Masonry Opening
- W.H. Window Height
- S.H. Sill Height
- C.L. Centerline
- B.O. Bottom Of
- O.A. Over All
- C.H. Ceiling Height (or put the measurement in an oval which signifies it indicates ceiling height)
- A.F.F. Above Finished Floor

It is usual to measure to the centerline of a window and then measure the width of the window. Another industry standard is to put ceiling heights in an oval. List objects measured in a consistent order: first by length, then by width, and finally by height. Wear protective clothing and comfortable shoes or boots. (You never know the condition of the existing building. You may find yourself crawling into a dusty attic or wading through unexpected ponds on the roof.) Figure 2.11 is an example of a field measurements document you might create.

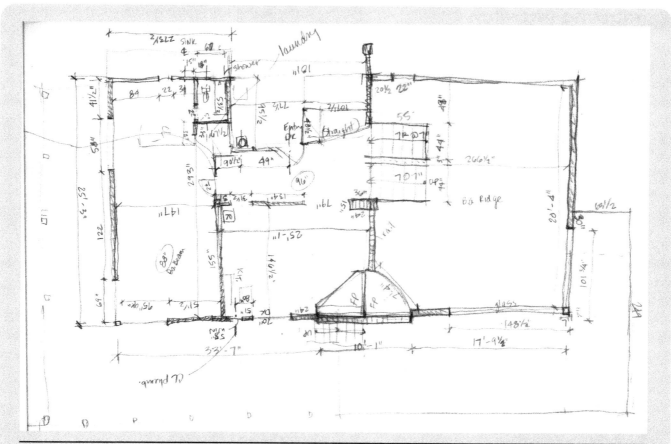

Figure 2.11 Example of hand-drawn site measurements.

many cases you will be asked to fill out a form requesting the original designer's permission to copy the files. Allow time for this process to occur, as it can take up to 30 days.

If these documents are not available through the city's records department, brainstorm about who might have these documents. Contractors, consultants who worked on the project, or the building's owner or property management company may have them. If the property is for sale or lease, the real estate agent or leasing agent may have floor plans.

If none of these sources has the information you need, here are a few questions to ask yourself:

- Is the building historically significant? If it is, you may want to try your local historical society.
- Is the building part of the city's infrastructure of public services, such as a firehouse or a building within a city-operated park? Some city agencies

maintain records of their own buildings and would be able to supply you with a copy.

As a last resort, most buildings have a posted "Building Exit Plan" that would give you an idea of the shape of the building and the location of elevators, stairs, and exits. You could use this information as a starting point for creating your own documents from field measurements.

Even if you are able to get a complete set of construction documents, you should double-check the information in the documents against the actual field measurements to verify the accuracy of the as-built plans. Professional designers may refer to the information on the existing plans that were prepared by previous designers, architects, and engineers, but they are legally responsible for generating their own drawings based on field measurements taken by themselves or their staff.

Conducting Interviews

The interview process can be uncomfortable or intimidating. You may be afraid to ask questions, especially when dealing with people you don't know. However, interviewing people is *essential* to the field of interior design. Further, interviewing is a skill, not a talent. You can become more confident and adept at this process through continued practice and experience of what works and what does not work. Watching skilled interviewers, such as Oprah Winfrey or Katie Couric, can help you build confidence and pick up some of the nonverbal cues that help an interview succeed.

Conducting personal reports involves taking information directly from an individual or a group of people. An **interview** is a type of personal report in which two or more people discuss personal or professional matters, in which one person asks questions of the other. For the purpose of interior design, it means to query someone to obtain information relevant to a design project.

According to Patton (1990), there are six areas of inquiry that can be asked in past, present, or future tense:

1. *Behaviors*—About what a person has done or is doing or will. do
2. *Opinions/Values*—About what a person thinks about a topic.
3. *Feelings*—Note that respondents sometimes respond with "I think . . ." instead of "I feel," so be careful to note that you're looking for feelings.
4. *Knowledge*—What someone knows factually about a topic, occurrence, or area of expertise.
5. *Sensory*—About what people have seen, touched, heard, tasted, smelled, or experienced physically.
6. *Background/Demographics*—Standard descriptive or background questions, such as age, education, residence, or income level.

Information interviews are concerned with gathering information to discover meanings and to test theories. A *theory* is a description of reality, or a proposed view that seeks to make sense of the interrelation of phenomena. Preparation also involves making a list of questions, putting the questions in a logical order, and orchestrating the format of the interview—formal or informal. You might administer these questions aloud in an interview. Alternatively, you could print the list of questions and distribute the list to a larger audience of people to fill out—this would be called a survey (discussed later in this chapter).

Interior designers interview clients to find out their goals, wants, and needs. Sometimes designers use the term **client** to mean all possible users of the space. However, this textbook uses *client* to refer specifically to the owner, organization, corporation, company, or decision-making agent who is responsible for hiring the designer, making the key design decisions, and/or funding the project. Your design project has a real client or an acting client. What do you want to know from your client? Obvious question content will address budget, function, location, size, and expected number of end-users. In an interview, you must also ask questions to determine the client's underlying values, belief system, and goals, and the mission of the project.

Interior designers interview people to find out the choreography of how they will use the space. There are ordinarily different kinds of **end-users** in any project. For example, in a daycare center there would be administrative staff, full-time and part-time care providers, volunteers, and family members or caregivers who drop off their children—as well as the children themselves. It is also necessary to consider the maintenance and security staff, who might also be interviewed for their experience and opinions. Two subgroups of end-users would be the *participant* end-user, the current or actual user of the space, and the *potential* end-user, a person who possesses the characteristics of someone who would use the space in the future. In a museum project, identifying a potential end-user may involve asking questions of people who (1) frequent museums, (2) are interested in art, or (3) live in the neighborhood.

A **focus group** is a small group of potential users of a service, product, or space who have been prescreened for certain characteristics—for example, expectant mothers who plan to work (for a daycare center)—gathered together and asked a few questions. The goal is to obtain high-quality information that arises from an in-depth conversation among qualified potential end-users. Focus groups are most successful for projects like churches, schools, and community centers in which participants may have varying view points and vested interests in the outcome of the project.

Interior designers need to gain information on a topic or project type from relevant experts. For example, when designing a spiritual space, it may be important to ask questions of a member of the clergy, or when designing a dental office it may be important to interview a dentist, hygienist, or receptionist. Experts in a particular field will have insights and knowledge that will be essential to the success of your design. Interior designers often use interviews to gain information about a specific professional or technical skill related to the area of design. You could interview a structural engineer when designing a mezzanine in a retail space; a Leadership in Energy and Environmental Design (LEED)–certified professional when considering sustainable features in your project; or a woodworker about fabrication techniques, properties of wood, and joinery when designing wood furniture.

When considering arranging an interview, ask yourself the following questions:

- *Why am I conducting this interview rather than gathering information from other sources?*
- *Who are ideal candidates to be interviewed? A professional who works in the field? An academic who studies the issue? A published author who has already written books on the topic? A person in the local community who has dealt with this issue in his or her personal life? (Wheeler, 2008)*
- *Is the person available for an interview? How can I contact him or her?*—Keep in mind that most people are usually flattered by the attention and are willing to participate in an information interview, particularly if they know you're a student.
- *Do I have a solid base of knowledge about the topic that will enhance my credibility with interviewees?*
- *Have I addressed issues of confidentiality? Have I gotten written permission to use the information I receive from the interview?*

- *Can I get a site tour before the start of the interview?*—A tour may help inspire questions you hadn't thought of before.
- *Have I established myself as a trustworthy and reliable person to the staff or receptionist (the "gatekeeper"), and have I instilled confidence in the interviewee? Does my attire match the cultural expectations of my interviewee?*
- *Can I use a recording device without making the interviewee uncomfortable? Or should I plan to take handwritten notes?*

Interview Types

Interviews range in formality and structure, depending on the situation. Note the progression of interview types displayed in Figure 2.12. The most casual type of interview is the informal conversation, in which no predetermined questions are asked. A researcher happens upon the subject without prearrangement and asks a few warm-up questions; then, during the interview, the researcher "goes with the flow." For example, as you enter a building, you encounter a resident and ask how many people live in the building. In the elevator, you ask another resident about her experience living in the building. As you are leaving, you ask a person next door to tell you a little bit about the neighborhood. All of these interviews are chance occurrences that yield a cursory response from a singular subject which may align with your needs.

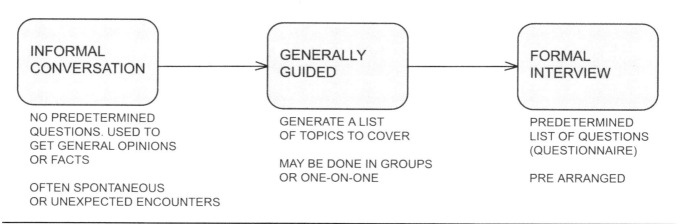

Figure 2.12 Interview types from informal to formal.

The generally guided approach uses a predetermined list of topics to be covered to ensure that you get more of the information you are looking for yet allows for a degree of freedom and adaptability in getting this information. For example, to determine the public's opinion about the way-finding/signage system currently used in a local hospital, you informally survey random staff members, patients, and visitors in the waiting room. You ask each person about (1) their ease in locating destinations; (2) their opinions of the signage, wording, graphics, mounting heights, and location; and (3) possible suggestions for improvement. You do not ask everyone the questions in the same way; you vary them depending on whom you are asking.

In a formal interview, a fully prepared list of questions is presented to an interviewee, typically at a prearranged time and place. The interview can consist of many types of questions, as outlined in the following section.

Question Types

There are different types of questions. A *primary* question introduces a topic. A *follow-up* question would be an attempt to elicit further information, as shown in Table 2.1.

Questions also range from *open-ended* to *closed-ended*, as in the following examples in Table 2.2. While closed-ended and yes/no questions might be appropriate at some points, typically limit the number of these kinds of questions. The main purpose of the interview is to acquire in-depth new knowledge from the interviewee's rich past experience. Questions that allow longer responses, and engage the interviewee in storytelling, can result in obtaining important details.

There are also certain types of questions to avoid, including *leading* or *loaded* questions and *compound* questions as well as *tagged* statements (see Table 2.3).

Sometimes, the most effective type of follow-up question is not a question, but a **probe**. "A *probe* is the interviewer's

---

TABLE 2.1

EXAMPLES OF PRIMARY AND FOLLOW-UP QUESTIONS

Primary Question	Response	Follow-Up
How did you first get interested in surfing?	My parents gave me a surfboard on my fourth birthday.	What happened then?
Are you satisfied with your office space?	No. I can't seem to get much work done.	Why do you think that is?
What is your favorite thing about being a teacher?	When they are struggling but then their eyes light up . . .	When did that last happen?

TABLE 2.2

EXAMPLES OF THE RANGE OF OPEN-ENDED TO CLOSED-ENDED QUESTIONS

Broad Closed-Ended	Narrow Closed-Ended	Yes/No	Moderately Closed	Closed-Ended
What don't you like about your kitchen?	How do you typically prepare a meal?	Will this stove meet your needs?	How many cooks use this kitchen?	Is this a one-cook kitchen or two-cook kitchen?
Tell me about a typical day in the office.	What is your role in the office?	Do you have enough privacy for meetings?	What are the qualifications for your position?	Would you describe your workspace as (a) excellent, (b) good, or (c) poor?
What made you decide to open a restaurant?	What made you decide to locate the restaurant in this location?	Are you satisfied with the layout of the dining area?	What are some of the issues raised by the staff?	Have you had more complaints about the lighting, the noise, or the size of tables?

prompting for further elaboration of an answer" (Zeisel, 2006). The most powerful probe is *silence*. Most people are uncomfortable with silence, so they will try to "fill" it by talking. As the interviewer, resist the inclination to talk; instead, wait for the interviewee to continue. You can increase the effectiveness of the silence with nonverbal cues such as a slight nod or an attentive, expectant facial expression and eye contact. Examples of probes and when to use them are provided in Table 2.4.

TABLE 2.3

EXAMPLES OF QUESTIONS TO AVOID

Questions to Avoid	Reason	Examples
Leading question	Implies you expect a certain answer	*Would you agree that safety is the first priority? Does this office seem too small to you? Are you ever going to organize this place?*
Loaded question	Implies an underlying negative belief	*Don't you think this color scheme seems dated? How do you get work done in here? Why wouldn't you want a window here?*
Tagged question	Inserted at the end of questions which tends to weaken or confuse	*You are planning to remodel your kitchen, aren't you? All children go through that, right? This color seems too bright, don't you think?*
Compound question	Two or more questions combined which does not allow each question to be answered separately	*What is the best part of your job and how often do you get to do it? Who usually visits the museum during the day and in the evening? How often do you get out of the office and do you go to the park across the street?*

TABLE 2.4

EXAMPLES OF PROBES AND WHEN TO USE THEM

	When to Use	Examples
Nudge	To encourage talking (enhanced by nod or raised eyebrows)	*I see.* *Go on.* *Really?*
Clearinghouse	To make sure you have all the information on that topic	*Is there anything else?*
Depth	To elicit greater detail	*Please explain*
Clarity	To understand the use of a word or phrase	*What do you mean by "uncomfortable"?*
Feelings	To explore emotions	*Why do you think you feel that way?*
Back on Track	To refocus conversation topic	*Let's return to your years as an editor.* *You began by talking about your lack of storage . . .*
Accuracy	To verify information	*Did you say that was in 1988 or 1998? How do you spell that? Did you say "old" or "bold"?*
Echo	An active listening technique that involves literally repeating back what was said.	
Summary	Paraphrasing a response to make sure you understand it	*So what I'm hearing you say is that you like the first option. Like you said, you need more privacy. Let me check to see if I understand all your points.*

Interview Tips

According to Carter McNamara (1999), question order is essential to getting the maximum benefit. He has a few additional tips:

1. *Ask about facts before asking about controversial matters (such as feelings or beliefs)*. With this approach, interviewees can more easily engage in the interview before warming up to more personal matters.
2. *Intersperse fact-based questions throughout the interview*. Long lists of fact-based questions tend to leave interviewees disengaged.
3. *Ask questions about the present before questions about the past or future*. It's usually easier for interviewees to talk about the present and then work into the past or future, especially if the topic is a sensitive or emotional one.

Upon conclusion of the interview, your goal is to leave the interviewee feeling positive and satisfied with the interview. The interviewer is responsible for signaling the upcoming conclusion, as with "My final question . . . ."

A final summary is a consolidation of the entire interview, and it provides a test of your listening and note-taking skills. As your conversation with the interviewee ends:

- Highlight key aspects and overall conclusions.
- Point out areas of agreement and disagreement.
- Ask the interviewee about the accuracy of your summary.
- Close your notebook, turn off the audio recorder, etc.
- If necessary, restate the confidential nature of the interview—and the purpose and use of the information.
- Be alert to other bits and pieces of information, as the interviewee may relax and relay important information as part of an informal chat.
- A sincere farewell marks the end of a post-interview discussion. And it is customary to thank your interviewee in a follow-up email or handwritten note.

There are several ways to compose a post-interview record. If the interview was audio-recorded, you may want to type a written **transcription**. If you took notes during the interview, you may want to write out the responses in full sentences *as soon as possible* while the conversation is still fresh in your mind. You may also summarize the interview in a report using direct quotes from the interviewee or paraphrasing what the interviewee said. Make sure to record information necessary to cite the interview, including the proper spelling of the interviewee's name, appellations, affiliations, and the date of the interview. In addition to documenting the interview, you may want to do a post-interview assessment. Your objective in this assessment is to evaluate the information you have just obtained for accuracy, relevance, and completeness. Can you verify the facts you have collected?

Alternative Interviewing Techniques— Image-Based Inquiry

Graphic representations were used in an interview setting back in 1921, with the Rorschach inkblot test, which evaluated the psychological interpretation of an inkblot, seeking to show the correlation between an image and the projection of the respondent's thoughts, emotions, and beliefs onto the image. During the 1940s and 1950s, the pioneer sociologist Robert Merton often used images and photos in "focused interviews" to help elicit feelings about war from war veterans, with the belief that people are sometimes moved more by an image than a word. In his book *Inquiry by Design*, John Zeisel (2006) also mentions using photos or drawings as a nonverbal probe—for example, to assist in getting a respondent to more clearly visualize something that happened in the past (such as showing a victim in a police interrogation a photo of the crime scene), or to get office workers to think more spatially about a room or an environment (for example, showing a photo of a doorway or a lock on the door).

The architectural researcher Edith Cherry pioneered the concept of participant end-user involvement. She writes extensively about involving end-users (schoolchildren) in the design process by having them participate in creative drawing exercises to envision their ideal school. The measure of the exercise is not so much in whether the ideas make their way into the final design, but did we have a good time? And did the kids feel that they had made a contribution? Did they get excited about their new school? Did we as designers form a commitment to do a good project for them? (Cherry, personal communication, June 4, 2008).

Sometimes a person is unable to answer verbal or written questions for a variety of reasons: age (too young or too old), mental or physical impairment, they speak a different language, or other social or cultural barriers that make it difficult for people to share intimate details about themselves. Sometimes people just cannot verbalize what they want or need. People tend to assign meaning to images. Therefore, designers may use images in the interview process to get interviewees to go deeper, into regions to which words cannot take us. To get a clearer picture of a client's mental images of style, a kitchen designer may ask the client to collect clippings from design magazines. The word *modern* may mean something different to a designer than it means to a client, so images tend to help clarify discrepancies in historical styles. Henry Sanoff, in his book *Visual Research Methods in Design* (1991), talks about extracting cognitive information by asking the participant to record **self-reports**. The form of these reports may be verbal, written (in a diary format), or visual (through photographs or artwork). Interior designers now make extensive use of **image-based inquiry**, even to supplement traditional interviews. There are two main methods: (1) the participant responds to, manipulates, or sorts photos that you provide or (2) the participant provides photographs or generates their own drawings.

One example is a common practice at many weddings of providing a place where guests can upload their digital photos. This is a good way for the wedding party to get an insight into the multiple subjective experiences of their guests. We can use similar techniques to gather information from our study participants, by having them photograph what is important to them about their environments.

The architect Jennifer Luce asked employees of a furniture showroom to photograph what was most important or inspiring to them about the products they sold and about their work environment. She collected more than 500 photographs that included details of the furniture, views of nature, and artistic interpretations of the existing workplace. She used them as a jumping-off point for her own ideas. "When you look at it all—there is the kernel of a really strong innovative and new idea" (J. Luce, personal communication, January 3, 2008).

Another type of self-report is for a client or end-user to compose something, either a drawing or a collage. Figure 2.13 shows a drawing of an ideal kitchen generated by an 11-year-old boy named Bernat. An interior design student, Esther, interviewed him as part of data collection for a family's house remodel. This drawing allowed the boy to express wants and needs in a creative way—he came up with innovative ideas to help his mother cook and serve, provided multiple games, a large area for homework, and a private loft with artificial turf for him to overlook it all. Esther analyzed the drawing to determine that the kitchen serves more than one function in a family home. The central island that Bernat drew represented the family coming together, with different areas on the periphery to support more individual functions.

A patented process for uncovering hidden concepts and distilling information into a design concept is called Zaltman Metaphor Elicitation Technique, commonly referred to as generating a ZMET Collage (http://olsonzaltman .com/zmet/). According to that website:

1. Participants collect a handful of images representing their thoughts and feelings about a particular topic.
2. Each participant is interviewed for up to two hours, using their images as a jumping-off point for discussion.
3. A trained, licensed ZMET® expert analyzes the interviews for surface-level and Deep Metaphors™ and distills them to reveal key insights.

Figure 2.13 Eleven-year-old Bernat draws his ideal kitchen.

Figure 2.15 Jordan produced this collage while interviewing Kristyn. "My client feels like her life is a high-speed tunnel. Family and her faith are the light at the end of the tunnel."

Figure 2.14 Chelsea worked with her client to produce this collage during an image-based interview and derived the following metaphors: "Heart-Centered Space: Seeking Inspiration in the Unexpected."

The interviews with ZMET result in composite images that represent the subconscious needs and wants of the interviewees. Researchers study the images, along with the participant's verbal explanation, to derive a **metaphor**. A *metaphor* is a poetic figure of speech that expresses an understanding of one concept in terms of another concept, to reveal some hidden similarity or correlation between the two—for example, "All the world's a stage." In this case, researchers seek to understand the wants and needs of the client on a deep, subconscious level, and they strive to create a mutual understanding through a combination of symbolic words and images.

Based on metaphors that evolve out of the interview process, designers can generate design concepts that guide the project during the schematic phase. Figures 2.14, 2.15, and 2.16 are examples of student collages that resulted from in-depth interview sessions with a classmate acting as a client. These collages were analyzed by the student designers to produce a concept for their client's personal retreat.

Figure 2.16 Interior design student, Elena, composed this collage with her client who views a home as a nest: She further explains, "A nest is made of a variety of materials much like a family is comprised of different personalities; love is what brings us together."

Conducting Surveys

In general, to **survey** means to query (people) to collect data for the analysis of some aspect of a group or an area. In an even more technical sense, to survey means to do a statistical study of a sample population by asking questions about knowledge, opinions, preferences, and other aspects of people's lives. For the purposes of interior design, to survey means to reach out to people to obtain information that is essential to the programming and design process. Like interviews, surveys attempt to get information from people using a list of questions—very often a written list, which is usually referred to as a questionnaire. Both interviews and surveys are a type of personal report.

You would use a survey when there are simply too many people for you to interview personally, or when you need to get the opinions of a majority of users. For example, you could interview a single student to get her preference of color to paint a classroom, but you would need to conduct a survey to find out what the *majority* of students at the school would like the color to be. You would choose to prepare and conduct a survey when your task is to turn qualitative information (opinions, feelings, and beliefs) into quantitative information (statistics). To do this, you must design a standardized questionnaire made up of questions that can turn opinions into numbers or percentages. It is not an easy task, but when it is done correctly it can yield very useful data for your project.

A **questionnaire** is a series of topic-related questions written to help you discover participant opinions (Sommer & Sommer, 2002). The reasons for using a *standardized questionnaire*—an identical series of questions distributed to a group of people—are (1) to survey as many people as possible with the most timely and efficient means and then (2) to be able to turn those people's responses (raw data/qualitative data) into quantities such as percentages or majorities. This numerical statistical data has a variety of uses, but primarily it is used to form a substantial basis for future design decisions. The following sections will take you from collecting the raw data by conducting a survey to communicating the results (including guidance on representing the data through graphic or visual means such as graphs, charts, and tables). We will also explore the process of analyzing the results and the different ways of interpreting the statistical data.

Types of Surveys

Are the employees of the company satisfied with their work environment? Can they offer any suggestions for improvement? An end-user questionnaire is aimed at uncovering raw data that would support or refute any preconceived notion or theory the client has about the experience of the users of the space. This kind of questionnaire must guarantee absolute anonymity so that the respondents can answer the questions honestly and without fear that giving a negative response would affect their job security or otherwise put them at risk. Many times an end-user has valuable information or feedback about the current space that would then require more in-depth study through direct observation or one-on-one interviews.

A target market questionnaire enables you to identify your end-user group when the group is not known. Who would most likely use your new facility? This kind of questionnaire helps you to generate a *user profile* in the written program (discussed in Chapter 4)—or to elaborate on a user profile if a vague notion of who would use the space has already been determined. For example, if your client would like to open an alternative birthing clinic, what are the characteristics of the target audience? Obviously, the target audience would be pregnant women or women who are planning to become pregnant, but how can you more fully detail your user profile to design a space that would cater to this user group's specific needs and closely align with their sense of aesthetics?

If you have already identified your target market and you know the user profile, you might use a *focus group questionnaire* to gather opinions about potential users of the space, such as visitors, patrons, or customers. As previously discussed in this chapter, the group of potential users you would assemble for a group discussion is called a *focus group*. The primary benefit of a focus group is to generate new knowledge or greater understanding about opinions through discussion among the members which can be audio-recorded and transcribed. A focus group can also be a type of informal, yet guided interview of multiple people. It is often in familiar surroundings, such as a company break room. Participation can be encouraged by serving food or light snacks.

To evaluate client satisfaction, we can also set up a list of questions to be answered at the completion of a project. Usually, this list of questions is referred to as a *client satisfaction survey* or *exit poll*. This information could be used to improve customer service or collect references for future projects.

Questionnaire Design and Distribution Methods (The Act of Surveying)

The graphic layout of a questionnaire is very important. The questionnaire should not appear long, intimidating, or confusing. It should be clear, concise, and inviting to the respondent. Several items must be stated clearly at the outset: (1) why people are being surveyed, (2) how long the questionnaire should take to complete, (3) instructions on how to fill out the questions (with pencil or pen), and (4) what to do with the completed questionnaire.

You might offer incentives for completing the survey, such as a coupon for a free coffee or snack, or a gift certificate, or the promise to be entered into a raffle for a prize. Professional survey companies often have respondents earn points for completing surveys.

A questionnaire can be written, oral (the researcher can ask the respondent the questions and record the respondent's answers), or electronic (distributed via the Internet or through email). Written surveys can be mailed to the respondents, or distributed via mailboxes at work, or they can be left in a public area along with a drop box for returning completed surveys. It is important to get permission when distributing a survey in this last manner. You cannot simply go into a classroom or wait outside a business without securing permission. In fact, it is important to understand the difference between private property and public spaces. While free speech is protected under the U.S. Constitution, interfering with business could be a complicated issue; so it is important to obtain written permission from the businesses you may affect when you're attempting to collect information from subjects in a survey.

Once you've completed the first draft of your questionnaire, it is advisable to test the questionnaire (1) for the length of time it takes to complete and (2) for clarity. "Make a few copies of your first-draft questionnaire, and then ask at least three readers to complete it. Time them as they respond. . . . Discuss with them any confusion or problems they experience" (Axelrod & Cooper, 2008, p. 699).

Consider assembling a focus group just for the purpose of pretesting the questionnaire. Did you get the kind of responses you were seeking? Did the group misunderstand any of the questions? Review the group's answers with them to determine whether the intent of each question was clear. Keep in mind that you may have to revise the wording of a question, the order of the questions, or the type of question. You may have to add further instructions. For example, a questionnaire recently distributed at a school failed to tell respondents what to do with the survey after they completed it! Believe it or not, this kind of error occurs quite often because the researcher is so caught up in the content that simple logistical tactics often go overlooked.

The most popular and promising method of distribution is through the Internet. Websites such as SurveyMonkey.com and Wufoo.com offer students a way to customize a questionnaire and distribute it to a list of email addresses. The respondents are ensured anonymity and can respond at their own convenience. The limitation to this method is that you can collect data only from persons who have an email address or access to a computer.

How can you reach your intended audience? Distributing or conducting a survey involves a certain degree of salesmanship and optimism, as well as an abundance of energy and courage. Doing a survey in person requires a great deal of time and legwork. For example, if you are trying to collect information about shopping habits in a grocery store, you may need to stand outside as people are entering or exiting in order to ask your questions. If you are planning to survey students in the student lounge, you must prepare a sign and a drop box and plan to be there to answer questions when the lounge is full of students.

It is often difficult to overcome people's suspicions about how you are going to use their information. So you must establish a rapport with your survey subjects. Whether by speaking to potential subjects personally or by writing a clear and compelling introduction to the survey, you need to (1) establish that you are a student, (2) assure their anonymity and confidentiality, and (3) pinpoint your project goals.

Types of Survey Questions

Survey question types should be mostly closed-ended, because a large number of people are being consulted and it is easier to quantify information that has a limited number of choices. You must know *exactly* what you are trying to find out and what your goals for the questionnaire are, so that you ask questions that are specific and you quickly get to the point of what you are trying to accomplish. You may want to use different types of questions to verify an answer. Asking a question in more than one way will help limit the chance that your results will be skewed because your audience was confused by a particular question. Your questionnaire not only needs to present your questions, it needs to identify the characteristics of the subject so that you can more easily see whether you are reaching your end-user or target market. To achieve this, make sure you integrate the following kinds of identifying questions in your questionnaire.

Qualifiers are questions that test whether the respondent fits a list of certain predetermined qualifications. You may want to ask these questions up front, because they will determine whether the respondent fits the user profile of the population. You'll need to collect simple **demographic data**—such as age, gender, education level, occupation, and mobility/ability levels—that would qualify the subject as a member of your defined population. Qualifiers can also be questions about the person's lifestyle, habits, and preferences. For example, if you are looking for people who frequent hair salons more than once a month, you may have to compose two questions: one that asks whether respondents have ever been to a salon, then a follow-up question regarding intervals of frequency—less than once a month, once a month, and more than once a month.

Open-ended questions should be used only when the sample population is small or as a follow-up to a series of closed-ended questions as an opportunity to get clarification or elaboration. It is generally too difficult to translate the many answers generated by open-ended questions into statistics that would identify trends. Imagine tallying election results if all the candidates were write-ins!

Multiple-choice questions can come in two varieties: forced-choice and check-all-that-apply. When giving a person a multiple-choice question with only one response required, you want to make sure that the categories are mutually exclusive—that is, that your categories do not overlap. This can be a simple yes/no question. Or it can have different categories, as in age ranges. For example, the age categories "under 11, 11 to 20, 21 to 40, 41 and over" are mutually exclusive (Zeisel, 1984, p. 164). Determining how to partition responses into groups is called **coding** (Zeisel, p. 164). There is an art to dividing up possible answers, as there are several different types of data: nominal, interval, and ordinal.

Nominal categories are different possible answers based on *names* of things, such as kinds of furniture (chair, table, or desk); or *descriptive* words, such as "curved, active, or busy"; or *adjectives* to describe the way a space feels, such as "intimidating, powerful, or comforting." If you wanted to know the types of activities that a person does in a room, you could generate a list for the respondent to choose from, such as "Sleep, Eat, Study, Entertain, Relax, Play, Work. . . ." When a question is a list, you want to make sure it is *exhaustive*—which means that you have listed all of the possible responses. This mistake is often found in questionnaires developed by students. If respondents can think of another option as a response to a question, they may become annoyed or frustrated. In addition, your data will not be accurate. To make an incomplete list exhaustive, researchers add an "Other" category (Zeisel, 1984, p. 164).

Interval categories involve numbers, such as the example of age ranges used earlier. Some additional examples are number of hours, size of office, or ranges in income level. Usually the items are divided into increments that make sense to the user.

When you want responses that indicate frequency, intensity of feeling, or degree to which respondents agree or disagree with a statement, you will want to use a *ratings scale*. Usually the question type involves creating categories along an *ordinal scale*—a ranking of measurement that ranges from "low to high," "least to most," or "agree to disagree." A typical example is the **Likert Attitude Scale**. This is a widely used scale in which respondents are given a list of statements and asked whether they "strongly agree," "agree," are "undecided," are "neutral," "disagree," or "strongly disagree." These are used to measure attitudes (Fraenkel et al., 1999). It is a good idea to group these questions together under a single heading so that the respondent becomes familiar with the scale and can move more quickly through the questions (Zeisel, 1984). Should there be an odd number of divisions or an even number of divisions? An odd number of divisions gives a "neutral" center value, while an even number of divisions forces respondents to take a non-neutral position.

Another type of question that uses an ordinal scale is ranking in order of importance or priority. These types of questions are often difficult to answer. To make ranking questions conceptually easier, you could vary them by, for example, allocating a percentage or a fixed amount to each category. For example, "what percentage of your total budget do you envision spending on each of the following kitchen components? Must total 100 percent." Another variation would be to have respondents select the "top three categories" that correspond with their priorities. It may be less intimidating to the respondent to just choose a few items from a list.

Sentence completion questions are open-ended questions that give the respondent an opportunity to answer in a creative way. These questions can be used judiciously to spark a different kind of response that might influence your design immensely. Or they can be used as a fun, light-hearted way to establish a rapport with an unknown respondent—to humanize the anonymous responses. For example, you could ask, "The most important item in my kitchen is_____., or "I could never live without _____."

Visual interpretation questions allow respondents to respond to an image (a photograph, drawing, or diagram) or to choose from a series of photographs. For example, one student wanted to explore what types of space were most conducive to studying. Using her knowledge of environmental psychology, she selected photos of spaces, each with one variable: size of room, ceiling height, amount of sunlight. She posed questions that had a choice of three photographs each, and she asked the respondent to select the photograph whose content was most conducive to studying. She then increased the complexity by showing photographs of furniture pieces and asking which would accommodate the respondent's needs for studying. She found that most students surveyed preferred to use a bed rather than a chair and desk for studying.

You may find yourself using a combination of these question types in your survey as in the sample shown in Figure 2.17. You can explore an issue through a series of questions or overlapping questions to test the same concept.

There are, of course, some question types that you probably should avoid. The first type is simply *weak questions*. For example, "What is your favorite color?" is a weak question because there are too many ways to interpret or apply the question. It is not specific enough to yield a valid answer. Are you asking a person about her favorite color for a wall in an office or her favorite color for a cocktail dress? This example illustrates an important part of composing a survey: Specificity! Answers would differ depending on the context and the object that is to be colored. Another type of question to avoid is one that *assumes there is a universal meaning to subjective words*, like design terms and adjectives. A good example would be the use of the word *comfortable* in a question. For some people, a "comfortable" space is open, free of clutter, streamlined. Other people would describe "comfortable" as plush, cozy, and full of personal items.

You may not be able to use answers that come from *questions about general likes and dislikes*. Questions like

Figure 2.17 A sample questionnaire using a variety of question types.

QUESTION TYPE	EXAMPLE
QUALIFIER MULTIPLE CHOICE FORCED CHOICE YES/NO	Have you ever gotten a manicure at a salon? Yes / No
CONTINGENCY MULTIPLE CHOICE INTERVALS	If you answered "Yes" to Question 1 How often do you get a manicure at a salon? Cricle one. Less than once/month Once/month More than once/month
MULTIPLE CHOICE NOMINAL CHECK ALL THAT APPLY	What words would you use to describe an ideal salon experience? Circle all that apply. Modern Creative Elegant Natural Sterile Tropical Cozy Indulgent Clean Sensual Eclectic Organized Friendly Fun Other _____
FOLLOW UP OPEN-ENDED	How could a salon make your visit more enjoyable? _____
RATINGS SCALE	I look forward to getting a manicure at a salon. Agree Neutral Disagree
RANKING	Which is most important when choosing a salon? Select only three. ___Cleanliness ___Short wait time ___No wait time ___Professionalism of staff ___Ambience ___Price ___Reputation ___Proximity to home or work ___ Friendliness ___Other (please indicate_____)
SENTENCE COMPLETION	The most annoying part of a salon visit is _____. The most enjoyable part of a salon experience is _____.
VISUAL INTERPRETATION	Which of the following images MOST reflect the feeling you would want in a salon experience? Circle one.

"Do you like your job; why or why not?" and "Do you like to drink wine?" leave too much room for misinterpretation, because they combine feeling, thoughts, beliefs, and actions. Rework these questions to ask about *behavior*. For example, you can ask, "Do you drink wine?" followed by a contingency question about how often or in what situations the respondent drinks wine. Then you can ask specifically about a feeling or belief about alcohol consumption.

Finally, avoid *questions that make assumptions* or lead respondents to take an obvious side on an issue. An example would be "Wouldn't you recycle more often if bins were provided in the cafeteria?" Who would answer "no" to that kind of question?

ACTIVITY 2.4
Writing Questions for Your Interview or Survey

Purpose: To explore different question types to begin writing questions for your interview or survey. Using the template provided in Table 2.5, write two or three questions in each box. Refer to examples in this chapter if you get confused.

TABLE 2.5

QUESTIONNAIRE TEMPLATE TO GET YOU STARTED

Question Type	Purpose	Write Your Questions Here:
Qualifier	To determine whether participant is a good candidate to participate: you could ask about age, gender, . . .could be a yes/no question or categories	1. 2.
Qualifier	Follow-up to determine depth or extent of participant's prior experience	1. 2.
Open-Ended	To determine behavior or preferences	1. 2. 3.
Multiple-Choice	To determine behavior or preferences	1. 2. 3.
Ranking/Scale	To determine preferences	1. 2.
Sentence Completion	To collect innovative ideas	1. 2.
Visual Interpretation	To find deeply rooted or subconscious desires	1. 2.
Other	To collect additional data	1. 2.

Now test your questions by asking them to a fellow classmate. Record his or her responses. Did your question yield the type of information you were hoping for? Or do you need to adjust your question? Revise your questions as necessary.

Survey Sampling—Establishing a Sample

Population includes all the members of a particular group of individuals that you have decided to study or to describe. It is usually very difficult or impossible to study an entire population (Fraenkel et al., 1999). Consider these examples of *entire* populations:

- All persons who have a family member who has been diagnosed with autism
- All women who are experiencing or have experienced infertility
- All preteens in the United States who play video games
- All teachers, staff, and students of a particular school
- All persons who live or work in a certain part of town

A **sample** is a subgroup of a population that is thought or meant to be representative of the population (Fraenkel et al., 1999). An individual member of the sample group would be called a *subject*, a *respondent*, or a *participant*.

The most common method of selecting a sample group of subjects is a *random sample*: selecting people by chance. The idea is that each member of the population has an equal probability of being selected, which reduces the likelihood of a sample being biased (Fraenkel et al., 1999).

You could use the questionnaire as a standardized list of questions and personally survey your sample group. If you stood outside a grocery store to conduct your survey,

your sample population would be any shoppers who might stop to answer a few questions. This would be called a *convenience sample*, because the subjects were chosen based on the fact that they were the closest to you or easiest to gather (see Figure 2.18). If you approached only those people who looked to you as though they bought a lot of groceries or bought a certain item, you would obtain a *purposive sample*; that means the subjects were selected deliberately and therefore may not reflect the characteristics of the population as a whole (Fraenkel et al., 1999).

Whether you choose a convenience sample or a random sample or a *stratified random sample* (this last type is a sample adjusted for percentages), your goal is to reduce or minimize **bias** (a systematic mistake based on prejudice or assumption) and to represent the entire population as accurately as possible, identifying and adjusting for variables. Once again, see Figure 2.18 to see how this sampling technique compares to a convenience sample.

REPRESENTING THE DATA

It is important to keep careful records of your survey data. Most researchers recommend using a computer spreadsheet to help you sort and organize the data. Your questionnaire doesn't do you any good if you can't draw new conclusions from the data. After the survey is completed and the data collected, you'll need to assemble the results in some usable format that allows comparison within the subject group, between groups, or both.

Data can be represented in a variety of ways. The key is to select a visualization method that helps you clearly

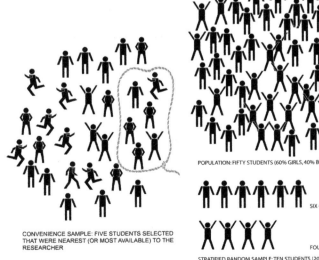

POPULATION: FIFTY STUDENTS (60% GIRLS, 40% BOYS)

SIX GIRLS

FOUR BOYS

CONVENIENCE SAMPLE: FIVE STUDENTS SELECTED THAT WERE NEAREST (OR MOST AVAILABLE) TO THE RESEARCHER

STRATIFIED RANDOM SAMPLE: TEN STUDENTS (20%) WITH PERCENTAGES REFLECTING THE PERCENTAGES OF THE POPULATION VARIABLE

Figure 2.18 Convenience sample and stratified random sample.

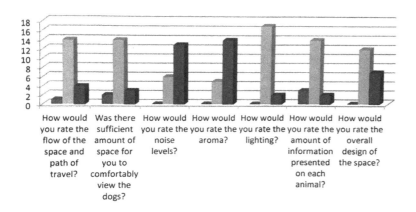

Figure 2.19 Interior design student uses a bar graph to represent how individuals he surveyed rated design elements of an animal adoption center.

■ Great
■ Fair
■ Poor

and powerfully communicate your findings to your intended audience. First, consider organizing the data into traditional charts and graphs. Use *line graphs* or X-Y plots to track changes over short and long periods of time. *Pie charts* do not show changes over time. Instead, use pie charts when you are trying to compare parts of a whole. Use *bar graphs* to compare items across different groups or to track changes over time. Figure 2.19 shows how one student used a bar graph to show data from a survey, how respondents rated design elements (great, fair, poor) in the design of an animal adoption center. We can see clearly that the features that received the lowest ratings were the noise level and aroma.

Next, consider more creative ways to express your data. Statistician and artist Edward Tufte has written four classic books on data visualization, which are incomparable resources for the design student: *Beautiful Evidence* (2006), *The Visual Display of Quantitative Information* (2001), *Visual Explanations* (1997), and *Envisioning Information* (1990). In them he shares graphic

design principles and innovative ways to display your data and other concepts in a visually compelling manner. In Figure 2.20, a student represented her findings as a color-coded map to show managers that the layout of the kitchen prep area caused servers to walk in inefficient paths of travel that often caused them to collide or infer with each other during busy times.

Statistics

Drawing conclusions depends on your interpretation of statistics. A **statistic** is a numerical characteristic of the sample that measures relationships, such as percentages, averages, and tendencies. "*Descriptive statistics* refers to a variety of methods that are used to simplify, summarize, organize, and identify relationships among quantitative data and sometimes to visually display such data" (Fraenkel et al., 1999, p. 20). As William Trochim (2006) explains, *inferential statistics* are used "to reach conclusions that extend beyond the immediate data alone." He continues:

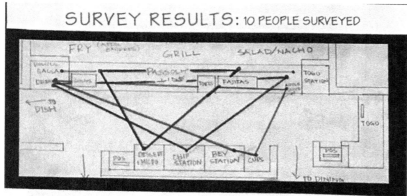

Figure 2.20 A visual summary of data by an interior design student showing how layout of the kitchen causes staff to move in inefficient paths of travel that overlap and conflict with one another.

For instance, we use inferential statistics to try to infer from the sample data what the population might think. Or, we use inferential statistics to make judgments of the probability that an observed difference between groups is a dependable one or one that might have happened by chance in this study. Thus, we use inferential statistics to make inferences from our data to more general conditions; we use descriptive statistics simply to describe what's going on in our data. (Trochim, 2006)

Summary Statements

The way that interior designers most often summarize their survey results is in a text format called a summary statement. A typical summary statement might be "Survey results showed the majority of workers ranked personal storage space as their highest priority and lounge seating as the lowest priority." When you prepare a summary statement, be specific, and acknowledge inherent weakness in your findings, if necessary. Let readers draw their own conclusions about the possible causes, or allow them, at the very least, to remain neutral about the possible cause or solution. Another sample summary statement might be "Out of 250 faculty, only 36 responded to the online survey. Of those surveyed, only three people, less than 10 percent, were satisfied with their workspace. One could infer that the remaining staff members were satisfied, but the few who were asked informally why they didn't take the online survey most often said they were just too busy."

Tips and Advice

When there are too many people for you to be able to interview each one personally, or when you need to convert the opinions of many people into a quantity or a statistic, surveys are an effective way to collect that information. In the interview process you gather introductory information that can help you create a survey. In a survey, you're trying to accomplish only a few focused goals or trying to get an answer to a very specific question. The interview helps you to understand what your question is, then your survey targets getting that question answered. Sometimes your survey must be immediately followed up with direct observation, as people's actions often speak louder than their words.

The quality of the information you gather depends on your data collection methods, your attention to detail, and your openness to learning something new. The next step will be to begin synthesizing all you have learned about the client, the end-users, the site, and the issues surrounding your problem to solve into a written document called a *program*. You will use the data that you have collected to describe the problems to solve in terms of programmatic concepts, names of rooms, sizes of spaces, numbers of fixtures and adjacencies, and many other programmatic concepts related to safety, lighting, and aesthetics and many more.

Conclusion

As we have explored in this chapter, there are multiple ways to casually and systematically collect data. Interior designers select from among these methods to customize their own research strategy for each project. It is always a good idea to triangulate your data, drawing from previously published literature to establish a generalized knowledge base, looking at previously built projects, and conducting your own data collection through observation, interviews, and/or surveys for information directly related to your unique project. The methods described in this chapter are meant to be a jumping off point, as you start to explore your own ways to collecting data and using it in your design process.

As you go on to the next chapter, keep this in mind: Although data collection has informed you about the issues to consider regarding end-users, clients, work flow or functionality, types of spaces, key elements, and/or aesthetic goals, it is up to you to analyze the information, and to decipher what it means and how it can inform your solution. Analytic tools are a critical step which separates interior design from the more decorative arts—the programming phase is not the end of research. Research can be used at each phase to enhance the end product of that phase.

References

Axelrod, R. and Cooper, C. (2008). St. Martin's guide to writing, 8th ed. Boston, MA: Bedford/St. Martin.

Fraenkel, J., Wallen, N., and Sawin, E. (1999). *Visual statistics*. Boston: Allyn and Bacon Pub.

Guerin, D. and Dohr, J. (2007). *Research 101: Part 3 research-based practice*. Retrieved May 15, 2018, from Informedesign.umn.edu.

Harris, D., Joseph, A., Becker, F., Hamilton, D. K., Shepley, M., and Zimring, C. (2008). *A practitioner's guide to evidence-based design*. The Center for Health Design Research Coalition.

McNamara, C. (1999). *General guidelines for conducting interviews*. Minneapolis: Authenticity Consulting.

Patton, M. (1990). *Qualitative evaluation and research methods*. Thousand Oaks, CA: Sage.

Sanoff, H. (1991). *Visual research methods in design*. New York: Van Nostrand Reinhold.

Sommer R., and Sommer, B. (2002). *A practical guide to behavioral research: Tools and techniques,* 5th ed. Oxford University Press.

Trochim, W. M. K. (2006). *Research methods knowledge base*. Retrieved May 2008, from http://www.social researchmethods.net/kb/statinf.php.

Wheeler, L. K. (2008). Research assignment #3. English Department, Carson-Newman College. Retrieved April 20, 2008, from http://web.cn.edu/kwheeler /researchassignment3.html.

Vickery, C. G. (October 22, 2014). *Research tools for healthcare design*. Retrieved April 14, 2018, from http://www.healthcaredesignmagazine.com/trends /perspectives/evaluating-right-healthcare-design -research-tools/.

"The Work of Edward Tufte and Graphics Press," (n.d.) Retrieved May 27, 2018, from https://www .edwardtufte.com/tufte.

Zeisel, J. (1984). *Inquiry by design*. New York: W.W. Norton & Co.

Zeisel, J. (2006). *Inquiry by design: Environment/behavior/ neuroscience in architecture, interiors, landscape and planning*. New York: W.W. Norton & Co.

http://universaldesigncasestudies.org/ [retrieved May 18, 2018]

https://humancentereddesign.org/ [retrieved May 18, 2018]

https://www.architecturalrecord.com/topics/306- building-type-studies [retrieved May 18, 2018]

http://psc.dss.ucdavis.edu/sommerr/pg5/pages/contents .html [retrieved May 18, 2018]

www.healthdesign.org [retrieved February 2018]

3 INFORMATION ANALYSIS AND PROGRAMMATIC CONCEPTS

When the blackbird flew out of sight, it marked the edge of one of many circles.

—WALLACE STEVENS, *Thirteen Ways of Looking at a Blackbird* (Stanza IX)

CHAPTER OBJECTIVES

When you complete this chapter you will be able to:

- Understand and implement the five steps and four considerations of the programming process for your interior design project.
- Identify and use programmatic concepts.
- Analyze existing conditions, and express programmatic ideas and project requirements using a variety of diagramming techniques.

WHAT IS PROGRAMMING?

In *Programming for Design*, Edith Cherry (1999) uses the following definition: "Programming is the research and decision-making process that defines the problem to be solved by design." As discussed in Chapter 1, programming is the first phase in the interior design process, and it serves as a bridge between research and design excellence. The more thorough your programming process, the smaller the gap between programming and design. This void between the completed project program and the resulting creative design solution is referred to as the **synthesis gap** (Karlen, Ruggeri, & Hahn, 2004, p. 4).

While there is one main synthesis gap that exists between the defined problem to solve and a potential design solution, there are several other cognitive "leaps" that occur between each step of the programming process. The phrase "jumping to a conclusion" acknowledges that space that exists between the known and the unknown, the observed and the proposed. Any time you transition from one step of the programming process to the next, between looking at what exists and describing what it means, is an opportunity to pause and reflect. The first gap exists between looking at data and determining what that information means. Determining the problem is a form of synthesis. It is thoughtful consideration that requires you to construct or explain what you have observed, through your own filter of experience.

According to Glesne (2011) a *theory* is "the latest version of what we call truth" (p. 37). Although your programming process may not be *explicitly* driven by a particular theory or theories, as discussed in Chapter 1, your viewpoint is always situated within a theoretical perspective. Everyone has underlying beliefs that contain their assumptions. For example, your prior knowledge and experience cooking and eating may influence your design of kitchens. Your theories about the purpose, function, and nature of cooking underlie each design decision:

materials, layout, equipment, storage needs, etc. Quite often people are unaware of their assumptions until they come across a kitchen design that is unfamiliar to them, such as one from another culture or geographic location.

According to Guerin and Dohr, components of a theory are called **constructs**. Constructs can be based on *empirical* or *objective* evidence that has been gathered using a scientific method, and can be measured directly, such as hue, chroma, and value in color theory. Constructs can also be more *subjective*, something difficult to measure directly, or be the result of many things, some of which are not observable, such as level of comfort or convenience. Established rules or relationships between theoretical components are called **prepositions**. For example, according to the accepted ideas in biophilic design theory, we use organic patterns (construct) in a blue/green color palette (construct) to enhance our perceived connection to nature (preposition). Constructs are most useful in a theory when we can define them in operational terms, specifying the procedures used to measure them, and methods we use to employ them. Our goal in the programming process is to successfully **operationalize**, or put to use, the constructs through innovative use of relevant and appropriate prepositions. Simply put, we need to express or define what we see as the problems to solve with detailed descriptions of specific methods by which functional, aesthetic, and economical goals will be put in to buildable form. Before we can confidently and successfully state the problem, we must determine what the data means, and oftentimes, acknowledge and question our unspoken assumptions.

Sometimes the interior design problem is obvious to everyone involved. Often, however, it takes some investigation on the part of the interior designer to sift out the actual problem and separate it from the symptoms of the problem. There are many ways a designer might do this. After reading or observing multiple instances of something, you may recognize a pattern, a trend, or a contradiction. These abstract issues may catch your eye as needing more attention, or further study, to gain insight. You may realize there are things you need to know that you cannot learn by just reading about it or watching a video. You may need to observe for yourself, ask questions to an expert, or survey people who have personal experience with the subject matter.

For example, you notice that in your apartment complex, single socks are left in the communal laundry facilities. You see a need to unite the sock with its missing counterpart. You conduct a survey to find out how many people have experienced this issue, ask several people who do laundry there about their experience, and you spend hours observing people doing laundry. Based on your findings, you discover there are two main problems to solve. One is to reunite the lost sock with its owner, and the other is how to prevent this problem from occurring in the first place. Both can be accomplished through thoughtful design solutions.

How you interpret the data will lead you to define the problem differently. And how you define the problem will influence how you solve it. If you see the problem as local to the laundry, you may decide the problem is the need for a location to store and retrieve the sock. So your design solution is a box marked "Lost and Found Socks." If you see the problem as a social issue, you may solve the problem by creating an app, taking a photo of each sock, and distributing them digitally to all the people in the complex. If you see the problem as behavioral, you may want to create *awareness*, *access* to lost socks, and a *system* for relocating them. You may design an attractive, interactive feature that puts single socks on display in a common area for people to retrieve as they pass by.

A deeper investigation might reveal how to eliminate the problem altogether. Through examination and analysis of the data collected through surveys, interviews, and observation, you conclude that lost socks are left in the dryer due to multiple reasons: dryers are placed too high so most users cannot see into them, socks fall into the space behind a folding counter, and people don't see white socks against a light-colored countertop. The solution could be lowering the dryers to a universally accessible eye height, sensors that issue an alarm when an item remains in the dryer, eliminating spaces behind the cabinetry, and providing a countertop with a darker color for visual contrast against pale clothing.

As you can see from this example, there is a gap between information and problem solving that requires an intermediate step. This step is more of a process that involves being surrounded by data, thinking abstractly, and reflecting on multiple considerations of what your data may mean. The next section of this chapter will address that process. Chapter 5 will address the second synthesis gap, which exists between the problem definition and a potential design solution. Closing the synthesis gap between program requirements and design implementation involves three main skills: brainstorming while immersed in information, fluency in diagram techniques for synthesis, and following a strong research-based design concept.

Programming: The Five Step Process

According to the widely accepted method presented by Peña and Parshall in *Problem Seeking* (2001), programming is a five-step process with four major considerations (p. 12). Each of the steps involves a cycle of collecting, analyzing, and synthesizing information. These five steps are:

1. **Establish goals**: What does the client want to achieve? (collection) What are the central issues? (analysis) Can we craft a mission statement with clearly outlined achievable objectives? (synthesis)

2. **Collect and analyze facts**: What do I know about the client, end-user, site, and budget? (collection) What have I learned from previously published sources about issues related to this project type? (collection) What have I learned from examining how other designers solved, or attempted to solve, these types of problems? (collection) How do these facts relate to this project? (analysis) How can I apply these techniques to this specific project? (synthesis)

3. **Uncover and test programmatic concepts**: Do I see patterns emerging from the data? (analysis) Can I identify and describe the underlying abstract ideas that seem to be arising? (synthesis) What are the performance requirements such as issues of safety, security, privacy, aesthetics, and so forth? (analysis) How can I explore these concepts further? (synthesis) Do I need to share them with stakeholders of the project for confirmation? (collection)

4. **Determine needs**: How can I distinguish what the clients need from what they want? (analysis) How can I set priorities balancing these needs with budget and other project constraints? (synthesis) What is possible given the circumstances? (synthesis) What does the client or end-user really need? (synthesis)

5. **State the problems**: How can I separate symptoms of the problem from the actual problem? (analysis) What are the problems to solve? (synthesis) What should be included in the project in terms of quantity, quality, and relationship? (synthesis)

NBC Nightline video "The Deep Dive" (1999) documented the product design firm IDEO redesigning a supermarket shopping cart, illustrating how an innovative design team follows the five-step programming process. First, they look at the existing cart, consider its shape, cost, and features to determine the direction of their inquiry or project *goals*. Then they look at previously published statistics about shopping carts, *collecting the facts*—that many children are injured using shopping carts, and that many carts are stolen. "Safety" and "theft" emerge as important concepts. After *uncovering these concepts* they ask experts who make, use, and repair shopping carts about theft and safety. They observe shoppers using carts and expand areas of improvement into two more categories: ease of movement (which they call "getting through the traffic jam") and navigation (which they call "finding what you're looking for"). These researchers have successfully synthesized the information into *needs*, and stated the *problem to solve*—in abstract, yet inspiring terms that offer a designer a jumping off point for a creative solution.

Similarly, when interviewing a client you may hear her say, "I need more space." This is, technically, a want. She *wants* more space. But does she *need* more space? It will be up to you to determine that. Perhaps what she needs is more efficient use of space, or access to views so that the space, psychologically, seems larger.

Stating the problem is an art. Be mindful of the words you use. Try to use performance requirements in place of physical design solutions. For example, a client may request a new master bedroom. A bedroom is actually a design solution—a room with a bed in it. What performance requirements does a bedroom solve? Try viewing it as solving a need and state the problem to solve as "acoustically private sleeping accommodation for two people." When you state the problem, you are not the designer. You are the programmer. A bed, a table, a chair, a window, are all physical design solutions. If you list those items in your project program, that's what you will get from the designer. State the problem in such a way as to leave the problem to solve open. In the future, when you are a professional interior designer, you will get project programs that list: two desks, two chairs, a window, and so on. A good designer will simply provide those items. But a truly great designer will question or restate the program using programmatic concepts, to help them come up with a truly innovative solution. Of course, you are not always allowed to do this; it depends on what role you are playing in the process.

The Four Considerations: Form, Function, Economy, Time

In *Problem Seeking* (2001), Peña and Parshall suggest that in each of the five steps of the programming process (outlined earlier) you should consider form, function, economy, and time.

- *Form* concerns the existing conditions of the site and building, the physical shape or configuration of the interior space, and the quality of materials and construction.
- *Function* pertains to how people will be using the space, the activities to be performed in that space, the relationship of spaces to each other, and psychological impact of the interior environment.
- *Economy* concerns the initial cost or budget, as well as the environmental impact of construction, use of resources, and maintenance or operating efficiency of the project over time.

- *Time* is an important global, or all-encompassing consideration, referring to ideas of past, present, and future as they affect not only the five steps but also how they relate to the previous considerations of form, function, and economy. For example, considering the history of the site or the origins of the organization could be instrumental in establishing goals for the project. Considering the current conditions of the site could greatly influence the timing of the project schedule. Considering the organization's plans for growth; how materials will wear over time; how items will be maintained, repaired, or replaced are examples of future considerations. Time can also be used to divide the project, so that the design can be implemented in phases.

As illustrated in the matrix Table 3.1, at each step of the programming process, you are considering function, form, economy, and time. Functional considerations have

---

TABLE 3.1

PROGRAMMING MATRIX: FIVE STEPS WITH FOUR CONSIDERATIONS

Considerations	Step 1 Establish Goals	Step 2 Collect and Analyze Facts	Step 3 Determine Needs	Step 4 Uncover Concepts	Step 5 State the Problems
Form	What do you (or the client) envision in terms of form (shape, texture, color. . .)?	What forms have been used in the past? According to your research which forms are best?	What forms will work best for this project?	What human factors or functional patterns or relationships arise related to form?	Summary of goals, facts, needs, concepts regarding form.
Function	What do you hope to achieve in this project?	What functions take place? Are they well supported?	What functions need to take place?	What patterns or relationships arise related to function?	Summary of goals, facts, needs, concepts regarding functions.
Economy	What is the budget and scope?	What resources are available?	What can you do given the budget restrictions?	What patterns or relationships arise related to cost?	Summary of goals, facts, needs, concepts regarding budget and resources.
Time	What is possible considering the past, present, and future goals?	What is the history? What are present conditions? What are future plans?	What is needed now? What needs to be implemented in the future?	What patterns or relationships arise related to past, present, and future?	Summary of goals, facts, needs, concepts regarding past, present, and future.

to do with what you imagine people doing in the space, and how the objects (fixtures and furnishings) in the space support the behaviors or interactions. Form has to do with size and shape of rooms, materiality, and other physical aspects of the built environment. Economy is, of course, budget considerations, and using resources wisely and efficiently. The last one is the concept of *time* in which you consider the past, present, and future. You can look at things that happened in the past, like the history of the place or organization. You can also focus on the present. What is ideal in this current technological or social environment? And you can think about projecting in to the future. How do we grow the organization? Can this space expand or respond to changing needs in the future? What if this technology becomes defunct? Will the space be flexible enough to accommodate new technology?

Table 3.1 is a matrix of possible considerations at each step. When you are looking at data, analyzing it, and turning it in to program requirements, you are always operating somewhere within this matrix. In school you might choose to highlight a few that are important to your project and focus on those. For example, when you are collecting facts about people, you may be looking at "user characteristics," which is a very important part of our program document. What are the characteristics of the end-users? What age, gender, or socio-economic status does the end-user population belong to? How far do they have to travel to this facility? Do they need parking? Do they need wheelchair access? Are there special needs? What do visitors need, as opposed to staff? If you are collecting facts about the form, such as the existing site, consider the views, and the path of the sun over the course of a typical day, and throughout the year. Which walls are load bearing, are fire-rated, or contain plumbing? Which walls can be removed while still maintaining the structural integrity of the building? You can choose to consider any or all of these factors. This matrix is a tool to remind you to consider multiple aspects of a design problem as you articulate your project's unique collection of program requirements.

EXPLORING PROGRAMMATIC CONCEPTS

As seen in the previous section, programmers develop *strategies* for solving a problem. For example, after defining an issue as "theft," the design team at IDEO decided to make the new shopping cart worthless, so that no one would want to steal it. If you find out that most carts get stolen, a variety of solutions are available to you. For example, you could make the cart wheels freeze up if someone tried to take it outside the parking lot. How many other design solutions can you think of? Most likely, you can imagine a few other ideas. Perhaps you can come up with an idea no one has ever tried. Therefore, if you embed a design solution into a program without its corresponding functional performance requirement, you are limiting the creative input of the designer. In other words, if you determine the design solution in the program, that's what you're going to get. Sometimes, it is a good idea to write the program in such a way as to define the problems to solve without necessarily determining the design solution. So, if you include the issue of theft in your program, and one of the design problems is to prevent the cart from getting stolen, you leave it open for the designer to come up with an appropriate and creative design solution.

According to Cherry and Petronius (2016) some examples of common categories of programmatic strategies include:

- *Centralization and decentralization*: Which function components are grouped together and which are segregated? For example, in some offices the copying function is centralized, whereas in others, there are copiers for each department.
- *Flexibility*: What types of changes are expected for various functions? Do facilities need to change over a period of a few hours? A few days? A summer recess? Or is an addition what is really needed?
- *Flow*: What goods, services, and people move through the project? What is needed at each step of the way to accommodate that flow?
- *Priorities and phasing*: What are the most important functions of the project? What could be added later? Are there ongoing existing operations that must be maintained?
- *Levels of access*: Who is allowed where? What security levels are there? Are some areas always open to the public and other areas only accessible at certain times?

A **programmatic concept** is a written description of an abstract strategy for achieving a performance requirement, or satisfying an aesthetic or functional need. Programming concepts summarize issues that may emerge when you study a complex problem. They are useful for getting to the essence of the underlying problem to

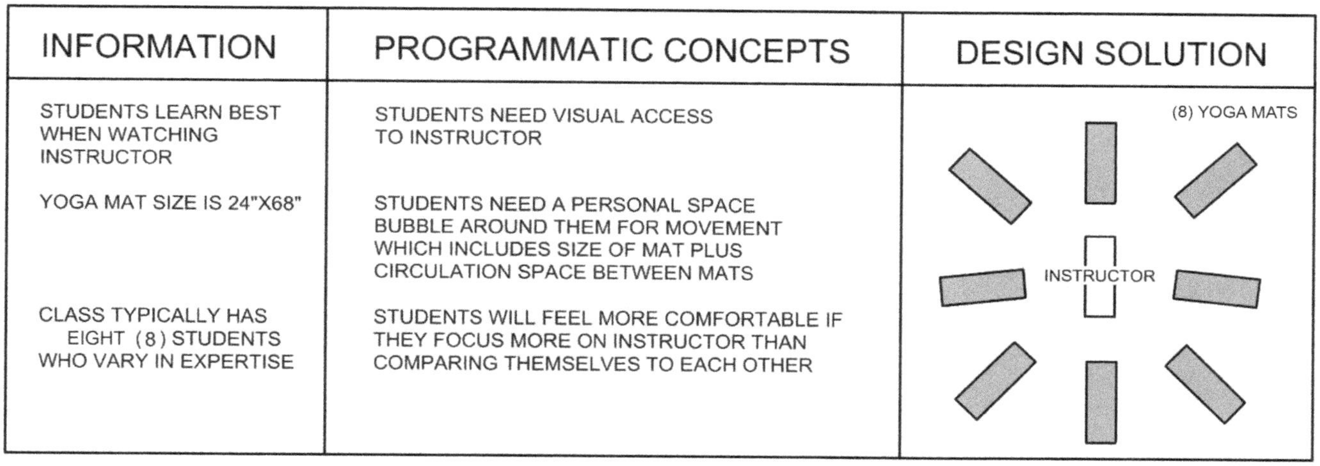

Figure 3.1 Yoga classroom example: Information gathered, programmatic concepts uncovered, and a radial layout of yoga mats around an instructor as a potential design solution.

be solved. It is important to understand the difference between programmatic concepts and design solutions. Ballast (2006) explains that a programming concept is not a physical solution, but rather a performance requirement related to methods of solving problems or satisfying a need. A design solution is the specific physical response that attempts to achieve a programmatic concept. According to Peña and Parshall (2001), "programming deals with abstract ideas known as programmatic concepts, which are intended mainly as operational solutions to a client's performance problems, without regard to the physical design response" (p. 95). They refer to this as the "principle of abstract thinking." This is the most creative part of programming. It is where you take your insights about the problem and develop descriptions of the possible solution.

Programmatic concepts are typically qualitative, although they can contain quantities. They can be related to technology, associated with the building itself, related to evidence-based human factors, or to the experiential aspects of the spaces. They can be functional or activity based. Aesthetic programmatic concepts most often

include reference to design elements and principles, but also may refer to a particular mood or architectural style. See Table 3.2 for an introductory list of some common programmatic concepts you can use in your project program.

Can you describe the performance requirements of a room or object without a direct reference to a physical design solution? Figure 3.1 will help you visualize the difference. Activity 3.3 at the end of this section will help you practice. Once you are aware of the difference, you will have ample opportunity to practice.

Part of programming is to predetermine the activities that will occur within the building. Keeping in mind the emotional responses and feelings that might be evoked in the user, you provide the spaces in which these events occur. In other words, like the choreographer of a dance performance, you are orchestrating movements and behavior within the spaces you program. Programming should not be seen as a process of guiding the project in a direction that will give it many exciting opportunities along that path. "A problem statement which is too limited inhibits creative ability" (Adams, 2001, p. 32).

TABLE 3.2

EXPLANATION OF TYPICAL PROGRAMMATIC CONCEPTS

Programmatic Concept	Explanation/Example
Access/Adjacency	Refers to a person or other entity being able to enter, use, and to travel easily from room to room, or from exterior to interior space. Typically is used to describe entry points, reception, and public areas.
Accessibility/ Adaptability	Refers to ability for people with disabilities to use the space with little or no additional effort than people without physical disabilities.

TABLE 3.2

Comfort	Hold various interpretations, but mainly applied to environmental systems or factors related to human comfort, such as temperature, relative humidity, light and sound levels, supportive furnishings, and balance of personal and social space.
Communication	Allows people to connect verbally, physically, or through assistive technology to support the exchange of ideas or to get work done.
Community	Sense of connection provided by character of the space. The idea that the space is welcoming and encourages participation in social activities, or inspires awareness that one is part of a larger group.
Control	Allows or limits individuals using the space to change aspects of the environment to suit their needs such as exit and enter freely, move furniture, adjust temperature or light levels, or through a combination of factors, feel like they can reach their highest potential. Maslow's hierarchy of needs would call this state self-actualization.
Character	Concerns the image the client wants to project, or the existential quality of the space caused by a number of aspects to produce an emotional effect on the end-user. Could also describe desired mood, aesthetics, or style. A theater could have a dramatic effect due to high ceilings, low light level, and intricate architectural details. A spa can have a relaxing effect due to neutral colors, soothing sounds, and use of natural materials.
Density	Can be low, medium, or high. Refers to the number of people or elements per unit of measure for the space. A computer lab at your school may be high-density while a studio classroom may be low-density (fewer number of students for same amount of space).
Flexibility	Refers to ability for people to use the space in a variety of ways or to change elements in the space to support changing needs over time. A multipurpose room would have this programmatic concept.
Flow	Refers to movement having to do with work routines or traffic patterns. Flow can be linear or sequential, mixed, circular, separated, nodal, networked, radial, and so on. Also refers to circulation patterns in a building.
Hierarchy	Refers to spatial or elemental sequence in which the occupant realizes that some are more important than others. Could be used to exercise authority as in a courtroom, and can be expressed using symbols of authority such as flags, badges, imposing furnishings, or high fences.
Interaction	Could refer to socially or physically interactive elements such as a café space or an information wall with touch screens.
Narrative	The underlying "story" that unfolds as a person moves through the space used for education, navigation, or entertainment purposes. A museum exhibit would have a narrative element to placement of artwork or choreography of visitor movement. A waiting room in a hospital could contain a narrative that inspires wellness.
Orientation/ Navigation	Usually refers to compass direction, or systems in place to prevent a feeling of being lost. Related to place legibility.
Phasing	Refers to implementing your design in different stages due to budget constraints or sequence of construction. You may determine that part of your design will be completed before beginning construction on another part. You may consider referencing that concept in your project program.
Place Legibility/ Way-Finding	The ability for people to "read" the space in terms of understanding where to go or which spaces are to be accessed. A very important concept for large retail spaces, healthcare, and transportation hubs like airports.
Priority	Evokes the question of the order of importance, ranking values among multiple, often competing, elements or options. A limited budget will cause programmers to give some items higher priority than others in a typical project.
Privacy	Could be visual, acoustic, or spatial separation to promote feelings of individuality, confidentiality, or physical retreat. An important concept to include in work environments, activity, or people groupings, security to give a sense of home base or territoriality.
Safety	Provides for functional solutions that anticipate and reduce accidents, such as rounded corners, slip resistant flooring, handrails, good lighting, visual contrast, and ability to get assistance if needed.
Security	Varies from minimum to medium to maximum, depending on the value of impending loss. Used to protect property and human life. Guides or controls movement of personnel, restricts access of visitors, and provides surveillance.
Sterility/ Cleanliness	Different levels of cleanliness exist in most healthcare, hospitality, and some specialty commercial projects. Environmental health codes and agencies will typically issue permits based on sanitary conditions and require inspections. A project involving food, beauty or health services, animals or high-density residential or institutional use may involve this programmatic concept.
Transparency/ Visual Access	Provides view or sense continuity between two spaces that are not necessarily physically connected. Typically refers to glass or other open materials that allow light or view.

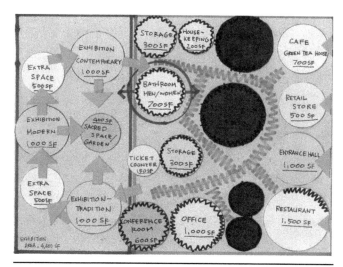

Figure 3.2 Example of bubble diagram using a flexible system of paper cutouts arranged, analyzed, and digitally photographed.

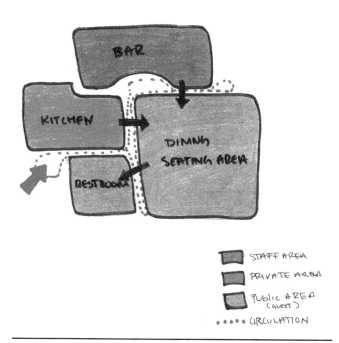

STAFF AREA
PRIVATE AREA
PUBLIC AREA (GUEST)
••••• CIRCULATION

Figure 3.3 Relationship diagram used for analysis, separate from a building shell.

DIAGRAMS USED FOR ANALYSIS

When translating text or verbal information into an abstract form, nothing is more powerful than a diagram. You may start out with a graphic representation of information to start making sense of what you have learned. This process involves *analytical* diagrams. When you start using your knowledge to create something new, we use diagrams for *synthesis*, which will be explored in Chapter 5. The following is a list of some diagrams used for analysis in the programming process.

The **bubble diagram** is very useful for representing the relative *sizes* of spaces and desired *adjacencies*. This diagram type places each space name in its own circle and often uses colors to differentiate program areas. When it is color coded for program, you can do a series of diagrams you can easily compare across changing relationships. Bold lines connecting the circles indicate direct adjacency and dashed lines often indicate convenient or indirect. No line may indicate there is no adjacency requirement between those two spaces.

This diagram is sometimes referred to as a *relationship diagram*. Figure 3.3 provides an example of relationships and adjacencies. Since this family of diagrams is mainly used to communicate an understanding of adjacencies, it may not be drawn to scale, and may be kept separate from the base plan and be included in the project program to inform the designer of the required spatial relationships.

Since the bubble diagram puts each space in its own "bubble," showing relative sizes and adjacencies, a downside is that each room represented by a bubble is considered a separate entity. You are forced to name

each one, and in doing so, you will likely find it more difficult to imagine that spaces can combine or transition without full-height walls and doors. Although the bubble diagram is primarily analytic in nature, it can be also used for synthesis or schematic design when drawn over an existing building shell (see Figure 3.4). Unfortunately, it does not lend itself to easy translation to a space plan because of the curved nature of the bubbles. And what about the awkward spaces in between the bubbles? Designers then tend to draw full-height walls at the edges of bubbles and doors where the lines of adjacency intersect. A bubble diagram is best kept not-to-scale and presented independent from the base plan, solely to show relative sizes, space names, and adjacencies. This is similar to the kind of information represented in an adjacency matrix, but in a more graphically relatable form for visual learners.

A variation on the bubble diagram is the **stacking diagram**, or layering diagram (see Figure 3.5). This diagram type establishes relationships between vertical elements in a multilevel project, between spaces on different floors that are "stacked" on top of one another such as a balcony overlooking a playground, an adult area supervising the children's area, or a mezzanine's relationship to a stage below. Other vertical functional relationships can be explored, such as plumbing that needs to be stacked, or a diagrammatic section that

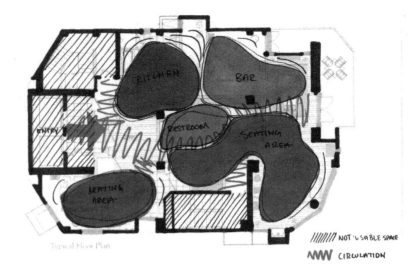

Figure 3.4 Bubble diagram as an overlay on an existing building shell, beginning to synthesize a design solution.

//////// NOT USABLE SPACE

WWW CIRCULATION

describes the roof's rainwater recapture system draining into the garden below. You may not want quiet areas to be placed over potentially noisy areas for sound transmission concerns. Noisy areas can be vertically stacked with other noisy areas, and quiet areas on top of other quiet areas. Stacking diagrams would also include vertical circulation, such as stairs and elevators.

A **corporate hierarchy diagram** graphically represents the way a company or organization is configured. It identifies each member and illustrates the relationships between them. It is often used to identify the decision makers during programming and the stakeholders during data collection. It is used along with the work flow diagram to inform the circulation or organization diagrams during design. Corporate hierarchy diagrams have been used to creatively depict a re-envisioning of the organizational structure. For example, one student team related departments of a health clinic to different types of bone cells, each building on and supporting one another, which appealed to the client. It was an innovative way of depicting a corporate structure.

Work flow diagrams, or activity diagrams, establish existing or ideal relationships between people or functions in an organization, to help determine the future circulation diagram. This diagram is typically used for describing an existing pattern or flow rather than generating something new. Notice the difference between analysis and synthesis. Does work proceed in a linear fashion, from one person or area to the next, or does it operate as more of a network? Does work originate from a central hub, radiating in different directions, or is it arranged in a loop, or in clusters? For example, a staff member may tell you, "When someone enters this clinic they immediately check in. We take their vitals in an adjacent exam room, and then they go to this room for further testing where we take a blood sample. If they test positive, we take them to this area for treatment. After they receive medication, we refer them to the psychologist for therapy. . . ." What they are describing is a linear work flow, proceeding from one area or activity to another. You could do a diagram that reflects your conversation with them about linear nature of the work flow. Alternatively, if the staff member says,

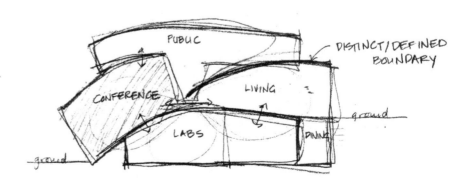

Figure 3.5 Stacking or layering diagram used to indicate required vertical spatial relationships and adjacencies.

"Typically people come in here for one of three reasons. They are either going to get tested, or they are going to have a procedure, or they are going to go to therapy." Then, your work flow diagram would be more radial, or nodal, representing the nature of choice from reception branching into three options of testing, procedure, and therapy areas. You can later use these diagrams to help create your new floor plan.

The *work triangle* in a kitchen is a kind of work flow diagram (see Figure 3.7). It describes a functional relationship based on a person's movement between the three main destination appliances or fixtures in a kitchen: the sink, the refrigerator, and the stove. Each of these three represents a physical design solution to the functions of prep, store, cook. And you would measure the different lengths of the sides of the triangle based on a view of a single person in the kitchen moving between three main appliances, which doesn't always translate to current kitchen design. But the work triangle could be used to check your design for efficiency in this capacity, rather than generate your design. Synthesis diagrams used for kitchen design will be explored in Chapter 5.

Usually done over the base plan, **functional analysis diagrams** analyze the existing conditions of a site for conditions that tend to overlap or contrast, such as *public* space versus *private* areas, *natural* light versus *artificial* light, *quiet* versus *noisy*, and for qualities that relate to compass direction, including sun path, prevailing breezes, or views. This diagram is flexible to accommodate any condition you wish to analyze the space for that may reflect the uniqueness or richness of the place, such as old (historic) versus new, staff versus visitors, or active versus passive areas. It can be combined with structural analysis diagrams and behavioral mapping/traffic patterns to provide a comprehensive site analysis.

Used for kitchen and bath or for projects on a smaller scale, the **zones of use diagram** is similar to a functional analysis. A good example of this diagram is when you want to represent the different functional zones that are found in a typical kitchen: prep, cook, store, clean-up, serve/entertain/eat. Maybe your client also requests a homework,

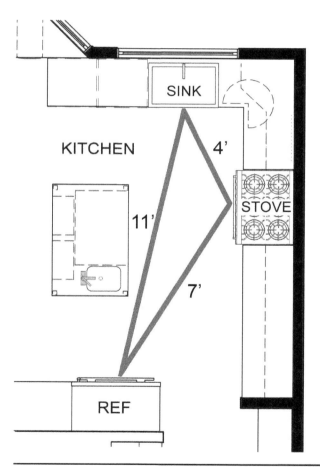

Figure 3.6 Work triangle diagram is an analytic diagram to determine efficiency in movement between three major appliance destinations in a typical kitchen. Each leg of the triangle should be between 4 feet and 9 feet in length. The sum of all sides should be no greater than 26 feet.

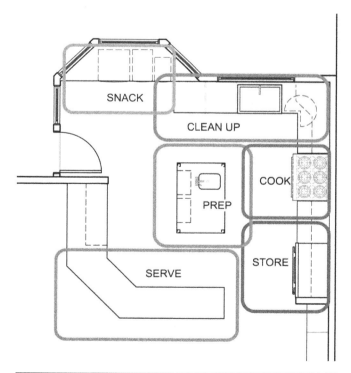

Figure 3.7 Zones of use diagram to visualize and analyze the various overlapping task areas found in a kitchen.

a bill-paying area, or a snack zone where children can help themselves. In this zone, other programmatic concepts such as safety and ergonomic issues (i.e., counter height) would be considered. When these zones are identified on an existing layout, one can tell if the zones are clearly separated or overlapping and if the location of the appliances, fixtures, and furnishing supports the zones of use. The intersection of each zone may indicate the ideal location to place fixtures and appliances that occurs between different zones or the need for two of them. For example, a sink is ideal at the intersection of prep and clean-up but if these two zones are not adjacent or are too far apart we may need two sinks, a prep sink and a clean-up sink. Between the cook area and the serve area may be a high counter made of a material that is resistant to heat. From there one could also measure the path from the refrigerator to the stove. We can use the work triangle as an analytical overlay on the zones of use diagram. As you will see in Chapter 5, zones of use diagrams can also be used for synthesis to generate a new design.

Structural analysis diagrams are usually part of the site analysis when the designer is looking closely at the building shell to determine constraints and possibilities. These diagrams create a visual record of the information gathered about the site, to establish possibilities and constraints. Usually done over the existing site plan or base plan, the designer might use them to highlight plumbing walls and describe the area adjacent to them as "wet," or use them to identify *load-bearing elements* that must remain. These diagrams can be done in section view, to make clear the structural column from roof to floor or the current pattern of movement of goods and services through the existing vertical circulation. They can also be three-dimensional, mapping a building's security system, electrical layout, or ventilation system.

Behavioral mapping or **traffic pattern diagrams** assist the designer by documenting the way people are observed using the existing space. Traffic, in this case, is not just about cars, but can be about other ways people arrive to the site such as by public transportation, walking, biking, scooters, wheelchairs, strollers, etc. Behavioral mapping captures activities observed in the location. What are people currently doing in or around the space? Do they tend to be sitting in the sun or in the shade? Are they walking, playing, working, or reading? Are they socially interacting in pairs, in groups, or acting individually? Look at the existing waiting, corridors, restrooms, programs

areas to determine how people are using the spaces. You can analyze the site as it exists in order to make a case for proposing changes. Or if you are looking at a case study, you can look at traffic patterns of that facility in order to apply what is working to your project. Very similar to the kitchen work triangle, these kind of diagrams would be used to analyze the spaces for efficiency or to make conflicting uses more apparent.

Locating existing doors and corridors can also indicate possible traffic patterns. These diagrams are a visual record of information gathered about the way people use a space over time; they help identify conflicts and they can influence the way a space is planned during schematic design. Figure 3.8 presents the traffic pattern analysis in a residential space occupied by the family's grandmother, after the designer observed the family interacting one afternoon.

There are a host of *culturally specific analytic diagrams* an interior designer may employ when reviewing an existing space or site. Many cultures have specialists who view space and landforms through the lens of a metaphysical theory or spiritual practice. Clients may request this to be done before the design can occur due to their beliefs that the environment influences their health, well-being, and prosperity. As shown in Figure 3.9 superimposing a *bagua map*, or eight-sided diagram, is common in the practice of *feng shui* to study the movement of *chi* or *life energy* through a space. *Vastu* is another system arising from a Hindu worldview that all materials (including human beings) radiate both positive and negative energies that need to be balanced with celestial energies to align our design with cosmic order. Native American traditions honor the *four directions* which refer to compass direction, and sacred symbols such as the *medicine wheel*. In fact, many traditions look to the natural world to inform placement, shape, color, and material of the built environment, so analysis of the surroundings, including the occupants themselves, is often critical to the programming process. You may need to consult outside resources and experts to assist you with this process.

A composite site analysis consists of a combination of diagrams previously discussed in this section. In landscape design, "the end product of the site analysis phase of the design process is a composite analysis map (sometimes referred to as an opportunities and constraints sheet). This is developed through an overlay process delineating the most suitable and least suitable areas of the site for each analysis factor" (McBride, 2006). Using an overlay

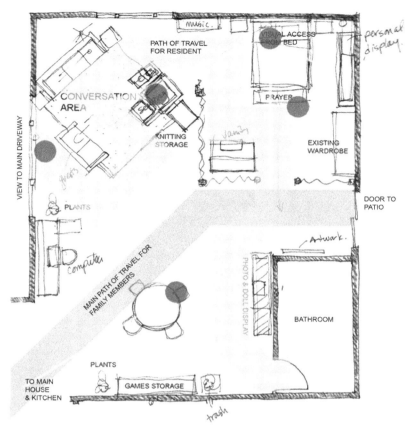

Figure 3.8 Behavioral map showing how an elderly resident used her residential space. The dots indicate locations she was observed spending the majority of her time.

technique, begin your site analysis diagrams with what you know; then continue to add layers of information. Start your structural analysis by identifying the columns and walls that would be difficult, or structurally infeasible, to remove. You can develop your own "language" through color, hatch patterns, and symbols. For example, you could mark the structural elements with a red marker. Then, identify existing plumbing locations, perhaps using a blue hatch to indicate plumbing walls and areas around piping, including the shafts and vents that contain the unseen piping. If the interior has other physical aspects that you want to document—such as condition of finishes, the feeling of the space, the view from the space—you can use color, hatch patterns, or text to communicate the site condition. The goal of these analyses is to identify the constraints or limitations of the site as well as its potential or possibilities. These layers of information may eventually become more speculative than factual. There is a moment when documentation becomes interpretation, and continued diagramming will help you reach a design solution during the schematic phase.

As you can see, the programming process for interior design has many diagramming techniques for helping with the analytic process that precedes schematic design. It is not recommended to jump from data collection to schematic design without this intermediate step of analysis. That intermediate, analytic step is the interpretation of the data collected, which sometimes involves multiple overlays of diagrams. It is important to document your findings in a visual form, through diagrams. Figures 3.10 and 3.11 in the accompanying activity presents illustrations of the step-by-step method interior designers can use to transition from information gathering to analysis.

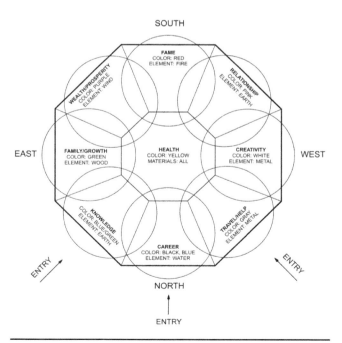

Figure 3.9 Cultural analysis example: Bagua diagram to be superimposed over floor plan derived from Black Hat Sect or Western *Feng Shui* principles.

Figure 3.10 Site analysis diagram showing topography, sun path, views, and prevailing breezes.

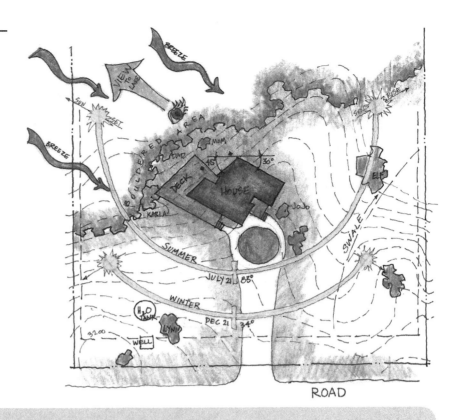

ACTIVITY 3.1
Analyzing Your Site with a Site Analysis Composite Diagram

Purpose: To practice analyzing an existing condition through a series of overlays.

First, review Figure 3.11 as an example of a completed site analysis. Then analyze your own building shell for the same features. You can use the building shell that is given as part of your studio assignment or use one that you have chosen. Sketch the floor plan. Document the space with additional photographs or video. The following tasks should be drawn over the base building shell or existing plan, each on a separate sheet of trace paper.

1. Identify components of the STRUCTURAL SYSTEMS (columns, walls, overhead beams) using a *red* marker.
2. Identify WET areas (plumbing walls, fixtures, risers, or stacks) of the building using a *blue* marker.
3. Identify the areas that receive NATURAL LIGHT with a *yellow* highlighter.
4. Identify QUIET and NOISY areas based on perceived sound levels using text notations or a hatch pattern as shown.
5. Identify ACTIVE and PASSIVE areas based on kind of activity using text notation or hatch pattern as shown. For example, activities such as reading, writing, studying, sleeping, or listening to lectures would be passive, while activities using gross motor movements, such as running, playing, or exercising, would be active.
6. Identify PUBLIC, SEMI-PRIVATE, and PRIVATE areas with regard to the existing functions, occupant types (visitors and staff), or program areas. Use text notations along with color or hatch pattern for the visitors and a different color or pattern for the staff.
7. Identify TRAFFIC PATTERNS to on the site, using one color for pedestrian traffic and one for vehicular traffic. Mark entry points with red arrows.
8. Create a BEHAVIORAL MAP to identify different activities or behaviors you observed taking place in the location. Use text notations, color, and pattern as necessary to record your observations.
9. Identify the view(s), locate the SUN PATH as it travels from east to west, and note the direction of prevailing breezes. Note any source of smells or sounds that you experienced.

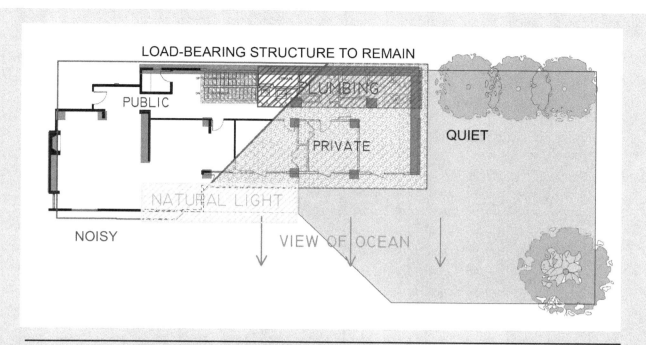

Figure 3.11 Example of a composite site analysis diagram.

ACTIVITY 3.2
Describing What You Have Learned in a Site Analysis Summary

Purpose: To summarize your site analysis findings in a text description. To practice describing qualitative information to determine if the existing conditions support the functional requirements of your program.

1. After you have completed Activity 3.1, overlay all of the diagrams and study them.
2. Write a summary of what the site analysis diagrams revealed to you about the possibilities and constraints of the site.
   - *Feeling of the site*, inside and out (qualities of the space, including sounds, smells, safety issues, your emotional response to visit)
   - *Neighborhood* and regional context (climate, demographics of local residents, adjacent uses or nearby amenities such as parks or landmarks, and character of neighborhood)
   - *Exterior and site conditions* (the style or character of the building, location of parking or pedestrian walkways)
   - *Interior configuration* (structural system and other existing systems)

See the following example of a site analysis summary to help get you started.

This site is located in a residential neighborhood, at the north end of a small community park in southern California, one block south of a main thoroughfare with access to public transportation. There are two separate structures on the property. Both buildings were built in 1969 as a senior center, and together they provide approximately 8,000 SF.

The west building has a slab-on-grade foundation with two main steel columns in the center and a perimeter load-bearing wall with large headers on all four sides. It has a suspended ceiling system under a hip roof that allows for 9-foot high ceilings. It contains a kitchen, restrooms, offices, and a multipurpose/meeting room.

The east building is one large open steel structure that contains multiple shuffleboard courts. Columns are spaced 16 feet 8 inches on center with 4-foot-high trusses overhead that span 60 feet. From the concrete slab foundation to the underside of the trusses measures 20 feet high. This floor-to-ceiling height will allow for a mezzanine or a full second floor. The spacing of the trusses allows access through the roof for skylights or natural ventilation. We can also take advantage of the flat roof of the east building for a green roof or a roof deck.

The property is surrounded by streets on three sides, but the long south side is immediately adjacent to the park. The 100-year-old trees provide shade and filtered natural light. The north side of the building has a loading zone for drop off or delivery. Dumpsters are located on the east side. There is a view of the ocean looking west from the roof.

The building is now abandoned. I was struck by the many tall trees and landscaping which supported local wildlife such as hummingbirds, butterflies, and squirrels. I would like to preserve as much of the vegetation as possible. We noted many people walking their dogs around the building, enjoying the peaceful surroundings and families having picnics in the park. There is an iconic, historic water tower across the street that is visible from many miles and serves as a community landmark.

3. When you've finished, create a PowerPoint or poster presentation that documents your findings. Present it to the class. Use this as an opportunity for an open discussion about its potential as an appropriate location for your future project.

ACTIVITY 3.3
Identifying Programmatic Concepts

Purpose: To read through an interview transcript and identify programmatic concepts.

In this final section we will follow a commercial designer, Bill Britt, through his programming process, as he determines the parameters for a small office project. We will illustrate the use of programmatic concepts and analytic diagramming techniques. Although the project scope is small—office space for five staff members—the basic process can be applied to larger projects, as well as projects that are smaller in scope, such as a grouping of furnishings, a singular piece of furniture, or the design of a product.

The following is an interview transcript. As you read, think about how you would translate all of this information into program requirements. Note that programmatic requirements that are quantitative or physical design solutions are underlined, and qualitative programmatic concepts are italicized. Answer the three questions located at the conclusion of the transcript.

Bill Britt describes the project he recently completed:

"SDCOE San Diego County Office of Education Master Control Room is where two engineers monitor the video quality of our broadcast. They need to be able to respond to and address any issues that they see so they need to be *in close proximity to these television screens*. That space, I was told, was also going to be shared by the programmer and two editors. So there's going to be five people in the room. My boss requested that there also be space for an intern or visitor to come in and use a computer if need be. So those were the initial parameters.

The first thing I noticed in that room (which was empty at the time) was that the monitors were already mounted on the wall just off to the side, so I thought, we have four people: the two engineers and two editors that are pretty much going to be looking at monitors all the time. And my boss had expressed that *it would be "cool,"* in his words, *if you walk in to that room and you see a wall of monitors because that's what we're all about*. So that meant that *these editors and these engineers had to be all facing that wall* and how can I do that *and separate* them?

My boss wanted a "wow factor." I wanted it to fall *somewhere between a home environment and a work environment and that meant it was definitely going to be all about the lighting, that you can control in terms of intensity and sometimes when you start your day you don't want to wake up that fast, you want to have a nice low lighting. If you want to change it as the day progresses, that's up to you.* The lighting had to be controlled in those edit bays, by them, as opposed to the main part of the room on one dimmer. They all had to be dimmable LEDs. *A dimly lit room for one person may be too bright for another. They needed to control their own lighting.*

I know from past experience that *editors like working in caves.* They like the room to be dark because they're very intent on studying the quality of the picture. They also like very few distractions. So I didn't have to worry about wall art, posters or how I was going to have to decorate it. They didn't need anything on the walls. *If they want to put something up, they can.* But that will be because they know it's not something that's distracting to them. *Surroundings should be dark and not distracting.*

So *I came up with the idea* of having *those program monitors or "air" monitors that the engineers watch to be in the center of the room* since they're the biggest and then have the editors on either side of that. So then it became a matter of measuring off that space to *divide it such that the editors didn't feel like they were in a closet.* So I had to make each of the rooms as wide as possible. So what I did was basically have the two large screens in the middle on the wall and then measure the distance to the left of them and to the right and say ok this is going to be the editors' space.

I knew at this time that programming was going to be on the right-hand side of the room. The left-hand side of the room is what's called the "machine room" where all the decks and servers and that sort of thing is separated by a glass sliding door. *No one wants to work on that side of the room. People are coming and going. There's noise.* Bottom line is programmer's desk is on the right side of the room. (Refer to Figure 3.12 to see Bill's bubble diagram.)

Each editor has two monitors—for all intents and purposes, the "raw materials" are on the left and the "finished product" is on the right. *Editors are deciding what edit they want to make [on the left]. On the right side is the finished video.* Also from experience, I know that *what helps them feel less crowded is when the producer can sit back* and see that finished product on the right-hand monitor is also reflected on a big screen above both of them. I knew that they would have to be *completely closed in with doors, because I didn't want them to have to wear headsets all day long.* They need to be able to close the door and turn the volume up so they could hear it. If they want to turn it up louder to hear minute details, [they could do that] with headsets on.

The engineers that are watching for quality control in the center—they don't need to have [the volume] cranked up. Their concern—*probably the only concern I could not meet. I kind of met them half way.* They wanted to be completely closed in as well, because they said "sometimes we need to turn our monitors up." Well, after watching them work, I came to realize they didn't want to be closed in so they could turn up their monitors. They wanted to be closed in *because they don't want you to see what they have on their computer screens when they're goofing off.* So I came up with the idea of a room divider that is portable, that could be moved, that's high enough where when

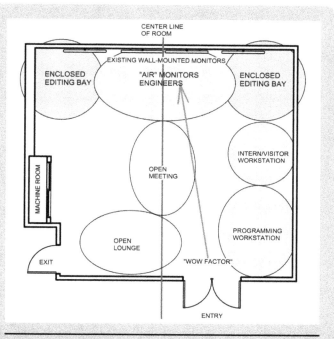

Figure 3.12 SDCOE Master Control bubble diagram overlaid on existing building shell.

you first walk in you can see the whole wall of video but you don't see their personal monitor until you walk more than half way across the room.

Once I figured that problem out I was left with figuring out how to arrange the programmer's desk. The [furniture] company I was working with came up with a plan to have <u>a partial privacy wall on top of his desk with fabric, wrapped around his desk</u>. I liked that for a while, but the more I looked at it I just felt like it was *this cumbersome thing, that, as you looked at the room from left to right and your eyes go around, it's kind of like a nice flow and then you'd get to his desk and there's this bump.* So I was talking to one of the engineers about it, and he looked at it and said, *"Well you designed everyone else's desk to be U-shaped. Why don't you do the same with his?"* So that way, he's kind of facing the corner, and so is the other desk.

There're only five people in here working which leaves a lot of room and there's one or two other offices that have sort like *a little lounge area or at least an area where clients can come in and sit and talk.* So I thought a <u>loveseat and two chairs and a small conference table</u> for working. Initially I had the loveseat and two chairs in the middle of the room and it looked inviting but I realized it would be *much more efficient to have them off to the side and have a table in the middle of the room so you could actually sit and work. Also the loveseat and chairs invites people to sit and chatter right on the other side of the partition where the engineers are sitting and figured that would be distracting.* (See Figure 3.13 for the final layout.)

The rest (of the design process) is just about materials and colors. I like earth tones, but I didn't want browns so I went to greens because *green is a favorite color* and it was a matter of finding a green that wasn't distracting. *It needed to be soft.* I knew the entire back wall was going to be a dark neutral gray because the monitors were going to be in front of it. I knew the *work surfaces could not be light colored, because that could reflect light onto their monitors, so everything had to be a darker shade than you would normally find in an office environment. Not shiny, and not rough.* Work surfaces needed to be smooth because they were going to be writing and taking notes. One of the biggest challenges was the carpeting. I didn't want something solid. I wanted something *interesting, but not distracting.* And I didn't want

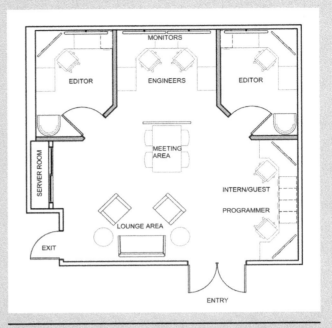

Figure 3.13 SDCOE Master Control floor plan showing new walls and furniture layout.

Figure 3.14 SDCOE Master Control photo of finished space.

something to look dated. I knew it was going to be <u>carpet tiles</u> so they could be replaced (if they got worn or soiled). My first choice, the one I was really set on, after thinking about it for a week, (I thought) *I don't know if this is going to look as cool or as hip as you think it is ten years from now. This is going to be here for a long time.* That's a great crazy geometric thing that's going on, but ten years from now, I don't want someone saying, "remember when that was something that was cool?" Like bellbottoms . . . I didn't want bellbottoms for carpet!

 My boss wanted a "wow" factor when you first walked in. I think I've achieved that because when you walk in your eyes instantly go to that back wall. In my rough drawing, the way I had it layed out, in the different layouts, I showed to my boss and he goes, *"this is very star-trekky looking. . . . I love it"* (Bill Britt, Personal communication, June 29, 2018).

Please answer the following questions:
1. How did the designer, Bill, separate wants from needs?
2. What bits of information helped shaped the design?
3. Refer to the list of programmatic concepts in Table 3.2 and see if you can identify which concepts they refer to, such as issues of privacy (both visual and acoustic), hierarchy, priority, comfort, and control, to name a few. Note how the accompanying analytical diagrams translate the designer's words into graphic form. Notice how the programmatic requirements were satisfied in the design solution.

Conclusion

Now that we have gone through each of the first four steps of the five-step programming process: established goals, collected facts, uncovered concepts, and determined needs, we are ready to state the problems to solve. We will continue to consider form, function, economy and time. We have also examined our assumptions and considered theories as we interpreted the information we have collected. And we have used a variety of techniques to visually, and verbally express our findings.

 Surrounded by this rich information, programmers typically begin to state the problems to solve by describing space types needed and/or the activities to be performed in those spaces. Problem statements can be simple, or extremely detailed, depending on the type of facility and the thoroughness of the programmer. Programmers document the problems to solve using quantities (numbers of people and sizes of space) and qualities desired in a project program. The format and content of a project program will be explored in Chapter 4.

References

Adams, J. L. (2001). *Conceptual blockbusting: A guide to better ideas.* Cambridge, MA: Basic Books.

Ballast, D. K. (2006). Interior design reference manual: A guide to the NCIDQ exam. Belmont, CA: Professional Publications, Inc.

Cherry, E. (1999). *Programming for design: From theory to practice.* New York: John Wiley and Sons.

Cherry, E. and John Petronis, J. (November 2, 2016). *Architectural programming.* Retrieved July 22, 2018, from https://www.wbdg.org/design-disciplines/architectural-programming.

Glesne, C. (2011). *Becoming qualitative researchers: An Introduction* (4th ed.). Boston: Pearson.

Guerin, D. and Dohr, J. (2007). *Research 101 tutorial.* InformeDesign, University of Minnesota. Retrieved December 25, 2007, from http://www.informedesign.umn.edu/

Karlen, M., Ruggeri, K., nd Hahn, P. (2004). *Space planning basics.* New York: Wiley.

Koppel, T. (editor). (July 13, 1999). Deep Dive [television series episode]. In James Goldston (executive producer), *ABC News: Nightline.* New York: American Broadcasting Corporation.

McBride, S. B. (2006). *Site planning and design.* West Virginia University. Retrieved May 16, 2009, from http://www.rri.wvu.edu/WebBook/McBride/section3.html.

Peña, W. M. and Parshall, S. A. (2001). *Problem seeking: An architectural programming primer.* New York: John Wiley.

4 THE PROJECT PROGRAM

I do not know which to prefer, the beauty of inflections or the beauty of innuendoes, the blackbird whistling or just after.

—WALLACE STEVENS, *Thirteen Ways of Looking at a Blackbird* (Stanza V)

CHAPTER OBJECTIVES

When you complete this chapter you will be able to:

- Synthesize information you have gathered to define problems to be solved through design.
- Differentiate between programmatic concepts and design concepts.
- Generate research-based design concepts.
- Develop space-based and activity-based programs.
- Determine space allocation through a variety of techniques.
- Organize and complete a detailed project program.

WHAT IS A PROGRAM?

The end product of the programming phase is a written document called a **project program**, *programming document*, or *design brief*. This document assimilates and organizes the information gathered by the programmer into a form that is usable by the designer. It is the document that will be the basis for their schematic design. The program may also be used by the client agency to manage the project, in terms of time and cost, or to communicate internally with all departments, to confirm personnel, furniture and equipment, and space needs. Your presentation of the program to the client tells them you have listened to them, have correctly identified their wants and needs, and have also "identified broader issues related to the project, such as human factors, environmental responsibility and social and cultural influences on the design" (Ballast, 2007, p. 1). Upon acceptance by the client, the project program serves as a guide or manual throughout the rest of the design process.

Programs may be written in a variety of forms that vary according to project type, design firm, and client requirements or expectations. In fact, there is quite a bit of variety in the scope and length of project programs. Similar to a contract or legal agreement, a written program may be a simply worded summary or it could be an elaborate, multidimensional document. For a residential project, it might be a list of spaces and furnishings to be included in each room. On a larger project, the program might be a bound volume, with multiple sections, used by all team members to guide not only current needs of the project and organization but future needs as well. The length of a project program varies, as does the format and type of detail.

Through text, numerical quantities, spreadsheets, diagrams, matrices, and images, a project program describes the project requirements that have been distilled from information gathered throughout the programming process. The written program is a stand-alone document that summarizes the project's mission, goals, client, end-users, or target audience. It provides a list of spaces needed, or activities to be accommodated, the size of each space, attributes or qualities of each space, and desired adjacencies. A program also includes quantities and sizes of furnishings, fixtures, equipment (FF&E) or the functional requirements of items that need to be in each room or area. A more detailed program may include technical details about integration of technology, power requirements, and clearances for critical equipment. It may also include site information, if a site has been chosen, or context requirements to help determine an appropriate site for the project. A program can be written independently from a site. A "siteless" project is one that can be located anywhere, or applied to multiple locations, such as emergency housing or a retail outlet that could be placed in any airport. Regardless of length or level of detail, the written program acts as an agreement between client and designer. It documents salient facts and contains an "analysis of the project goals and objectives, aesthetic considerations, organizing concepts, the existing building, activities and relationships, space needs, adjacency requirements, code review, budget requirements and scheduling requirements" (Ballast, 2007, p. 6).

The programming document should be viewed as separate from the design solution. A program can have multiple solutions; as many solutions as there are designers. Any designed or built project that arises from the programming document represents one interpretation of the countless ways the problems can be solved as each designer or project team brings their unique point of view to the program requirements. Therefore, a program should be viewed as an objective guide to be used by any designer. The knowledge, passion, and vision you have for a project and all you have learned must be embedded in the program, or you run the risk that your ideas will be lost in translation from programming to design.

An *activity-based program* focuses on the tasks to be performed in each space and across multiple spaces, either sequentially or concurrently, by the people envisioned to be using those spaces. Similar to writing a performance specification, activity-based programmers tend to describe the functional requirements (what activities the space has to support) rather than the furnishings (physical design solutions typically associated with a function). For example, instead of writing that a space needs a 36 inch x72 inch table and six chairs, the activity-based programmer would write that the space needs to support flexible, individual seating and work surface for six people to meet. Emphasis on the problems to solve in the program allows the designer more freedom to choose the physical aspects of the design solution. Figure 4.1 is a graphic produced by commercial furniture company, Knoll, which categorizes workplace spaces based on type of activity. Primary or "home base" workspace is for independent work (which gives a sense of *territoriality* or *personalization*), while "go to" activity spaces vary by number of expected participants and type of interaction. *Refuge spaces* are for private work away from the primary workspace. *Enclave spaces* are for two to four workers to conduct informal group work. A team meeting space is for up to ten people to plan or strategize. An assembly space is for large group presentations.

Furniture company, Herman Miller, takes a similar approach with what they call the "three branches of ergonomics," a checklist of physical, cognitive, and social human factors guidelines to help designers with activity-based programming for workplace design. Does the environment provide *physical* support and adjustability in terms of seating posture, work surface height, and task lighting? Does the environment support *cognitive* health in terms of views, natural light, appropriate sounds level, and organization? And, finally, does the work environment balance "autonomy and choice"—does it provide an optimal environment for necessary *social* interaction as well as address need for privacy and areas for personalization.

Many facilities or owners tend to use a *space-based program*, meaning that they define spaces based on a commonly accepted or preconceived notion of what spaces that project type *should* hold. For example, a typical space-based program for a residential project may be a living room, kitchen, dining room, two bedrooms, and two bathrooms—a list of commonly found spaces in a home. In fact, most people tend to define their needs in terms of what they have seen before. In the design of a restaurant, for example, the owner may ask for a "hostess stand" rather than asking you to help him define a check-in system for guests. A homeowner may ask for a "master bedroom suite," rather than areas that support sleeping, bathing, and dressing. While a space-based program is ultimately what you may end up producing, it should always be informed by activity-based programming to help overcome assumptions and create an innovative research-based project.

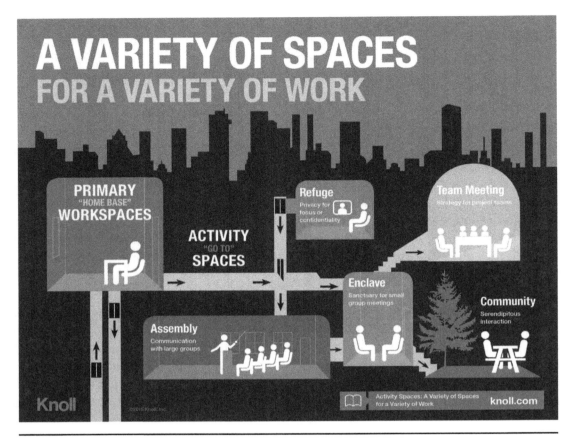

Figure 4.1 Activity-based guidelines for workplace design by Knoll.

ACTIVITY 4.1

Exploring and Identifying Your Program's Activities

Purpose: To begin to develop an activities-based program for your project.

Consider all the information you have gathered about your project. Then, write down thoughtful responses to the following questions:

1. How many different activities take place within the project, both inside and outside of the building? What are these activities? Make a thorough list.
2. What are the *primary activities*? These are the activities that occur on a full-time, frequent, and regular basis. How often is the activity performed? Specify number of times per day, week, month, or year. At what time of day or night does the activity take place (hours of operation)?
3. What are the *secondary activities*? These are the activities that support the primary activities and may occur on a part-time, infrequent, or irregular basis.
4. What is the nature of each activity? Is it public or private? In small groups or large groups? Noisy or quiet? Active or sedentary? Work-related, recreational, educational, or other?
5. Who is involved in each activity?
6. Are there any special *environmental requirements* for any of the activities—access to outdoors, views, natural light? Task lighting, dimmable lighting or darkness? Ventilation, acoustics, plumbing, slip resistance, and so forth?
7. Are there special *security requirements* for any of the activities?

It is not always possible for designers to write their own programs for the projects they are designing. In many cases, the client will supply the project program to the designer. "According to standard AIA agreements, programming is the responsibility of the owner. However, the owner's programmatic direction can vary from vague to very specific. In some cases, the owner does not have the expertise to develop the program and must use the services of a programming consultant" (Cherry & Petronis, 2016). Even though a program may be an owner's responsibility contractually, a designer can step in and assist with programming, or specialize in programming as a consultant.

In the professional arena, a program is often written by someone other than a designer, such as a facilities manager, an owner, or a professional programmer. You may see a program for a school include classrooms filled with tables and chairs, but not know the functions of the rooms, or the abilities and needs of the students and teachers. Or you may have a client who supplies you with a list of appliances she wants in her new kitchen without letting you know anything more about how she imagines using the kitchen. On a regular basis, interior designers must reinterpret space-based programs by looking through the lens of human factors theories and programmatic concepts as discussed in this book.

In school you may have been given a project program to follow by your instructor. Now, you are writing your own program. Even if you are ultimately the person designing it, the rule of thumb is that you should write the program as if someone else will be designing the project. Ask yourself the following questions: Have I embedded all relevant information into the program? Have I articulated my client's values, end-users' abilities, variety of activities, and functional and aesthetic goals? Would a designer who is unfamiliar with my research, or the intimacies of the project type, be able to design the project from this document?

Programmatic Concepts versus Design Concepts: The "What" versus the "How"

The programming document is a description of *what* is to be designed. However, if we gave the same written program to a hundred different designers, we would get a hundred different solutions. Why is that? One explanation is that each designer may have their own design concept.

As discussed in Chapters 1 and 3, a *design concept* differs from a programmatic concept in that it is not a view of the problem to solve but rather an abstract idea or strategy for *how* to solve it creatively. While the program informs you about the functional requirements, the design concept will help you make decisions about the aesthetics of the space. The size of the space and its relationship to other spaces are stated in the program, but the design concept will help you articulate *how* the space is configured or shaped and *how* it relates to the adjacent spaces. The design concept creates a framework for evaluation. It is the poetic image of the project, an idea held in the mind, and it serves as the basis for your design decisions.

Your subsequent design decisions (choice and placement of lighting, flooring, wall colors, furnishings, etc.) either will support your concept or not support your concept. Every solution you come up with during the design process must be run through the design concept to see how that solution reinforces your concept. A strong design concept will help you answer the major questions, such as circulation pattern or overall organization, as well as address the details, such as flooring pattern, style of furnishings, or accent colors (see Figure 4.2).

A research-based design concept arises from or is inspired by information gathered during the programming phase. For example, in Chapter 3, the designer Bill Britt mentions several bits of information that could be turned in to viable design concepts. He talks about how editors like "working in caves," and that his boss commented that his initial design was "very star-trekky looking," which he liked. These two statements involve a metaphor. As discussed in Chapter 2, a *metaphor* is an abstraction or symbol used for poetic reference, which is a powerful tool for communicating design intent and selling the project. Viewing the design as reminiscent of "the bridge" on the Star Trek Enterprise, positioning the engineers with full control to oversee, and incorporating elements that support a cave-like environment for the editors support the design concept.

Design concepts help designers to frame a design project to appeal to the end-users in a way that is deeper than on a functional level, in a similar way that poetry affects the reader differently from reading prose. We will see later (in Chapter 5) that Bill decides to put artwork in the communal space based on a concept derived from his love for photos of nature that include elements of technology, such as clouds behind a satellite dish. The concept was confirmed after one staff member said, "what

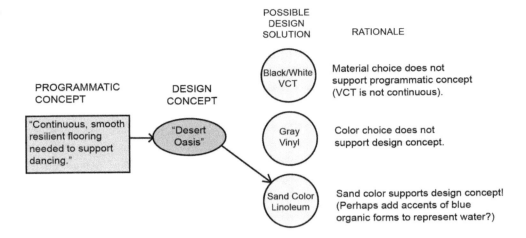

Figure 4.2 Role of the Design Concept.

if you laid them all out in a strip side by side, just like a line going across [the room] . . . like a film strip." The design concept of "nature complementing technology" was born.

In Chapter 5 we will further explore the types of design concepts, and how we can use them in the schematic design phase. For now, a design concept in the program can be used to help guide the layout of the cover page, compose a name for the facility, and a motto or tag line, generate a logo, and be embedded in a concept statement or marketing image strategy commonly referred to as **branding**.

Program Content

The next section explores what to include in each component of a typical program document. Please refer to the template provided in Appendix A and sample program in Appendix B as visual references to accompany the text descriptions and to help create your own written program.

Cover Sheet

The cover sheet of a program sets the tone for the project's identity. It will include the name of the facility, logo of the facility (if applicable), the client or organization the program is prepared for (typically who will be funding or sponsoring the project), date of preparation or submittal, and the designer or programmer's name. Figure 4.3 shows an example of a logo composed by a student for their project. You may also include some photos of end-users, concept imagery, and explanation of the design concept, if developed as part of the programming phase. The design concept or imagery can be presented separately, or as a separate section within the body of the program.

Figure 4.3 Logo for a facility by student designer as part of the cover page of the project program.

The Project Proposal

The project proposal generally includes a **mission statement** that summarizes your understanding of what the client seeks to accomplish with this project. It could include a list of goals, who will be served by the project, and other expectations such as when the project is anticipated to be constructed and where. In addition, you will have a section or at least a few paragraphs that describes the site and project context. This information typically accompanies a vicinity map, satellite view, site plan, or plan of the existing building shell or tenant improvement space. The site analysis diagrams and site summary discussed in the previous chapter can also be inserted here.

A detailed description of the client or client organization, called a **client profile**, explains the history or background of the sponsoring agency or owner, the relevant details pertaining to values and goals, or size of the firm. It may include specific personnel such as the director or stakeholder's photos, backgrounds, and areas of expertise. It would also be helpful to include an organization chart to show decision makers and the hierarchy of the company, or different departments and their key personnel.

ACTIVITY 4.2
Creating a Project Identity

Purpose: To assemble and organize elements that may appear on your project program's cover sheet.

Using the project program template included in Appendix A as a guide, assemble the following elements to compose your cover page.

1. What is the name of your facility? Many projects already have a name which is established by the client or your instructor, however you may have an opportunity to choose the name or modify the project name. When choosing a name, consider your target audience and be creative. List three possible project names here:

   _____

   _____

2. Does your project have a logo? Can you modify the logo to reflect your design concept? Or do you have the opportunity to create a new logo? Jot down your ideas here, with sketches as necessary.

   _____

   _____

3. Oftentimes an interview or observation sparked an "aha" moment that could contribute to your design concept. Have you been able to derive a metaphor from information gathered about your project? Write down at least six words or phrases that stood out as possible poetic references or sources of inspiration:

   _____

   _____

4. Reflect the words you have written down in step 3. Find at least three images or photos that express those words or phrases nonverbally.

Writing about your understanding of your client's values can be difficult to do. It is not unusual to see programs containing a list of requirements but omitting the essence of the project, which would be the key to its most impactful solution. "This search for values is a programming, *not* a design, activity" (Hershberger, 1985, p. 42). For example, during the programming phase for the Salk Institute for Biological Studies in La Jolla, architect Louis Kahn quoted his client, Dr. Jonas Salk, as saying he wanted to "create a facility worthy of a visit by Picasso." The client's appreciation of modern form, and his view that scientific pursuit could benefit from creativity as exemplified by a visit from an artist, was at the heart of the design solution. How can you embed the ideals of your client into the aesthetic and functional goals of the project? This information must be stated clearly, in some form, so that the designer can make choices in keeping with the client's wishes—ones that may not fall into the typical categories of furniture, fixtures, and equipment, or space sizes, but something more ethereal, such as mood or feeling. This idea will be further explored in Chapter 5.

An **end-user profile** outlines the target population of the project, typically including the age range, abilities, and other demographic information such as the special needs of the people who will be served by the project. The term *end-user* encompasses a variety of categories of people, such as patients, staff, visitors, volunteers, guests, board members, students, faculty, workers, doctors, nurses, caregivers, children, and so forth. It is important to separately describe the needs of each type of end-user. For example, nurses will have vastly different needs than patients, such as resilient flooring to reduce back pain, acoustically private areas to discuss patient treatment with other medical professionals, and good task lighting when disbursing medication. You may ask yourself about the needs of different types of patients, as well. Are there some patients who are particularly sensitive to light or noise? Do they use mobility devices? And the variety of visitors such as families with small children. Will they need stroller parking, an area for daycare, or access to a changing station? A sense of empathy and consideration for human factors considerably improves the quality of an end-user profile. A good end-user profile will include statistics from a literature review, a summary of salient points gleaned from past studies, as well as references to original data collection such as quotes from an interview or findings from a survey. You can also make your end-users come alive with photos taken from experiential activities, observation, or case studies.

In a residential project, the client or owner may also be the end-user, but not always. An owner of a housing project may have a certain type of end-user in mind for their rental property, or a residential homeowner may be designing the addition for their aging parent to move in. In that case, the client and the end-user are different and that should be made clear in the project program.

List of Spaces

The core of the written program is a list of required spaces, open areas, or enclosed rooms. One can then turn the list into a spreadsheet format with additional columns as shown in Table 4.1. The *short program* is a concise, "at-a-glance" expanded list of the project program areas containing essential information for an initial layout or diagrammatic space planning. This summary of information is used to select an appropriate building shell for the project or to help determine if the chosen building shell meets the space needs for the program.

Table 4.1 illustrates how you might begin to format the short program in a grid or spreadsheet. Once you have identified all room names, number of units, and the square footage per unit, you can add up your total square footage. Use this total *program area* to estimate the amount of circulation area that may be required. Add the program area and estimated circulation to get a total square footage requirement for the project. The requirement column in the short program itemizes key project requirements such as numbers of anticipated occupants for seating and other furniture components. This column can also include a brief explanation of desired adjacencies, and other programmatic requirements related to an initial space planning such as access to a particular view, or the desired degree of visual or acoustical privacy of the space, flexibility, level of security, and other issues regarding human comfort.

Well-organized lists of spaces show grouping of similar or adjacent spaces with subtotals of net assigned space, estimate the percentage of circulation required, and the total square footage needed. All of these numbers can help you to identify preliminary code issues such as use or occupancy, means of egress, minimum number of exits, and minimum number of restrooms required.

In a *long program* you provide more description of the activities, functional requirements, and types of people using the space to define the areas. The long program emphasizes relationships between spaces as well as between people and spaces. Your long program should use clear, expressive, yet technical language. Be careful not to provide design solutions in your long program, but only programmatic concepts and strategies, as discussed in the previous chapter. For example, a company occupying two floors in an office building might need a way to travel between floors (*the design problem*). The programmatic requirement would be "vertical circulation," which may encourage many different design solutions, such as a stair, an elevator, an escalator, a rope ladder, a firefighter's pole, or even a jet pack. This flexibility allows you, as the designer, to select the most appropriate design solution in the design development phase. If "flexible ergonomic seating that allows for movement" is the *programmatic concept*, what would you select as the design solution? Here's a hint: Have you ever seen office employees sitting on a yoga ball as their office chair? Consider an example

TABLE 4.1

SHORT PROGRAM FORMAT

Room Name or Space Type	Number	Space Allocation (SF)	Total Area	Requirements and Other Notes
Waiting	1	350	350	• Seating for four. • Visual access to reception desk. • Access to natural light without glare or heat gain. • View of park or other positive distraction. • Convenient to restroom and snack lounge.
Offices	2	120	240	• 36 inch x 72 inch worksurface. • Lockable storage cabinet. • (1) office chair. • (2) guest chair. • Visual access to waiting area. Acoustical privacy from waiting area. • Security/control of entry door. • Area for staff personalization.

from the offices of a well-known Internet company. With a large office space, the company had to solve the problem of productive time lost walking back and forth from space to space. What was their design solution? Scooters and "Segways" to move people along the corridors twice as fast and with twice as much fun!

Long programs may utilize **room data sheets** that specify architectural, mechanical, electrical, and plumbing requirements as well as security measures and special requirements. Room data sheets may also contain sample layouts of key equipment showing sizes and clearances to help the designer visualize work flow. Room data sheets are typically used on large-scale healthcare or other highly specialized institutional projects.

Space Names

In a written program, each space or area is given a name. Naming each space may seem like a simple thing to do, but it is very important to understand the significance of naming each space. A room's name determines many assumptions or preconceptions about that room's design and function. A codes official will often base his entire evaluation of the code compliance of the room based solely on the room's name shown on the resulting plan. For example, when you name a room a "bedroom," the

codes official will assume that people will sleep there, and will therefore require operable windows with a minimum dimension as a means of escape in case of fire. If a room is named a "kitchen," you will not be permitted to exit through that room as one of the means of egress.

Even beyond the codes issues are other preconceptions. For example, if you name a room a "bedroom," your resulting design will most likely be a room with a bed in it. If you name that room "private sleeping accommodation for two," you may end up with a completely different design solution. Subtle changes in language may also help you later to think outside the box. Consider the different connotations of the following room names: "cafeteria," "dining hall," "staff lounge," "eatery," or "snack area." Can you think of areas in your program that would benefit from reinterpreting (or reinventing) the room names?

In writing a program for a children's daycare center, interior design student Machiko Ichimaru considered her end-users to select room names that would inspire children. She called the large motor skills play space "the power room," and dubbed the snack area "the refueling station." Names such as these also helped the guest critics at her presentation to understand the playful nature of the space and the student's willingness to explore innovation beyond a typical daycare program.

Space Allocation

Determining space allocation is a skill that generally gets easier with practice over time. Eventually you will have an instinctual sense of the difference between 100 square feet, 500 square feet, and 1,000 square feet. In the meantime, this section includes some tips to help you make educated square footage calculations. There are some terms to be familiar with, and general consideration for allocating square footage. Is the area you are proposing an estimate, a minimum, or a maximum (not to exceed)? Is it net or gross? Does it include space for circulation (corridors, hallways, and aisles)? Does it include space for equipment or ancillary spaces associated with the main space, such as a mechanical room for an elevator or storage for a classroom. Or is this space listed separately? Architects differentiate between **net square feet (NSF)** or *net assignable square feet (NASF)* and **gross square footage (GSF)**, which is the total area of the building including wall thickness. Architects Edith Cherry and John Petronis also recommend using the client's existing facility as a resource for comparison and point of reference when talking to the client about your new program, as "people can relate to what they already have" (Cherry & Petronis, 2016).

A percentage for "tare" space is added to the total NASF. **Tare space** is the area needed for circulation, walls, mechanical, electrical and telephone equipment, wall thickness, and public toilets. Building efficiency is the ratio of NASF to gross square feet (GSF). The building efficiency of an existing space used by a client can inform the selection of the net-to-gross ratio . . . some space within an office is considered circulation, even though it is not delineated with walls. We call this circulation, "phantom corridor." (Cherry & Petronis, 2016)

A good rule of thumb here is to estimate 10 to 20 percent of the net assignable area as corridor and ancillary space as a line item and then add it to the program areas to get an estimate project total. See sample short program included in Appendix B for an example.

Five Methods for Calculating Square Footage

Method 1: Use Prototypical Space Sizes from a Similar Project. Architect and architectural programmer Edith Cherry (2016) recommends studying plans of a similar project, or case study, and doing an **area take-off**, a construction term for cost-estimating purposes for materials such as carpeting or roofing. You can use the polyline area in CAD to get these numbers or print the plan to scale and use an architectural scale and calculator. An example of a color-coded area take-off of a hospital floor plan is shown in Figure 4.4.

The areas have been identified in terms of the various types: patient rooms, waiting area, administration

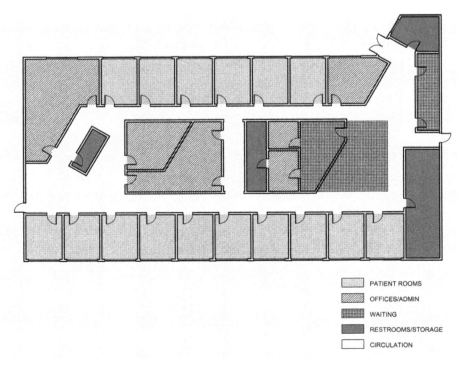

Figure 4.4 Area take-off of hospital floor.

PATIENT ROOMS
OFFICES/ADMIN
WAITING
RESTROOMS/STORAGE
CIRCULATION

offices, ancillary or support areas such as restrooms and storage, and circulation. The area of each of these types is calculated and used as a guideline or comparative case for your program in terms of proportion.

You can use information from your case studies (refer back to Chapter 2) to identify prototypical or appropriate sizes for spaces that are similar to those you are creating. Study the floor plans of other projects to see how the designer has used space. You could confirm your findings by interviewing people within the existing space and ask if the size is appropriate for the function. Keep in mind that you are looking for the most appropriate amount of space for the activity, which may, in fact, differ from the prototype.

Method 2: Identify and Use Standard Dimensions. Some spaces, such as a basketball court in the United States (Figure 4.5), are based on accepted or required standard dimensions. Whether you are designing for a half court or a full court, there is a culturally established set of rules for the space that you will need to abide by. In fact, almost all sports have standard sizes for spaces related to the game. There are standard dimensions of swimming pools, tennis courts, and bowling lanes to name a few. *Time Saver Standards for Interior Design and Space Planning* (2001) by DeChiara. Panero and Zelnik, and is an excellent resource to find standard dimensions of prototypical spaces, as well as the *AIA Architectural Graphic Standards*, edited by Dennis Hall, which is currently in its 12th edition.

Method 3: Use Equipment Size, Clearances, and Human Factors. Another excellent way to determine the size of a space is to research what kind of equipment or furnishings must be in the space and find out the dimension of those objects. Calculate the square footage required to accommodate required equipment or furniture in the space. Don't forget to account for the required clearance around the equipment. For example, a massage table may be 30 inches wide and 72 inches long, or 15.6 square feet. But you must also include the 3 feet of open circulation space required on all sides of the massage table which allows the masseuse to move easily around the table in order to give a massage. So, in practice, the square footage requirement for a massage table is actually 8.5 feet wide by 12 feet long, or 102 square feet. That's a huge difference!

Knowing the sizes of the equipment and any existing or required furniture will help you develop your calculations. This is a great approach for commercial kitchens with large appliances, medical spaces with bulky equipment, and office spaces that will be using systems furniture. The book *Interior Graphic and Design Standards*, by S. C. Reznikoff (1986), is a great tool for finding typical sizes of equipment and furniture when using this approach.

Next, consider the impact of human factors on space allocation. **Anthropometrics** is the study of comparative sizes and ranges of ability in human bodies, whereas **ergonomics** focuses on the interaction of the body with tools and furnishings while engaged in activity or work. *Human Dimension & Interior Space: A Source Book of Design Reference Standards* (1979) by Panero and Zelnik is a classic reference for this kind of information. As you may assume, a person in a wheelchair takes up a different amount of space than a person who is standing, but also consider that there is a difference between static dimensions and dynamic dimensions. Think about your seat in one of your classes. You take up a different amount of space

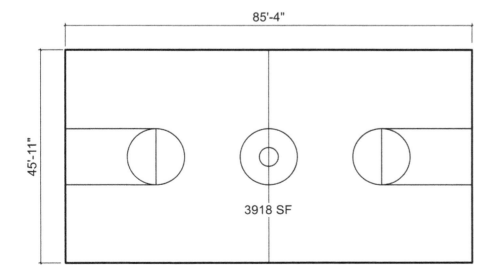

Figure 4.5 Standard dimensions of a basketball court.

depending on whether you are (1) sitting up in your chair, paying attention, or (2) lounging back, with your ankles crossed out in front of you, staring at something outside the window. Another example: When you are focused and working hard at your drafting table, you take up much less space than when you are frantically rallying about your desk, trying to make the deadline for a final presentation. When you are calculating square footages, you should consider not only the static dimensions within the space but also the dynamic dimensions; then accommodate for that heightened level of activity. In the same vein, as espoused by Edward T. Hall in *The Hidden Dimension* (1966) there are invisible personal space bubbles around people, which vary due to their culture and relationship with other individuals in that space. Consider these varying *proxemic* relationships as well when allocating space in both public and private areas. This human factors theory is further discussed in Chapter 6.

Method 4: Multiply or Scale Up from Occupancy Classification and Load Factors. In this method, we use some simple math and code compliance as the minimum basis for space allocation. Start with the number of people you envision will be using the space. This is based on what your research has indicated, and/or what your client has requested. Determine the minimum number of square feet required by code for each occupant. In the *International Building Code (IBC)* each **occupancy classification** or use has a corresponding **load factor (LF)**. An occupant load factor is the maximum floor area allowance per occupant to calculate *occupant load* (which is the number of people allowed to safely occupy the space). The load factor also represents the minimum number of square feet per person

required by code for an occupant in that space. For example, current IBC lists the load factor for Education Occupancy as 20 square feet/person net. This means code has determined that a student needs 20 square feet of space in a classroom setting. If you intend to have a classroom with 30 students, for example, you would multiply 30 students by 20 square feet net each to determine a minimum square footage of 600 square feet (excluding the furnishings or built-ins). Contrast this quantity with the load factor for Assembly, Unconcentrated (Tables and Chairs), which puts the minimum area for someone in a restaurant at 15 square foot/occupant net. If you wanted to accommodate 30 people you would only need a minimum of 450 square feet (excluding the furnishings or built-ins). This is discussed at length in Chapter 6. Please refer to the Table 6.5 for standard occupant load factors. Determine the occupancy classification of that space. Find the appropriate occupant load factor in the table. Multiply the load factor by the number of people expected to use the space, and this gives you a *minimum* required square footage as a place to start.

Method 5: A Holistic Approach Based on Spatial Hierarchy or Priority. This final method is useful if you are designing a project type that is so innovative that you cannot find similar examples, or it is a school capstone project in which you are writing your own program from scratch or have full control over the space allocation. If you already know the overall available square footage for the project or are using a building shell and know how much space is available in that structure, you can use an understanding of your priorities or spatial hierarchy to determine how you want to divide the space. For example, if you are designing a 10,000-square-foot Buddhist retreat, you determine, based on your research, that 50 percent of the square footage, or 5,000 square feet, should be dedicated to the meditation space; 25 percent, or 2,500 square feet, dedicated to a retail space such as a bookstore; and the remaining 25 percent, or 2,500 square feet, dedicated to back-of-house services such as offices, employee locker rooms, and storage (see Figure 4.7). Another way to use the hierarchy or priority approach is to determine how prominent or accessible a space would be. Perhaps, in this same example, you decide that a meditation space is important to be centrally located, or visible upon entry into the building. Therefore, even if you just allocated 10 percent of the total space, or 1,000 square feet, you could show its significance by making a requirement that it be located directly adjacent to the entrance, or at least visually accessible from the entrance, and directly accessible by all other spaces in your adjacency diagram (see Figure 4.8).

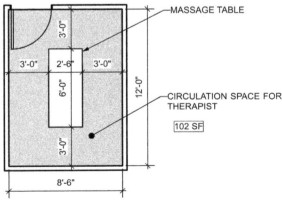

SIZE OF MASSAGE TABLE + CIRCULATION SPACE FOR MASSAGE THERAPIST = MINIMUM SQUARE FEET

Figure 4.6 Massage room based on size of table, storage, and clearance for use.

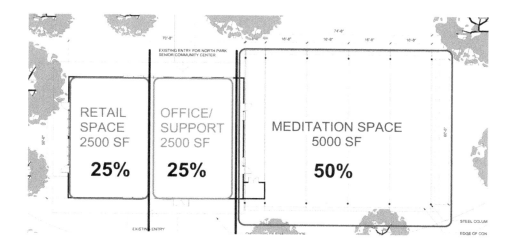

Figure 4.7 Diagram showing one option for Buddhist center using "percentage of the whole" method to allocate space.

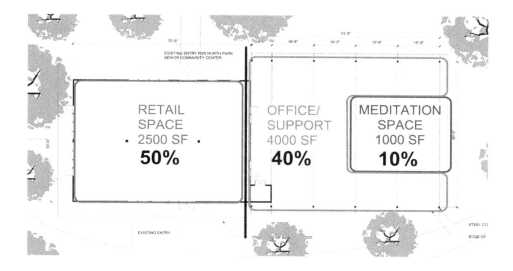

Figure 4.8 Diagram showing alternative option for Buddhist center using "percentage of the whole" method to allocate space.

Use a combination of the above methods to complete your space allocation. After finalizing your calculations, verify your results with the client, or your instructor, before moving forward.

ESTABLISHING RELATIONSHIPS: ADJACENCY MATRIX AND DIAGRAMS

To achieve the functional objectives and work flow for a project, you need to decide which spaces should be directly adjacent, or convenient to each other, to facilitate the relationships among people, objects, and activities. Then you need to communicate that information in your program. There are a few ways to do this. One way is to indicate adjacency requirements in a text or narrative format in the "notes" column in the short program. For

example, when describing a programmatic concept for a nurse's station you could write "must be adjacent to patient rooms," or "must have visual access to patient rooms."

Another method is to graphically indicate the relationships. *Relationship diagrams*, like the one shown in Figure 4.9, are a great way to identify (1) the location of critical spatial relationships and (2) the types of relationships between spaces, from immediately adjacent to no adjacency required. The relative sizes of the bubbles reflect the size of the spaces. Include a key that determines which line type shows *direct adjacency, convenient access,* or *no-access*. You can use lines of varying weight, colored lines, or dashed lines. Unlike a bubble diagram used for synthesis, the relationship diagram is independent from the base plan and never drawn to scale. A well-thought-out relationship diagram will help you to shorten the gap between programming and schematic space-planning.

Purpose: To practice estimating sizes of spaces you experience in order to help you determine appropriate space requirements for your project.

1. Close your eyes and guess the size of the classroom (or room) you are in right now. Write that number here in terms of measurement (length ? width) and/or square footage:

   Guesstimate: _____

2. Verify this guesstimate by counting the number of ceiling tiles, floor tiles, or other modular units in the space. For example, standard ceiling tiles may be 24 inches x 24 inches or 24 inches x 48 inches, and resilient flooring tile tend to be 12 inches x 12 inches and carpet tile may be 18 inches x 18 inches. Or measure the space using a tape measure and calculate the square footage. How close were you?

   Actual size: _____

3. Now go out into the world and try to guesstimate spaces you find yourself in this week.
   - How many square feet is your bedroom?
   - Guesstimate: _____ SF
   - Actual size: _____ SF
   - A local coffeeshop?
   - Guesstimate: _____ SF
   - Actual size: _____ SF
   - A gym or yoga studio?
   - Guesstimate: _____ SF
   - Actual size: _____ SF
   - A supermarket?
   - Guesstimate: _____ SF
   - Actual size: _____ SF
   - One other space: _____
   - Guesstimate: _____ SF
   - Actual size: _____ SF

Use modular units you find in these spaces, such as bricks, ceiling tiles, and flooring tiles to verify the size of the space mathematically. Or bring your tape measure with you. What spaces surprised you in terms of size? Which ones did you think were bigger than they turned out to be? Which ones were smaller? Why do you think that is? After a while you will get a good sense of the size of spaces and your guesses will become pretty accurate!

Many interior designers also use a matrix—either an **adjacency matrix** or a *criteria matrix* that includes an adjacency portion—to document required spatial relationships. An adjacency matrix focuses solely on the nature of spatial relationships, while a criteria matrix also addresses needs and requirements for each space, such as electrical or natural lighting needs (see Figure 4.10). An adjacency matrix or criteria matrix is commonly included in a project program.

The adjacency matrix in Figure 4.10 helped an interior design student develop a bubble diagram over the existing floor plan in Figure 4.11 and then on to schematic design in Figure 4.12.

For your own project, create a relationship diagram and adjacency matrix to help you explore the critical relationships in your project.

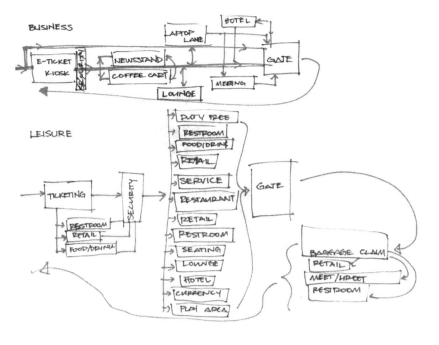

BUSINESS

LEISURE

Figure 4.10 Adjacency matrix for an airport project by interior design student.

■ ADJACENT
☒ NOT ADJACENT
☐ NEUTRAL

	SQUARE FOOTAGE	NON-PASSENGERS	SEATING	MANDATORY TO USE	COMMENTS
TICKETING HALL	80,000	YES	Y/N	Y/N	PROVIDE HUMAN INTERACTION AND KIOSKS
SECURITY	21,000	NO	NO	YES	SEPARATE AREA FOR PAT-DOWNS
RETAIL/SERVICE	50,000	YES	NO	NO	BEFORE AND AFTER SECURITY
CONCESSIONS	20,000	YES	YES	NO	BEFORE AND AFTER SECURITY, VARIETY OF TYPES
CONCESSION SEATING	7,500	YES	YES	NO	SEPARATE AREA OFF CONCESSION AREA; MEETING SPACE
RESTROOMS	15,000	YES	NO	NO	BEFORE/AFTER SECURITY; FAMILY/ASSISTED ACCESS
CONCOURSE	375,000	NO	YES	YES	INCLUDES MOVING WALKWAYS
GATE LOUNGE	275,000	NO	YES	YES	AIRLINE COUNTERS AND PASSENGER LOAD/UNLOAD AREA
CUSTOMS/IMMIGRATION	24,000	NO	YES	Y/N	NEAR ANY INTERNATIONAL FLIGHTS
BAGGAGE CLAIM	50,000	NO	NO	NO	AREA FOR CARTS
MEETING/GREETING HALL	10,000	YES	YES	NO	INCLUDES GIFT/FLOWER RETAIL SHOPS
STAFF/OFFICES	110,000	YES	YES	NO	AREA FOR EMPLOYEES, ACCESS TO CONCESSIONS/RETAIL
HOTEL	100,000	YES	YES	NO	ONLY FOR PASSENGERS
DEPARTURES CURB	35,000	YES	NO	YES	ACCESS TO TICKETING; CHECK-IN AREA
ARRIVALS CURB	35,000	YES	YES	YES	SEATING FOR WAITING PERSONS

Tips and Advice

• View the written program as a living document that can change when new information becomes available. A program is never really finished; it can always be made clearer or include more information.

• Have a trusted colleague read your program and give you written feedback with regard to the following questions: Do they understand the mission statement? Can clarifications be made to the end-user profile which elaborates on the special needs of the target population which may affect multiple spaces? Are there any spaces that you have not included that should be considered? Even seasoned programmers may forget to include a staff break room or janitor's closet.

• List primary spaces first and then consider the secondary spaces which serve those spaces. For instance, consider all of the possible uses of a primary space such as a multipurpose room. If it could be used as a lecture hall, a yoga room, or to host a fundraiser with dining and dancing, ancillary spaces for those uses might be a large storage room, serving kitchen, recycling/trash area, coat check room, and lockers.

• See Chapter 5, Activity 5.4 "Testing Your Written Program through Peer Review," as a way to further revise and clarify your programming document.

Figure 4.11 Bubble diagram for an airport design by interior design student.

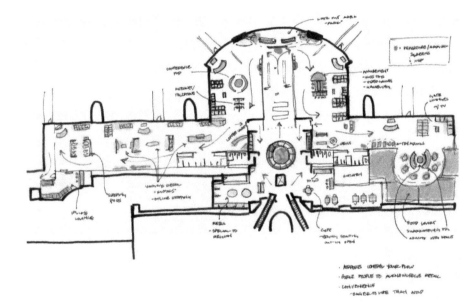

Figure 4.12 Schematic furniture layout for an airport design by interior design student.

Conclusion

In summary, your written program should integrate all of the information you have gathered for a project, as that research has guided your programmatic decisions. In many cases, your program is a living document which aligns with the design process. It is inherently flexible, responding to the evolution of the design, evolving with further information, and subject to change with the client's (or your instructor's) approval. The programming process itself is evolving. According to professional architectural programmers, Edith Cherry and John Petronis (2016), some of the emerging issues in the discipline of architectural programming include:

1. Development of standards and guidelines for owners that build similar facilities frequently. These efforts include:

   a. Formalizing (computerizing) building facility requirements for Web-based consumption—for example, the National Park Service has developed Facility Planning Model Web-based software to assist park superintendents and other staff in the development of space and cost predictions for legislative requests. The intention is to make budget requests more realistic and more comprehensive.

   b. Facility programming to make early predictions to aid in early capital budgeting.

2. Client-owners are increasingly requiring verification that the design complies with the program.

3. New technologies are generating a need for types of space that have no precedents. Basic research on these technologies is required to determine standards and guidelines.

4. As more clients require measures for building energy and resource conservation standards (LEED, Green Globes, etc.), the programming process needs to reflect these requirements in goals, costs, scheduling, and process.

5. The supply of facility programmers is smaller than the demand. More professionals need to consider this sub-discipline as a career path (Cherry & Petronis, 2016).

References

Ballast, D. K. (2007). *Interior design reference manual: A guide to the NCIDQ exam (4th ed.)*. Belmont, CA: Professional Publications, Inc.

Cherry, E. and Petronis, J. (November 2, 2016). *Architectural programming*. Retrieved July 22, 2018, from https://www.wbdg.org/design-disciplines /architectural-programming.

DeChiara, J., Panero, J., Zelnik, M. (2001). *Time saver standards for interior design and space planning.* New York: McGraw-Hill.

Hall, D. (2016). *AIA architectural graphic standards (12th ed.).* Hoboken, NJ: John Wiley & Sons.

Hall, E. T. (1966). *The hidden dimension.* New York: Anchor Books/ Doubleday.

Herman Miller. "Fundamental Human Needs," company confidential, March 2015.

Hershberger, R. G. (1985). Values: A theoretical foundation for architectural programming. In W. Preiser (ed.), *Programming the built environment.* New York: Van Nostrand Reinhold.

Knoll Workplace Research (2012). "Activity Spaces: A variety of spaces for a variety of work." Knoll, Inc.

Panero, J. and Zelnik, M. (1979). *Human dimension & interior space: A source book of design reference standards.* New York: Random House.

Reznikoff, S. C. (1986). *Interior graphic and design standards.* New York: Whitney Library of Design.

5 RESEARCH-BASED SCHEMATICS

*I know noble accents and lucid, inescapable rhythms;
but I know, too, that the blackbird is involved in what I
know.*

— WALLACE STEVENS, *Thirteen Ways of
Looking at a Blackbird* (Stanza VIII)

CHAPTER OBJECTIVES

When you complete this chapter you will be able to:

- Identify different types of design concepts.
- Understand how research can inform your design concepts.
- Use research-based design concepts throughout the schematic design phase.
- Employ ideation and synthesis diagrams to explore multiple design solutions.
- Present your research-based schematic design to instructors, clients, and fellow colleagues.

Upon completion and acceptance of the program, an interior designer then moves on to the second phase of the design process: schematics. Books about research and programming often stop at the end of the programming or pre-design phase. But research and programming principles are used at every step of a research-based design process to ensure research-based design solutions. An interior designer may be handed a program and begin the process of design at the schematic design phase. A conscientious interior designer will thoroughly examine, analyze, and reinterpret the given program, incorporating evidence, theory and best practices, before proceeding to schematics. Throughout the schematic design phase, research assists the designer in translating the problems to solve into potential, viable solutions. It may seem that using research may limit a designer's creativity, but incorporating research can, in fact, assist you to be more creative, and offer solutions that exceed a client's expectation.

The purpose of the schematics design phase is, first, for the designer to be fluid in thinking and to generate many viable solutions. Why? In a professional environment, the answer is simple: you have been hired for your ideas. When you generate many ideas, your flexibility in thinking allows new, previously untried solutions to emerge. Roberto Rengel, in *Shaping Interior Space* (2014), and other educators call this process **ideation**. Ideation, an active process that searches out all the ways of getting to the major goals, involves intuition and leads to alternatives (Koberg & Bagnall, 1976). The product design firm IDEO calls this process "The Deep Dive"— an immersion in the problem at hand, with all of the data gathered around them to create a collaborative state of informed chaos from which multiple ideas emerge. Dave Kelley, the founder of IDEO and of the Hasso Plattner Institute of Design at Stanford University, states, "Routinely coming up with good ideas is what leads to innovation" (Koppel, 1999). Kelley believes that you need a language, a process, and a framework in order to design (2001). He recommends reading *The Art of Innovation*, written by his brother (Kelley & Littman, 2001), which explains IDEO's unique process of brainstorming while surrounded by information. This process for generating new ideas involves a highly collaborative and speculative series of tasks: sketching, sharing, building prototypes, and testing them with potential end-users.

A deadline is often necessary to achieve an outcome, because the process of design could be endless. The word **charrette** is used in design schools to indicate a concentrated effort to create a viable solution in a limited amount of time. It was derived from the Beaux Arts tradition in France when students would be furiously sketching ideas in the horse-drawn cart (or French *charrette*) on their way to school. The modern-day charrette prepares students to generate many ideas—practice "ideating"—as quickly as possible. Withholding judgment during this process is essential. Time limitation also helps. Dave Kelley says, "Without time constraints, you would never get anything done. Because design is a messy process; it can go on forever" (Koppel, 1999).

GENERATING RESEARCH-BASED DESIGN CONCEPTS

In addition to creating a nuts-and-bolts list of *what* your project entails, which is clearly stated in your program, it is also important to establish *how* you are going to achieve these goals. As touched on previous chapters, the *design concept* plays a central role in the translation of the written program to a design solution by giving the client an idea of how their finished design is going to look and feel. Design concepts help you "sell" your project to the client. Design concepts also act as aesthetic filters while you are in the schematic phase of design. Interior designer Laura Metcalf states, "The design concept drives the bus!" She says that having a clear and compelling design concept means that you can go through an entire library of fabrics and quickly select exactly the right one. She says, "Keep the design concept firmly in the front of your mind as you search for the appropriate fiber, color, pattern, texture, and watch how easily you will be able to determine whether a fabric aligns with, supports, further enhances, or conflicts with your design concept" (personal communication, August 23, 2018).

As you will find about most tasks in interior design, generating a good design concept is more of a skill than a talent. It is a skill that can be perfected over years of practice. But a few pointers about developing concepts can help a great deal. One key point is to make it memorable for anyone who hears it. A good design concept, like a good poem, song, or work of art, evokes an emotion or excitement in the viewer or listener. So try saying your design concept to friends, family, and colleagues, to gauge their reaction.

In previous chapters there was some discussion of design concepts. This chapter will delve deeper into the role that the design concept plays in the evolution of your design, as well as explore ways to incorporate research into your design concepts. As discussed in Chapter 3, design concepts differ from programmatic concepts. While the program will describe *what* needs to be in the space in terms of functional requirements, the design concept will help you decide *how* to put it there in terms of configuration and aesthetics. Your overarching design concept serves as the *basis for your subsequent design decisions.*

As we discussed in Chapter 1, design concepts can be *imposed on* the project, as with an art-based concept, or can be *derived from* information gathered during the programming phase. A research-based design concept, one that uses quotes from client interviews or surveys, appeals to clients mainly because they may feel they are "being heard." One client of the author reports, the designer did a "good job of listening to us and trying to understand our culture. My best advice would be to make the designs personal to the client." Another client, the head of a religious facility, warns future interior designers, "(do) not allow (your own) belief systems to interfere with professional and creative judgment. Always listen to the client and find the deeper meaning behind the words being spoken." This reminds us of the premise behind creating ZMET collages during the programming phase (discussed in Chapter 2). We need to uncover unconscious desires of the client and compose a metaphorical design statement based on these unspoken wants.

Out of research, metaphors emerge. A good designer relays back to the client what they require in simple and direct terms to manifest their inconspicuous needs. The principle of *abstract thinking* applies to this task at this phase of design. We can derive or distill design concepts from underlying stories, themes, or feelings we uncover, turning statements made during an interview or selections in a survey into an abstract summary. It is important that your design concept be communicated simply and directly to the client and, if necessary, the end-users. So, it is best if the design concept can be distilled to its essence, to a single word or phrase. Table 5.1 includes examples of very brief design concept statements in quotations.

Rengel (2014, p. 265) has defined the categories into which design concepts generally fall:

1. Philosophical (example: "less is more")
2. Thematic (example: a western bar)
3. Functional (example: a two-wing configuration)
4. Artistic (example: a balanced composition of bold colors)
5. Mood-Related (example: a place that induces tranquility)
6. Stylistic (example: a space that combines traditional and futuristic elements)

In Table 5.1 this list is expanded to include a few other categories of concepts, illustrated by well-known designers and student examples. This table also separates more comprehensive concepts (applicable to a majority of project types) from simpler concepts (applicable to limited project types.) A strong design concept is one that can answer a multitude of design questions, on many levels, such as spatial organization, sequence, hierarchy, furnishing types and layout, lighting levels, textures, patterns, color palette, and so forth. A concept would be considered weak if it just addressed an artistic or a stylistic concern—solely focused on colors or architectural detail.

An example of a *philosophical* design concept is the Vidarkliniken in Sweden, designed by Eric Asmussen. With its first location completed in 1992, it is a place of healing based on *anthroposophical medicine*, a "philosophy of healing the body, soul, and spirit" conceived by Rudolf Steiner. This philosophy sees "illness as a gift and healing as a conscious process of self-transcending spiritual development" (Coates, 1997, p. 148). The healing must engage the patient, as the patient is actively involved in the healing process. The design responds to the philosophy on every level of design—from the way the buildings relate to one another, interior circulation space, space plan, to the window locations, shape and detail, the furnishings, and the colors and finishes. Architecturally, the community of healing is expressed as a cluster of three buildings that complements the natural features of the site (Coates, 1997). The main circulation corridor has widened alcoves that alternately face the wild forest and the inner courtyard, a balance of the "turning inward of the life energies and a desire for isolation." The patient's gradual interest in returning to increased activity is "intentionally aroused by the corridors' rhythmically varied, naturally flowing spaces" (pp. 130–31).

The interior walls are painted by the "lazure" method, in which vegetable dyes are layered into a beeswax medium, resulting in soft, glowing walls. The color of the walls of the patient's room corresponds with the patient's illness: warm colors to balance "cold" illnesses such as sclerosis and cool colors to counteract "warm" illnesses such as inflammation (Coates, 1997, p. 131). Asmussen's placement and configuration of windows also support the mind–body–spirit connection, separating sky-viewing windows from earth-viewing windows, which emphasizes the separation of heaven from earth. The earthbound windows are configured with deep shelves to hold flowers, plants, and artwork.

Rudolf Steiner, founder of anthroposophy, Waldorf education, biodynamic agriculture, anthroposophical medicine, and the new artistic form of eurythmy . . . advocated a form of ethical individualism, to which he later brought a more explicitly spiritual component. He derived his epistemology from Johann Wolfgang Goethe's world view, where "Thinking . . . is no more and no less an organ of perception than the eye or ear. Just as the eye perceives colours and the ear sounds, so thinking perceives ideas." (https://www.waldorfsandiego.org/our-school/waldorf-history/, retrieved September 10, 2018)

TRANSLATING CONCEPTS TO FORM

In an article titled "Lines of Inquiry" (2006), architect Alan Phillips states, "Diagrams, in whatever visual form they take, represent a threshold moment in the creation of successful architecture." In *Space Planning Basics* (Karlen, Ruggeri, & Hahn, 2004), Mark Karlen refers to a "synthesis gap": that perceptible junction or moment between the end of research (information-gathering) and the beginning of design—the conceptual leap between the known and the unknown. This leap of faith at the onset of design is often a stressful moment for students. Or it can be a very exciting moment, if you are armed with the appropriate tools.

How do you go from a written program to space plan? How do you go from analysis to synthesis? How do you bridge the conceptual gap?

TABLE 5.1

COMPREHENSIVE DESIGN CONCEPT CATEGORIES FOR ALL PROJECT TYPES

Design Concept Category	Explanation	Examples
Philosophical	Based on a particular school of thought or practice	• Rudolf Steiner's *anthroposophical medicine*, a philosophy of healing explored in Vidarkliniken in Sweden • Rudolf Steiner's essay "Education in the Light of Spiritual Science" (1907), which describes the major phases of child development underlying Waldorf school design.
Scientific	Based on measurable or generally accepted principles	• "Aqua-Marine-Odyssey," an aquarium designed around the natural movement and physical properties of water, which result in ideal bio-habitats for the animals and their interaction with human visitors. • "Circadian Rhythm House," a residence in which the layout of the rooms correspond to the sun path, providing natural light to daily domestic functions to improve health and well-being.
Process-Oriented	Based on an observed natural or man-made occurrence, dynamic or change over time	• "Metamorphosis," a medical facility based on the concept of transformation as a natural biological process, from caterpillar to butterfly, or from sickness to wellness. • "Flip the Switch" a restaurant that gives owners the ability to change seasonal décor through use of technology.
Ideological	Based on the idea of a causal relationship between space and a desired social or behavioral response.	• "Hum" furniture system by Kimball, which uses cognitive ergonomics and environmental psychology to design workspaces in alignment with how our brain organizes information, and our need for privacy and social interaction. • A civic center based on the idea that "art unites," to encourage a sense of inclusion, and foster creativity and participation of community members.
Experiential	Based on the phenomenological/ existential idea to create a state of mind in the occupant through using their senses	• "Bluewater," an immersive museum that uses sound, texture, color, and light to create an underwater simulation to foster empathy in the viewer for sea creatures. • "A Monastery for Scientific Research" idea behind the Salk Institute for Biological Research in La Jolla, by Louis Kahn in which he envisioned scientists needing the silence and light typically found in secluded religious retreats.
Narrative	Based on a sequence of spaces that communicates a story, progression, or journey	• "Into the Woods," an outpatient clinic for children using the characters and plot of a fairy tale to help reduce stress or foster a transition from sickness to wellness. • "Our Story," a waiting room designed to portray the history of the organization and surrounding neighborhood.
Juxtaposition	Based on seemingly disparate, opposite or unrelated ideas put together for a unique contrast.	• "Ozark Gothic," the concept behind Thorncrown chapel by architect Fay Jones combined the spatial height of Gothic architecture with the wooded setting of northwest Arkansas. • An "East Meets West" concept for a medical clinic which combines the wisdom of eastern culture with western medicine practices.

(continued)

(continued)

TABLE 5.1

ADDITIONAL DESIGN CONCEPT CATEGORIES LIMITED TO SOME PROJECT TYPES

Stylistic	Based on visual details and elements of a particular architectural genre	• *Art Nouveau* • *Craftsman Bungalow* • *Romanesque* • *Baroque* • *Mid-Century Modern*
Formalistic	Based on the manipulation or use of artistic elements (lines, shapes, color and texture) and principles of design such as symmetry, unity, harmony, pattern, etc.	• "Twisting Torso" Santiago Calatrava's concept behind the structure of a high-rise building in Sweden • Eero Saarinen used curvilinear concrete forms evoking wings of a bird to capture the "Spirit of Flight" in the design of TWA airport terminal.
Functional	Based on solving the functional requirements, extended to the aesthetics of the space	"Granny Flat," a residence designed to support aging-in-place by using Universal Design principles that support human activity over the course of a lifetime.
Mood-Related	The desire to evoke a particular emotional response in the occupant	• A theater designed to evoke a sense of mystery or suspense. • A cathedral inspires awe and a sense of wonder. • A waiting room with a spa-like atmosphere intended to be relaxing.
Thematic or Image-Based	Based on simulating the sensory experience of a particular time period, genre, or cultural milieu	• A children's dental clinic based on the imagery of animals in a zoo setting. • Rides in Disneyland, such as *Pirates of the Caribbean* or *Mark Twain Riverboat*, offer a dynamic theme-based entertainment experience.

ACTIVITY 5.1
In Search of a Research-Based Design Concept

Purpose: To use interview transcripts to generate a research-based design concept.

1. Interview a friend—ask them to describe a recent pleasant event or experience such as a vacation or party.
2. Audio record and transcribe, or use "talk to text" function on your recording device to turn the interview into a transcription.
3. Go through the interview transcript and highlight any word or phrase that could be viewed as the starting point of a design concept using the categories listed in Table 5.1. For example, a friend may say, "It was like a dream" or "in my mind's eye." Natural speech is often full of poetic references, metaphors, and descriptive phrases.

    Write down several of them here: _____

    _____

4. Now, go through the transcript of an interview you have conducted during the programming phase of your project. See if you can find similar hidden gems: words or phrases that can be used as a beginning of a design concept.

    Write down several of them here: _____

    _____

One of the best tools designers use to transition from research to design are diagrams. In fact, diagrams could be considered the primitive or early *language* of design. They translate the words and phrases of the written program into visual forms. In *The Hidden Dimension*, Edward Hall (1966) sees language as a basis for perception. We often think it is the other way around, that we see things and then perceive them; but in fact learning words, even the sequence of words in our language, frames our perceptions and organizes our thoughts! For example, in the United States we name soup by the *objects* in the soup, such as clam chowder or chicken noodle. In contrast, the Japanese name their soups by what the *broth* consists of, such as miso. (*Miso* is the fermented soybean paste suspended in the broth.) If the soup contains vegetables or noodles, that information is added to the soup's name as a secondary aspect, as in "miso ramen." This also translates spatially, to the way people of different cultures experience space differently. "When Westerners think and talk about space, they mean the distance between objects . . . we are taught to perceive . . . and to think of space as 'empty.' The meaning of this becomes clear only when it is contrasted with the Japanese, who are trained to give *meaning* to spaces—to perceive the shape and arrangement of spaces; for this they have a word, *ma*" (Hall, 1966, p. 153). Diagrams are a way to perceive, analyze, and manipulate space, to give meanings to space.

The reason for bringing up the idea of language is to make a connection between diagrams and language.

Discussions of different kinds of diagrams in this chapter are intended to increase your design "vocabulary." We will start by introducing several different diagramming techniques, give examples of each, and encourage you to start using them on your own project. Each diagram type allows you to view and interpret information differently, leading you to new ways of configuring space.

DIAGRAMS

"It is very difficult to think of complex things being expressed in simple terms without the use of diagrams" (Phillips, 2006, p. 68). When scientists were racing to find the form and structure of DNA, "the diagram which emerged . . . the first sketch of the double helix made by Francis Crick, is very much an architectural sketch with soft lines swimming in space, an authoritative representation of geometry, and a confidence that could easily have come from the hand of Louis Kahn or Eero Saarinen" (Phillips, p. 68). (See Figure 5.1.)

Phillips (2006) further defines architectural diagrams as either *representational* or *abstract*. A representational diagram is a sketch designed to be interpreted visually and geometrically, while an abstract diagram represents an idea. He talks about *flow* and *system*—*referential* sketches in which the designer refers to past influences or previous experience—and the *doodle*, which results from thinking about something else while drawing. He also identifies

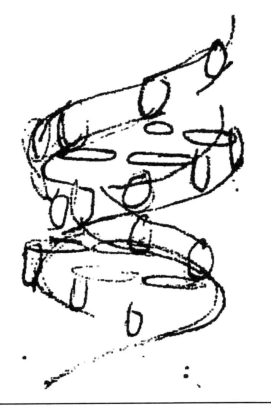

Figure 5.1 Francis Crick's first sketch of the double helix of DNA.

a *polemical* sketch, which is "sometimes presented as an irritable grouping of marks born of frustration . . . or awakening" (Phillips, p. 71). It is a drawing produced by the act of drawing and is not necessarily thought out first.

The "napkin diagram"—which documents communication between people in public places, at meetings, or attempts to illustrate a thought that one would have on an airplane or during a meeting—is an often underrated but valuable tool. Many designers rely on moments of inspiration that can come from impromptu yet meaningful conversations during a relaxed state of mind. Be prepared to put those ideas into a visual form at any moment.

> The first diagram is made in the mind of the author. . . . The beauty of the diagram "as imagination."
> . . . the mind-diagram contains a moral and ethical fingerprint, as to how the eventual building will provide the greatest good for the greatest number. . . .
> During the early stage of sketching, the diagram is required to fold the "self" into the drawing, so that

the link between the physical work, the imagination . . . and the ethical responsibility . . . are one and the same thing. (Phillips, 2006, p. 72)

Although many types of diagrams are used in science and architecture, two categories of diagrams are used specifically for interior design:

- **Analysis diagrams**, to document and ponder existing conditions or to represent the program requirements such as relative sizes of spaces and adjacencies as a graphic extension of the written program (discussed in Chapter 3).
- **Synthesis diagrams**, to quickly generate multiple possible configurations that meet functional or aesthetic requirements, or to simply propose something new.

Analysis diagrams represent the known, while synthesis diagrams may represent the unknown. In Chapter 3, we explored using some of these analytical diagramming techniques. The purpose of the next few pages is to review the function of previously learned diagramming techniques, to weigh the pros and cons of each, and to introduce new ones to expand your ability to perceive and manipulate interior space. (For a summary of diagram types, see Table 5.2.)

Diagrams Used for Ideation

Proposing something new is a leap between what you know and what you don't know, which often requires courage. Synthesis diagrams help you bridge the gap between what you know and what you want to create using lines or marks on a paper that allow you to ponder, speculate visually, and propose something new. Architect Steven Holl believes this is best accomplished by drawing by hand on a daily basis. He does ink sketches and watercolor paintings on 3 inch ? 5 inch index cards every morning to help him in this practice. When beginning a diagram, you can be guided by your program requirements of size, proximity, and location. Or you can be inspired by your design concept to draw something in a particular shape.

Parti Diagrams

"The word 'parti' passed into architecture via l'Ecole des Beaux Arts to represent that freehand sketch diagram that was at the tangent between idea and imagination. The parti

Figure 5.2 Freehand parti diagrams (drawn on a blackboard by author).

is the *threshold sketch*" (Phillips, 2006, p. 73). The term comes from the French verb *partir*, which means "to separate." Therefore, we can envision this diagram as freehand marks on a paper guided by the designer's thoughtful first expression of a conceptual separation of parts. This separation can be a distinction of parts or areas (such as an inner realm divided from an outer realm), or the idea behind an end-user's intended movement through the space (such as a spiral upward or through a series of concentric circles). A **parti diagram** can also be a *figural gesture* that unifies or makes the whole project work together. A few hand-drawn parti diagrams are shown in Figure 5.2.

A parti is the sketch of a designer rather than a programmer. The designer, in this moment, is temporarily suspended from the role of researcher yet still immersed in information while proposing something new. Now is the time to take that leap of faith, to take the written concept to a drawn form by calling upon subconscious or non-rational skills. You may use a hand-drawn diagram or you can create a parti using digital tools, as well.

One way to learn about parti diagrams is to look at examples. A classic parti underlies the design of a traditional catholic church (Figure 5.3) in which a person enters, moves along the nave toward the altar, but may turn at the crossing to the north or south transept. This parti creates a building that ends up in the form of a cross-shaped, or cruciform, floor plan.

Another famous parti is the Guggenheim Museum by Frank Lloyd Wright. In the mind of the architect, one views the gallery of artwork as an upward spiral along a continuous path or ramp. Wright also considered how one would enter by walking off the street or emerge from the parking garage in considering the placement of building forms on the site (Figure 5.4).

As suggested by architect Louis Kahn, architecture is the thoughtful making of space. Similarly, we can say that interior design must also contain *design thinking*, which is represented or manifested in the earliest sketch. In this way, you can view a parti diagram as simply a translation of your design concept onto the site. In research-based design, a parti is also guided by the data you have internalized about the site and the program as well. So the first poetic gesture is produced within a rich context of understanding. You may need to add some supplemental text to your parti diagram to express your thoughtful process as shown in Figure 5.5.

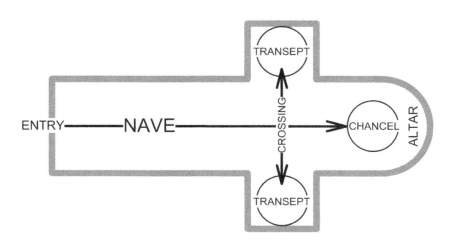

Figure 5.3 Example of a classic parti diagram: a church design that results in a cruciform floor plan (drawn in CAD by author).

Figure 5.4 Example of a famous parti diagram: Frank Lloyd Wright's Guggenheim Museum in New York City (drawn in CAD by author).

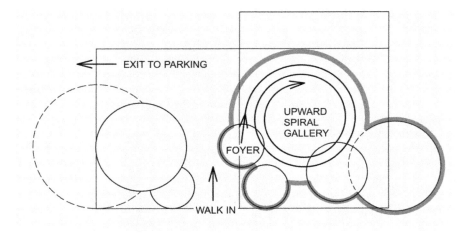

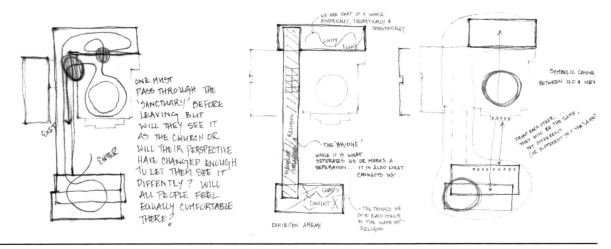

Figure 5.5 Example of parti diagram with supplemental text.

A client's logo, or other imagery inspired by the client's artwork or hobbies, can inspire a parti diagram as well, as long as you can identify the thinking behind the drawing. For example, a parti diagram of a flower can connect parts of your program using a powerful, yet simple, figural device. In a recent residential project that had a 180 degree view of the ocean horizon, the interior designer created a parti that envisioned entering the space as one would enter the bow of a ship, with a resulting "wake" of zones rippling on either side. The parti was successfully communicated to the client as he enjoyed the concept of his home being metaphorically associated with being aboard an ocean vessel. The parti diagram (in Figure 5.6) indicated why removing walls, adding a deck, a bow window, curved stair, and angled floor pattern would all support the design concept. In addition, subsequent design decisions, including the finish materials, color

palette, and furniture selection, will help maximize the panoramic view, support an underlying process-oriented design concept of nautical navigation, and a mood-related feeling of adventure.

Circulation Diagrams

This type of diagram focuses on the movement of people through a single space or through passageways that lead to destination spaces. We can also do a **circulation diagram** to identify different types of organization patterns or plan arrangements in an entire building. Main circulation patterns can be linear, radial, central, networked, or nodal (see Figure 5.7). Linear patterns may have variations, as in a continuous path that loops back to its origin or entry point. Networked patterns may have variations as well, as you may have to pass through one space to get to

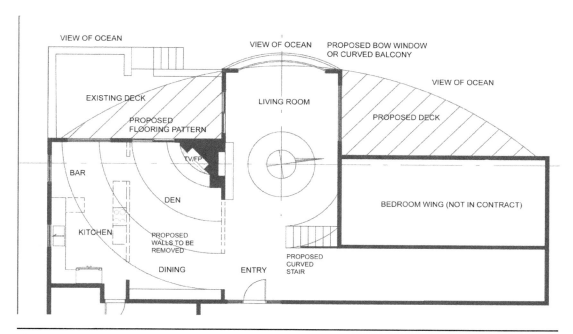

Figure 5.6 Parti diagram for a residential remodel envisions the home as a metaphorical bow of a ship. Note conceptual compass symbol in center showing north.

another (a French term, *enfilade*) in a linear format or in some other pattern like a triangle. Ballast (2013) also adds there can be a *grid pattern*, like the way the streets of New York City are organized, and an *axial pattern*, similar to traveling the streets of Paris.

The circulation diagram can often be derived from or informed by a previously completed analytic *work flow* diagram. If a patient has a series of places to go on a typical doctor visit, the circulation pattern may follow as a string of destinations off a central artery. If a visitor arrives at the entrance and has choices about which place to go, we may call upon a central or radial organization. The difference between a central circulation pattern and a radial circulation pattern is that in a central circulation pattern, the space that a person is standing in when deciding which way to go is a main space, such as an atrium or garden; and a radial circulation pattern may result from divergent corridors (which would not be a central space), as in a mall configuration that has major destinations, such as Nordstrom, Sears, and Macy's, at the end of each of the radiating main corridors.

Bubble Diagrams Revisited

As we have discussed in the previous chapter, a bubble diagram can be employed as a good visual representation

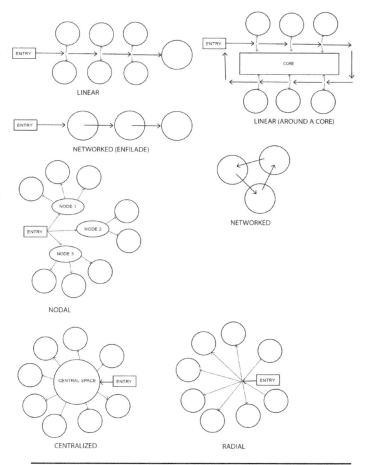

Figure 5.7 Circulation diagrams to be imposed on a floor plan.

of desired relative sizes and adjacencies of program areas, showing convenient, direct, and separated relationships between program areas when they are neatly assigned each to their own bubble. A bubble diagram is especially useful when it is color-coded, complete with a legend, and included in the program. Many designers then use a bubble diagram technique when initially locating the program areas on the existing building shell. When a bubble diagram is drawn over the existing building shell, the "direct" relationship line between two adjacent spaces (for example, the kitchen and dining) often becomes a doorway (or a corridor if it is an indirect relationship), and the edge of the bubble becomes a wall. In the worst case scenario, designers end up with curving walls. In this way, a bubble diagram may be seen as a weak method of translating the program to a schematic floor plan. You may want to supplement your design process with other types of diagram techniques listed in this chapter.

Block Diagrams

A **block diagram** has limitations similar to a bubble diagram in that room names are assigned to each area (see Figure 5.8).

However, it is easier to transition a block diagram into a schematic floor plan due to the straight edges and the ease of overlapping or intersecting blocks to achieve interesting spatial configurations that go one step beyond mere adjacency. According to Ballast (2013), there are four ways that spaces can be "adjacent" to one another: (1) they can be next to one another, (2) they can overlap one another to create an intermediary zone, (3) they can be convenient to one another through an intervening space, and (4) one space can be within the other. Direct adjacency can also include one space being partially embedded within another space, or a space being open to or combined with another. Figure 5.9 illustrates these six adjacency options.

A block diagram can be a final diagram that occurs as a result of an overlay over other types of diagrams such as a parti and circulation diagram. Try generating a parti, followed by a functional diagram (discussed

in the next section), then put a fresh sheet of trace paper over both diagrams to start placing your program areas (rooms). For example, a library fits nicely into the quiet, sunny, dry area. Reception would be located between staff and patient areas.

Multiple block diagrams, showing alternative options, give clients a choice, or an illusion of a choice. If you just show them one, they have nothing to compare it to. After drawing one viable block diagram, a good practice is to put it aside, and then come up with something completely different. Use a comparison to show the benefits of the preferred solution. A minimum of two block diagrams should be done for every project.

Functional Diagrams

This type of diagram offers a kind of flexibility that is not found in bubble or block diagrams. Instead of starting with each room in its own bubble or block, you can focus on a broader set of characteristics or spatial qualities, and then place program areas in the naturally supportive locations. **Functional diagrams** divide spaces not by room names but by other aspects such as type of activity. A designer can group activities into those activities that are passive versus active, quiet versus noisy, or individual versus social interaction. There may also be intermediate gradations of semi-private or semi-public activities. Areas can be categorized by type of occupant: visitor versus

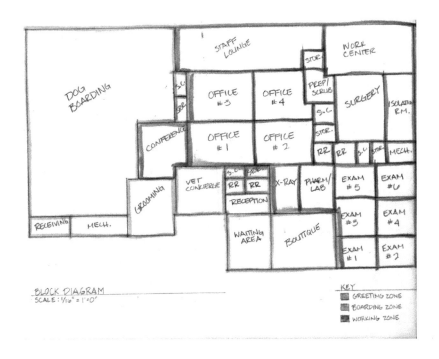

Figure 5.8 Example of a block diagram.

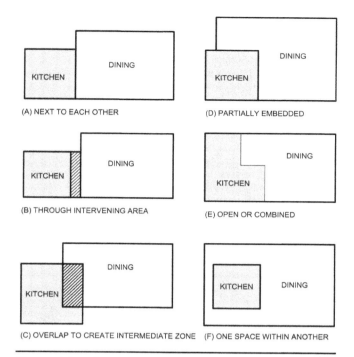

Figure 5.9 Adjacency options in a block diagram, adapted from Ballast (2013) and expanded by author.

employee, faculty versus student, adult versus children, or by age of child, to name a few.

In a healthcare project, for example, you may want to distinguish between sterile and non-sterile areas, patient versus staff, or outpatient versus inpatient. In other project types, such as hospitality or retail, functions will relate front-of-house versus back-of-house, or high-security versus low-security. In almost all projects, you will want to determine areas that need natural light (sunlight) and those that need to be dark, and areas that need to be quiet versus areas that tend to be noisy. A functional diagram may indicate areas with sound-absorptive materials and those with sound-reflective materials, or high versus low ceilings. In a place with a pool or other water elements, you will want to distinguish wet areas from dry areas for future consideration such as imperviousness or slip resistance of flooring materials.

Functional diagramming techniques can apply to spaces of any size, from an 80-square-foot kitchen to an 80,000-square-foot institution. For smaller spaces, this diagram may be referred to as **zones of use**. In kitchens designed by the zoning method, the functional spaces are typically designated as cook, prep, store, serve, and clean up. Thus, zones of use plans are conceived differently from those generated by the more analytic triangle method (which links a path between the three major fixtures: the refrigerator, the stove, and the sink).

Figure 5.10 is an example of a master bedroom suite planned around three zones for sleeping, bathing, and dressing. The first diagram is a color-coded functional diagram over a figural parti representing a fluid movement between the three spaces without a need for doors. The

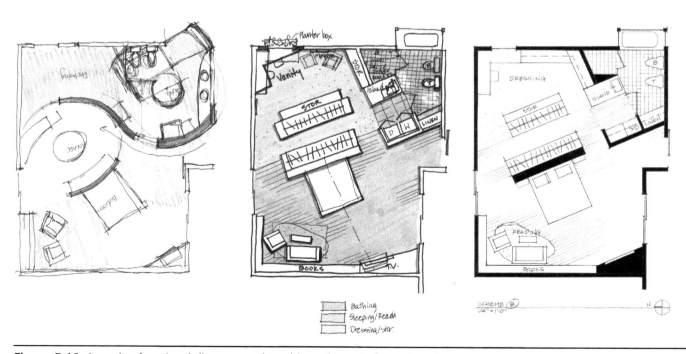

Figure 5.10 A parti, a functional diagram, and resulting schematic floor plan of a master bedroom suite.

second diagram further defines the three color-coded areas through change of materials and rectilinear partition elements. The series of diagrams allowed for flexibility of thinking which crystallized innovation and functionality into a schematic design solution on the right.

For larger spaces—such as an institutional or hospitality space, a library, a school, or a hotel—a functional diagram would correspond to your understanding and configuration of spaces on a gradation of noisy to quiet, age ranges, and active to passive (see Figure 5.11). In the design of a daycare center, for example, sometimes these levels of activity are listed by how much of the body is physically engaged in action—such as gross motor (running, dancing), fine motor (art, crafts), and sedentary (reading, napping).

Both *zones of use* and *levels of activity* can inform a functional diagram that would explore finish material possibilities. Flooring materials, for example, can be categorized into hard, resilient, and soft. For projects that have a "wet versus dry" functional diagram, the proposed finishes could be categorized by impervious and pervious. A functional category of seamless flooring could be an overlay on the functional areas previously marked as "sterile."

Rengel (2014) notes that one strength of a functional diagram is that you can develop your own graphic vocabulary using colors, hatches, line weights, dashes, and symbols to represent a variety of things you are interested in exploring. The graphic vocabulary for diagramming includes graphic symbols to differentiate bubbles for hierarchy; different line types, dashes, line weights, and arrow styles to indicate movement; and special symbols to indicate entry, destination, landmarks, and exits. Providing text labels, color coding and a key can help illustrate your thinking process and communicate that process to others (see Figure 5.12).

In a gym, the locker rooms can be viewed conceptually as the transition between "street clothes" and "barefoot" areas. In a supermarket, areas can be categorized into "frozen," "refrigerated," and "room temperature." Alternatively, the areas can be categorized as "produce," "meat," "dairy," and "dry goods." A specialized grocery can also sort the areas by "organic," "vegetarian," "vegan," and "raw"; or "local" and "shipped." On the shelves down an aisle, how many ways can you categorize how food is organized, such as "kid's eye height"? Think about how many ways there are to separate areas at a wine retailer. You can sort by country of origin, by type of wine, by price. How many other ways can you categorize the project type you are working on? A functional diagram is unlimited in its potential to categorize, sort, and group areas to help you envision myriad spatial configurations that all correspond to programmatic requirements.

The beauty of the functional diagram lies in the fact that there are no rules. It emphasizes activity or a programmatic concept over space names. Instead of thinking that kitchen and dining are two separate rooms, try thinking about the overlapping functional

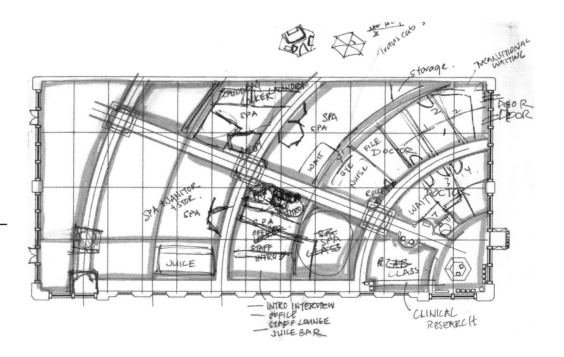

Figure 5.11 Example of a functional diagram showing gradations of activity types from waiting (public/noisy) to clinical (semi-public) to spa (private/quiet).

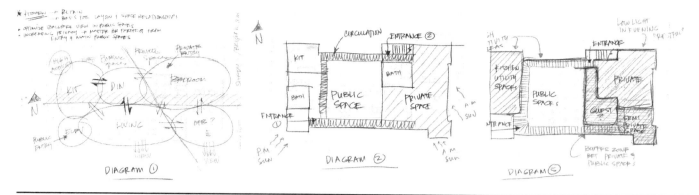

Figure 5.12 Example of a bubble diagram and two functional diagrams for a residential project.

performance areas of storing, prepping, cooking, serving, eating, entertaining, and clean-up. Then recognize groups of qualities such as spatial qualities, lighting levels, and materials that support those activities.

Composite Diagrams

Alan Phillips sees computers as a "quicker diagram management tool, replacing hundreds of paper overlays with click-on-click-off layer process." Take advantage of the layers, the scale, and the flexibility in computer applications! The computer has its strengths, just as hand-drawn sketches do. Use a combination of both, in a back-and-forth manner, until the revolutionary, or ideal, design solution emerges. Figure 5.13 represents the use of the computer to produce a structural analysis diagram that identifies which walls must remain and the potential for expansion, as well as the scaled

accuracy of the furnishings such as the bed, the depth of the hanging storage, and the toilet fixtures. The drawings done by hand explore movement, options, and design thinking behind furniture placement and materials. Note the additional, small elevation studies for cabinets in the margins. The resulting schematic reflects the layers of information incorporated into the exploratory, composite sketch.

Massing Diagrams

The **massing diagram** differentiates between enclosed space and open space, between objects and space, or between program space and support space. It is sometimes referred to as a *mass/void diagram*, as it shows the built space in relation to open space, or positive space in relation to negative space.

ACTIVITY 5.3
Developing a Functional Diagram of Flooring Materials

Purpose: To apply a functional diagram technique to a current project.

1. Put a sheet of trace paper over a preliminary space plan that you have begun in a studio class.
2. Assign colors or hatch patterns to three different categories of materials, such as "hard," "resilient," and "soft" or "patterned," "solid," and "directional" (or develop your own categories, such as materials that correspond with various elements: "wood," "earth," and "water," or gradations of cost, such as "very expensive," "average," and "inexpensive").
3. Define areas according to flooring material designations. Keep in mind that different materials may be used in a single room, or that multiple rooms may use the same material.
4. See if you can link areas conceptually by using continuous flooring or divide a large area by introducing more than one type of flooring. Materials should respond to programmatic criteria as well as support your design concept.

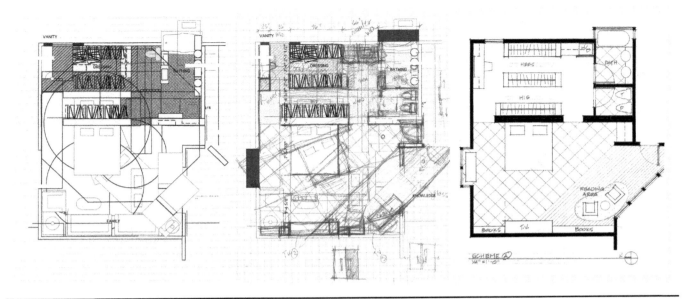

Figure 5.13 Example of two composite diagrams and the resulting schematic floor plan of a master bedroom suite, by author.

Massing can take a stacking diagram (discussed in Chapter 4) or a schematic section into three dimensions, making it volumetric. These volumes of space do not necessarily need to be extruded straight up from the plan, like cubes, but can be other shapes as well. For example, when you are trying to envision or create a courtyard, you can try it in multiple locations or shapes, which results in different shaped buildings or surrounding walls or elements. Deciding the location and shape of a loft area or how an elevator accesses an upper floor or roof can be explored using a massing diagram. An elongated cube can represent vertical circulation and how it intersects the upper floor or roof.

In Figure 5.14, an interior design student successfully translated three block diagrams into three massing diagrams which help her decide which solution makes the

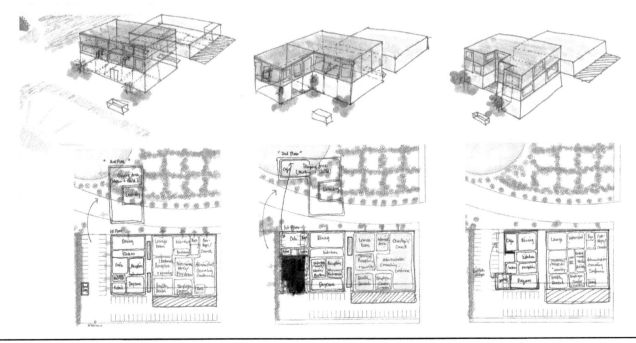

Figure 5.14 Example of three block diagrams with corresponding three-dimensional massing diagrams for a student's institutional project.

TABLE 5.2

DIAGRAM TYPES USED FOR IDEATION OR SYNTHESIS

Name	Use in Schematic Design Phase
Parti	An initial figural gesture to translate design concept onto the existing site, or poetic separation of parts
Circulation/Organizational	Proposed movement of various types of occupants (visitors, staff, etc.) onto the site which corresponds to program requirements
Bubble	Quick way to explore relative sizes and adjacencies of spaces by name (individually encircled)
Block	Preliminary space plan which places program areas (enclosed in flexible line work) onto site
Functional/Zones of Use	Locates and groups areas by type of activity or other common characteristics such access to views, natural light, plumbing, acoustics, or degree of privacy
Composite Overlay	Use of computer and hand drawing to create a multi-layer series of analysis and synthesis diagrams to generate a schematic floor plan
Stacking	A diagrammatic vertical section cut to explore relationships between spaces on different floors
Massing	A three-dimensional stacking diagram showing volumetric space configurations based on program requirements and design concept

best use of outdoor area. The third option in the series was chosen due to the pleasing three-dimensional quality of the courtyard dining space facing south (see Figure 5.14).

Table 5.2 shows a list of diagrams discussed in this chapter and their applicability or use during the schematic design phase. Not all projects require you to use all of the diagram types. The various diagrams covered in this chapter serve as a menu from which to choose considering the type of project and the depth of study during schematics. The following section includes examples of student work, as they translate their program and concept into schematic floor plan solutions.

ACTIVITY 5.4
Testing Your Written Program through Peer Review

Purpose: This activity allows you to get feedback and see how your program is interpreted by another designer.

Choose a partner to work with. After you have both completed a written program, swap with each other. Each of you will read the other's program, making notes in the margins with pencil to answer the following questions:

- Do you understand the design concept? Is the mission statement clear, as well as the client and end-user profiles? Can you offer any improvements? Is their site analysis comprehensive? What stands out as exceptionally useful? What still needs to be addressed?
- Go through their list of program spaces. Look for discrepancies or inaccuracies in size. Are there any spaces overlooked, such as a staff restroom or a janitor's closet, which need to be added? Does each space have clearly stated programmatic concepts which address number of people, lighting level, acoustics, furniture types, etc. Do you have any questions about the functional or aesthetic requirements of a particular space?
- Are the adjacency requirements clear? Do they make sense?
- Use one or more of the diagramming techniques discussed in this chapter to propose a creative solution.
- Present your diagram(s) to them. You will receive one in return.
- Examine their diagram of your project. It represents an interpretation of your written program through someone else's eyes. Is their design solution one you had in mind, or does it contain something you had not anticipated?
- Consider clarifying, correcting, or adding information to improve the written program.

SPACE PLANNING AND THE SCHEMATIC FLOOR PLAN

The final outcome of the diagram process is to arrive at a **schematic floor plan**. This process is often referred to as space planning, as you are deciding how to translate lines in the diagram into physical design elements such as walls, counters, flooring changes, and furniture layout. Schematic floor plans are used to conduct preliminary codes review and to communicate space planning to instructors, clients, and fellow colleagues. It is important to draw all existing walls accurately, differentiate existing walls from new walls (if applicable), identify areas by name listed in the program, and lay out furnishings in key areas.

   Schematic floor plans should align with program requirements in terms of quantities of square footage (size) of each space, adjacencies, and functional and aesthetic qualities of each space. Attention should be paid to clarity of line weights in the floor plan: *Bold line weight* for walls and structural elements such as columns that are cut through; *medium line weight* for low walls, built-ins, and furnishings; and *thin lines* for changes in level, stairs, changes in flooring materials, and flooring patterns. Medium-weight dashed lines are used to indicate proposed changes in ceiling height or the presence of ceiling-mounted elements.

Schematic plans also show wall thickness, which depends on the wall assembly, material, or acoustic properties. Wall thickness can range from a 12-inch thick concrete wall to a 4-inch thick stud and drywall partition. Glazing (operable and fixed windows) should be shown to indicate visual access to views, natural light, and natural ventilation. Doors and door swings should be located to indicate physical access and monitored restriction to adjacent spaces, entrances, and exits. Include a variety of circulation: *corridors* (by full height partitions, typically fire-rated), *hallways* (defined by full height partitions), *aisles* (passageways through areas defined by furniture placement), and *aisleways* (smaller areas of movement between seating and adjacent work surfaces).

Student Examples: Diagrams to Floor Plan

The following student examples show three students' approaches to schematic design, using a variety of diagram techniques. Figure 5.15 shows an innovative bubble diagram technique. In order to come up with multiple solutions and promote flexibility in thinking for her 14,000 square foot museum project, interior design student, Yuki Endo, cut out paper circles, wrote space name and size on each, and moved them around, taking photos of

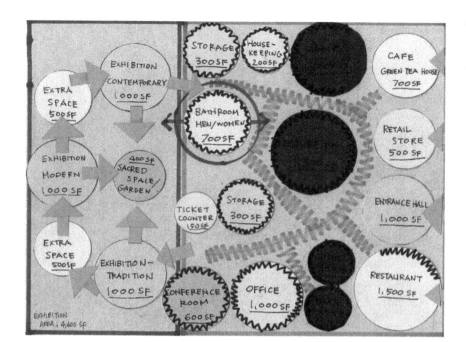

Figure 5.15 Innovative bubble diagram technique for museum project.

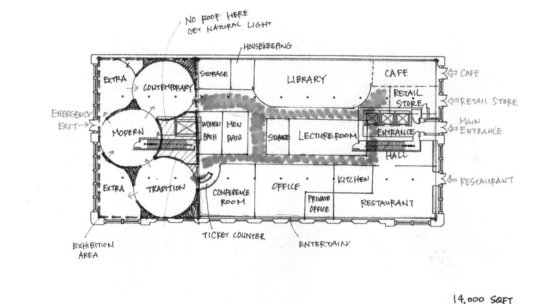

Figure 5.16 Block diagram for a 14,000 square foot museum.

each iteration. This process produced multiple adjacency solutions. The selected bubble diagram shows exhibition spaces grouped on the left and the more public support spaces on the right with restrooms, ticket counter, conference, storage, and garden space in the middle.

Bright yellow cut-out arrows show possible entry points into the building at café, retail, restaurant, and main entry, and primary circulation between main exhibition spaces, while gray marker indicates circulation corridors. In the resulting block diagram in Figure 5.16, Yuki finalized the

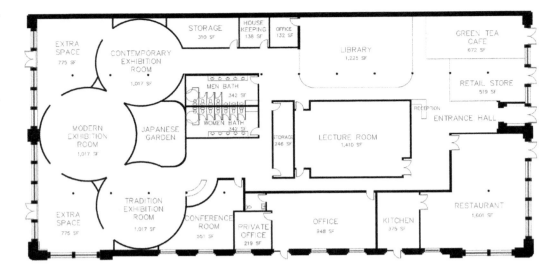

Figure 5.17 Schematic floor plan for a 14,000 square foot museum.

location of the café, retail, restaurant, and entrance on the east, showed the program areas located in relation to the glazed areas of natural light to the south and solid walls to the north. She shows a double loaded corridor around a core containing restrooms, storage, and lecture room. The ticket counter is placed at the entry to the exhibit spaces. The resulting schematic floor plan (Figure 5.17) shows the structural columns and walls (**poched** or filled in with black); all windows; thin lines showing flooring changes at the library, café, and retail; and door locations showing direction of door swings. All restroom fixtures have been included in this plan as well.

Figure 5.18 shows a progression of a student project development for a live/work project from a bubble diagram overlay on the building shell. He refined the relationship of adjacent program areas in the block diagram, showing a level change from dining to kitchen and an overhead arch separating the dining and living areas. His schematic floor plan further articulated the interior design elements, such as thickness of walls, floor material and pattern direction, type of doors and furniture layout. Now the plan is ready to present to the client for their feedback.

Figures 5.19 to 5.21 are three consecutive diagrams for a 12,000 square foot mental health outpatient clinic by student, Andrew Hunsaker. He first explored access to natural light, views of nature, and noise levels from the surrounding environment in a functional diagram. These aspects were important programmatic concepts. He followed this diagram with a sketchy block diagram, tentatively placing program areas to align with the functional diagram. Final schematic floor plan shows how he integrated outdoor areas and a domed garden space for waiting in the center of a circular, central plan.

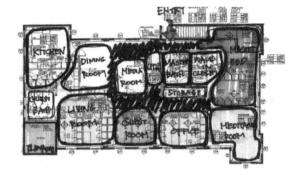

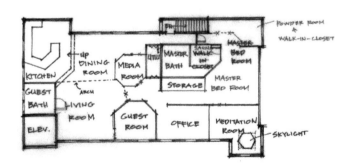

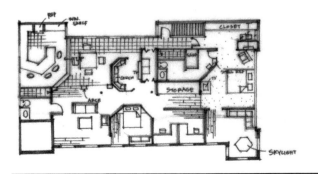

Figure 5.18 From bubble diagram to block diagram to schematic floor plan for a 4,000 square foot live/work project.

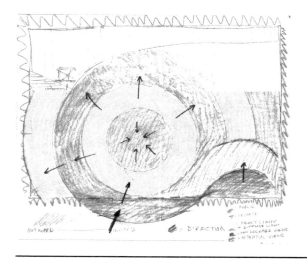

Figure 5.19 Functional diagram showing natural light, views, and degrees of acoustical privacy for a mental health clinic.

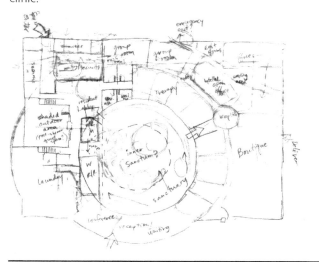

Figure 5.20 Sketchy block diagram drawn on a separate piece of trace over functional diagram aligns program areas with functional aspects of the plan.

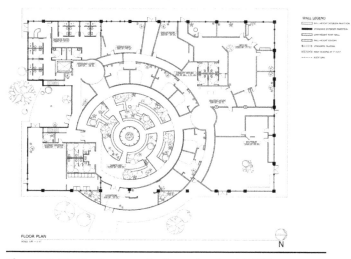

Figure 5.21 Final schematic floor plan for 12,000 square foot mental health clinic.

Presenting Your Schematics

The conclusion of the schematic phase is a creative response to what you have learned about the site, the client, the end-users, and program requirements. Your schematic presentation visually communicates, both in two dimensions and in three dimensions, several ideal solutions.

Further data collection will occur when the designer presents her schemes to the client at the end of this phase. In an academic environment, your schematic designs are presented to your instructor, fellow students, guest critics, or an acting client. Feedback from these individuals on your multiple design schemes is critical to helping you determine the final solution to take through to completion. In fact, a great way to look at the in-class critique is simply as another data collection method!

Preliminary Material Palette

An additional component of the schematic design phase is a sampling of colors, textures, patterns, and forms that you would like to be considered as an extension or embodiment of your written design concept. Figure 5.22 shows a collection of materials that not only supports a student's design concept but also satisfies programmatic requirements such as durability, sustainability, and budget.

This preliminary material palette should also work together to enhance a sense of place, comfort, safety, beauty, and a balance between consistency and variety. More about these issues, incorporating considerations of human factors, environmental psychology, and neuroscience will be discussed in the next chapter.

Figure 5.23 is a series of photos of an informal schematic design presentation. The interior design student presents her diagrams, concept imagery, schematic floor plan, and preliminary material palette to an acting client while fellow students look on. The color-coded functional diagram helped her to visually communicate the overall layout, while the labeled floor plan shows the client where each room will be placed. It is important to understand that the schematic plan represents a suggested, research-based layout subject to change with detailed input from the client and/or end-users. Concerns that a particular client might have should be carefully considered and incorporated into the final floor plan. Note how the student keeps a pad and pen nearby to record feedback during her schematic design presentation.

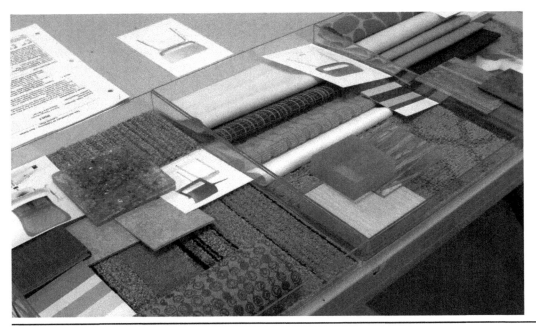

Figure 5.22 Example of preliminary material palette.

Figure 5.23 Student presents her schematic design in class.

Conclusion

This chapter has focused on the translation of data into a design concept and schematic space plan. The schematic phase in interior design can also include many other elements—preliminary color scheme, materials direction, lighting ideas, suggestions for furnishings, fixtures, and equipment, to name a few. Each of these areas requires considerable research with regard to function, sustainable features, durability, historic aspects, etc. Once a design direction has been established, further information gathering will occur with regards to the materials, furnishings, lighting, acoustics, and other important features and programmatic requirements of the project, including code compliance, sustainability, and integration with building systems. Chapter 6 will address these areas, as well as human factors, including Universal Design, environmental psychology, color theory, and design for special populations.

References

https://www.archdaily.com/66828/ad-classics-twa
-terminal-eero-saarinen (retrieved October 15, 2018).

https://www.waldorfsandiego.org/our-school/waldorf
-history/ (retrieved September 10, 2018).

Ballast, D. K. (2013). *Interior design reference manual (6th ed.)*. Belmont, CA: Professional Publications, Inc.

Coates, G. J. (1997). *Erik Asmussen, architect*. Stockholm: Byggforlaget.

Hall, E. T. (1966). *The hidden dimension*. New York: Anchor Books/Doubleday.

Karlen, M., Ruggeri, K., and Hahn, P. (2004). *Space planning basics*. New York: Wiley.

Kelley, T. and Littman, J. (2001). *The art of innovation: Lessons in creativity from IDEO, America's leading design firm*. New York: Doubleday.

Koberg, D. and Bagnall, J. (1976). *The all new universal traveler: A soft systems guide to creativity, problem-solving and the process of reaching goals*. Los Altos, CA: William Kaufmann.

Koppel, T. (Ed.). (July 13, 1999). Deep Dive [Television series episode]. In James Goldston (Executive Producer), *ABC News: Nightline*. New York: American Broadcasting Corporation.

Phillips, A. (January 1, 2006). Lines of inquiry. *The Architectural Review*. EMAP Architecture. Farmington Hills, MI: The Gale Group.

Rengel, R. J. (2014). *Shaping interior space (3rd ed.)*. New York: Fairchild Books.

6 RESEARCH-BASED DESIGN DEVELOPMENT

Icicles filled the long window with barbaric glass. The shadow of the blackbird crossed it, to and fro. The mood traced in the shadow an indecipherable cause.

— WALLACE STEVENS *Thirteen Ways of Looking at a Blackbird* (stanza VI)

CHAPTER OBJECTIVES

When you complete this chapter you will be able to:

- Gather information from members of a project team and specialists in design-related fields.
- Apply human-environment interaction theories to help articulate human-centered programmatic concepts in your project.
- Incorporate building codes and accessibility guidelines in your project.
- Consider building systems such as structural, mechanical, electrical, and plumbing in your project, including sustainable features whenever possible.
- Use research to inform and refine your furniture, fixture, color, and material selection requirements.

Upon selection of a scheme by the client at the completion of the schematic design phase, a designer will move on to the design development phase. This phase involves fully developing and articulating the design direction chosen by the client. One major goal of the design development phase is to make sure the design is viable, constructible, and code compliant, and that it protects the health, safety, and welfare of the public; supports the functions intended for the space; and achieves the programmatic requirements—all of this, as well as fulfilling the conceptual and aesthetic goals. This chapter will help you develop assessment charts to determine if your project meets all of the technical and human factors goals.

In the written program, you may have indicated the need for natural light in a particular room. In the schematic design phase, you may have created a diagram that placed the room along a south-facing exterior wall. In design development, it is time to choose the method for introducing natural light to the space. Will it be through windows, skylights, or via some other innovative design solution, such as light shelves or an engineered daylighting system? If they are windows, will they be operable or fixed? Will the glazing be opaque, translucent, or transparent? Will they be located below, above, or at eye level? What shape and size will they be? What material will they be constructed of? How will the occupants control the amount of natural light? It is during this phase that all of these decisions are made, about all of the elements involved in the three-dimensional interior design solution.

Questions regarding applicable codes; integrating and coordinating building systems; selecting appropriate finishes, furnishings, and equipment; and detailing interior design components typically arise during this phase. The client's feedback to you about their preferences and concerns may warrant further research. This may entail consulting with experts and assembling a project team to help you complete the project.

Table 6.1 shows a list of possible members of a project team, and sample questions you may want to ask

TABLE 6.1

QUESTIONS TO ASK PROJECT TEAM MEMBERS

Project Team Members	Questions You May Want To Ask . . .
Project Manager/ Owner's Representative	• What is the budget for the project? • What are the owner's goals for the project? • What is the project's schedule or timeline? • Who are the other members of the project team?
Contractor/Builder	• What is the project scope of work? Cost? Time constraints? • What is the project schedule? Sequence of construction? Milestones? Deadlines?
Architect	• What is the Authority Having Jurisdiction (AHJ) of the project? Zoning? Site constraints and possibilities? • How is building's structure and exterior being designed? Graphics? • What is the building's fire-resistive construction type?
Structural Engineer	• What is the structural system of the building shell? • What are the possibilities and constraints of the building's structure? • Would you help me size and/or identify load-bearing elements?
Mechanical Engineer	• What kind of Heating Ventilation and Air Conditioning (HVAC) system do you recommend? • How do the equipment, vents, ducting, or piping affect the interior space?
Civil Engineer	• How do the project's site, soil conditions, landscape elements, and grading affect the building? • What are current trends in sustainable landscape and hardscape strategies?
Licensed Plumber	• Where are drain/waste/vent stacks and laterals located? Where are supply risers? • What size is the supply line? • What are the limitations or restrictions regarding the type and placement of plumbing fixtures?
Codes Official	• Do you agree with my choice of occupancy classification(s) for the building? • Would you review my drawings for code compliance? • Means of egress? Fire resistance ratings between occupancies?
Electrical Engineer	• Would you help me calculate electrical load for circuits, locate panels, and comply with electrical code?
Acoustics or Audio Engineer	• Would you help me analyze the configuration of the auditorium for its acoustical quality? What materials would you recommend for sound attenuation for room acoustics or to reduce transmission from room to room?
LEED-Certified Consultant	• What is the approach to sustainability in the design of the building envelope and the building systems? • What are maintenance and other life cycle issues? • How does climate affect the design? How can we achieve the LEED rating certification we are seeking?

TABLE 6.2

QUESTIONS TO ASK DESIGN SPECIALISTS AND RELATED INDUSTRIES

Design Specialists	Questions You May Want To Ask . . .
Lighting Designer	• How can I achieve ambient, accent, and task lighting? How can I integrate the lighting into the architecture? • What color temperature lamps will be most suitable? • Ask questions about codes related to energy efficiency, output levels (lumens), illumination levels (footcandles), and wattage.
Kitchen/Bath Designer	• What are current trends in kitchen and bath design? Which products suit my client's needs in terms of price and quality? • What are the standard modular units of the cabinetry? What finishes and colors are available?
Historic Preservationist	• Is this property listed? What components of this project must comply with historic review?
Furniture Designer	• Is my design buildable? • All questions regarding materials, fabrication, cost, joinery, function, and aesthetics.
Fine Artist/Curator/Art Dealer	• What is the price point of the works you represent? What media do you have available? • Do you provide custom work?

Related Industries	Questions You May Want To Ask . . .
Manufacturer Representative	• How and where is this product manufactured? • What are the recommended uses of this product? • What are the recommended installation procedures? • What are the design possibilities of this product? Details? Specifications?
Product Vendor/Sales	• What are the product options, benefits, limitations, and warranties? • Can I obtain a sample? • What is the unit pricing for this item?
Specialty Product Designers (Kitchen & Bath, Cabinetry, Fireplaces, Window Treatment, etc.)	• What are projected product trends? • What problems do you see with my current design? • What are the costs involved with this design? • What options are available? • How energy efficient or sustainable is this solution?
Product Installers (Doors, Windows, Railings, Hardware, Appliances, etc.)	• What is involved with the installation of this product? • What has been your experience with this product? • What problems, if any, have you encountered with this product?
Sustainability Watchdogs	• How "green" is this material in terms of its impact on the earth? • Is this material renewable, recyclable, biodegradable, etc.? What is this product's embodied energy? • Where is the product manufactured? What materials and tools are associated with its installation?
Subcontractors (Masons, Carpenters, Painters, Upholsterers)	• How do you achieve this texture, color, or appearance? • How much raw material (paint, fabric, etc.) must I order? • What are the costs involved?

them. For example, you may need to include an audio engineer as part of your design team when designing an acoustically "live" theater or "dead" recording studio. This person (or company) will help you specify the proper equipment, place the speakers, and give insight into how to balance reflective and absorptive materials for ideal sound quality in the room. Table 6.2 is a list of design specialists and professional consultants in trades related to interior design, and sample questions you may want to

ask them. If you are working on a project that involves an old structure that needs updating to a particular time period, for example, you may have to consult an historic preservationist.

After enough practice, a designer will establish **benchmarks**, or develop a series of in-house standards that serve to inform future projects with similar programs, end-users, and/or clients. Experienced interior designers tend to stick with what they know, developing a library of details, and resources they can call upon for future projects without too much extra effort. Each project builds on the knowledge gathered from previous projects, and designers will tend to become experts at a particular area of specialization such as dental clinics, law offices, yacht interiors, public parks amenities, or a variety of other niche areas within the wide-ranging field of interior design.

Under the broad category of hospitality design, for example, designers can specialize in restaurants. There is a variety of issues particular to restaurant design that would allow a seasoned designer to stand out from novice designers: familiarity with accessibility compliance and requirements for food handling, safety and cleanliness (codes); mechanical, electrical and plumbing requirements for a commercial kitchen (building systems); and acoustics, lighting and ergonomics for eating and socializing (human factors).

This chapter deals with items that may have been left out of your project program, and need to be addressed,

ACTIVITY 6.1
Seeking Out the Experts

Purpose: To identify ideal candidates to interview for information during the design development phase.

1. Review feedback you received on your project program and your schematic design solution. What questions do you still have? What information do you need to develop your space plan and complete related tasks during the design development phase? Write down at least three questions here (you may have more!):

    1.

    2.

    3.

2. Identify individuals or groups who may have the information you need. Refer to Tables 6.1 and 6.2 for inspiration. Keep in mind that some specialized fields will not be on that list. What experts would be ideal potential interviewees?
3. Find three individuals who fit the description. You can use the Internet or the library, or you can make use of faculty contacts, colleagues where you work, or contacts provided by fellow students.
4. Provide the name, qualifications, and contact information (phone number, mailing address, email address, and/or Website) of each person you seek to interview.

    Question   Interviewee Name (Qualifications or Position)   Contact Information
    1.
    2.
    3.

5. Contact the interviewees, set up an interview, either in person, via phone, or email, and ask your question(s).
6. Record your experience with each interviewee, as well as their responses to your questions. How has this interaction added to your project program requirements or design solution?

    Experience with interviewee #1

    Experience with interviewee #2

    Experience with interviewee #3

or enable you to flesh out your short program by turning it into a longer, more detailed program. As mentioned in Chapter 4, a project program in school typically serves as a living document to be amended as students uncover additional information. In the professional arena, modifying a project program could be a legal issue, similar to making changes to a contract. But, no program is ever perfect; it can always use improvement, such as further clarification, more quantitative or qualitative detail, and increased technical information.

ARTICULATING HUMAN-CENTERED DESIGN SOLUTIONS

Linking Human Factors and Neuroscience to Your Project

Since the earliest writings about architecture by the Roman architect Vitruvius (27 BC), designers have sought to connect the built environment with the well-being of the occupants it serves. Human-centered interior design draws on a variety of theories to explore the power and potential of the built environment and as an underlying basis to create ideal spaces for people to live, work, and play. Theories that guide a designer come from a variety of perspectives and across multiple professions. Numerous fields of research have contributed to our understanding of how the built environment affects us.

Natural or "hard" sciences, such as biology and neuroscience, have taught us that people are physically affected by the environment. Our brains, once thought to be fixed, constantly develop new neural pathways and strengthen others depending on stimuli in the environment, throughout our lifetime. We are coming to understand which environmental features are optimal for nurturing our brains. Research from social sciences, such as environmental psychology, sociology, cultural anthropology, and education, inform us about the role of the environment in human behavior, social interaction, and cognitive development. We can base our design decisions on evidence produced by studies related to how lighting, color, materials, furniture placement, and so forth relate to human health and well-being.

Food and garden journalist Michael Pollan wrote a book called *A Place of My Own: The Architecture of Daydreams*. In this book he documented the process of building a small writing hut on his property. He described,

from initial idea to finish detail, how science-based theories, artistic principles, and cultural customs (such as *feng shui*) helped him decide on how to position the hut in the landscape, organize the interior, and detail built-in furnishings.

> At first it seemed uncanny to me that the three different perspectives I'd tried out on my site could have overlapped so closely. . . . Yet what confirmed me in my choice finally was no one test, but the very fact that all three perspectives—science, art and mysticism—had evidently concurred: (an) . . . alignment of theories and metaphors. (Pollan, 2008, p. 51)

Architectural theorists such as Esther Sternberg, Harry Francis Mallgrave, and Sarah Goldhagen have written extensively about the intersection of neuroscience (the way the brain responds to the environment) and design theory. There has always been a fascination about our innate (what we are born with) tendencies as living organisms and what we learn through personal experience, language, and culture. These authors recognize and explore the idea that our surroundings play a very important role in development of our brain, more closely than we had previously imagined.

Sternberg (2009) states, "we need to know what healing is, and what place is" (p. 14). She claims that *healing* is an action or series of actions from microbiological cellular level to macro organism level for "restoring the body to a state of balance" (p. 14). And *place* is a space that evokes "an emotional memory," which in turn triggers a biological or neurological response in the body. A *sense of place* is therefore a psychological and physiological sensation created in the brain as a response to the perception of the environment and is directly related to how we feel. Sternberg continues, "when we look at a scene, we not only hunt for . . . object clues but we also search for narrative, for a story that connects the objects together. If there is something in the scene that doesn't fit, the scene will feel unsettling or magical" (p. 32). In addition, patterns found in nature, with complexity and a bit of chaos, such as in waves, snowflakes, flowers, and seashells "are intrinsically satisfying to the human mind" (p. 35).

Mallgrave (2011) considers the two most important realizations about the human brain as *embodiment* and **neuroplasticity**. Scientists now not only see the brain as an embodied organ with neural extensions that allow it to see, feel, taste, smell, and hear but "a self-contained organism capable of spontaneous activity on its own" which not only processes sensory data but constructs its own reality (p. 135). Mallgrave continues, "plasticity is a biological term for the brain's ability to alter its synaptic networks." Our brains continue to develop over our lifetime through reinforcing pathways or patterns of neurons (memory) and weakening or disregarding others. All of this happens on a cellular and molecular level. Mallgrave concludes, "we are, in good part, the specific neural circuits or maps we build over the course of a lifetime" (p. 135).

Goldhagen (2017) confirms "studies reveal the human brain is dynamic, ever-changing in response to what we experience in our environments . . . our minds are changing and quite literally being shaped by our experiences in the physical environments in which we live" (p. xxxi). Goldhagen refers to this new understanding as **embodied cognition**, "an emerging, scientifically grounded paradigm" which places design of the built environment as the foundation for improving the lives of people (p. xiii). She urges us to

consider the shape of the room where you are sitting and the height . . . texture and construction of the walls. The softness or hardness of the floor surfaces. The views . . . air quality and temperature. The quality of the sounds . . . selection of furniture . . . types and levels of lighting. . . . All of this affects you. (Goldhagen, 2017, p. xxxii)

As interior designers we are familiar with *ergonomics*, which is design for the way our bodies work. A field of engineering, **cognitive ergonomics**, seeks to design products and environments for the way our minds work. Interior designer Liz Barry based her design for a real estate office interior on research produced by the furniture design company Kimball. She specified their *Hum. Minds at Work.* system, an open plan solution designed for individual focus while also encouraging creative thinking, because she was inspired by the way the design sought to echo the way our minds organize, coordinate, and collaborate.

We can selectively enhance desired visuals or filter out unwanted sound (noise). According to Sternberg, darkness removes visual cues (like before a movie starts) and according to architect Juhani Pallasmaa, silence is "the most essential auditory experience created by architecture" (Pallasmaa, 2005, p. 51). Good project programs will include mechanisms that will remind the designers of the importance of phenomena such as *silence* and *darkness* in the rooms that require this kind of attention or function. These phenomena are not prescriptive but

performance-related, and they are very closely tied to our cultural expectations, and norms.

Programming concepts, such as privacy, comfort, and sense of place, arise from our similarities as humans yet also from differences in how we may have been raised, our experiences, and even what language we speak. We call these **human factors**. In Chapter 1, we discussed how theories can be used as lenses through which we view data or design a study. Human factors theories can also be used to help enhance a design during design development by helping us examine spatial configurations, materials, products, and details from a scientific, humanistic, cognitive, behavioral, or cultural standpoint. Some of the most common human-environment theories used in interior design are summarized in Table 6.3.

We begin our overview of human factors theories with Abraham Maslow. In a nutshell, Maslow focused his studies on "self-actualized" people, those who seemed to be achieving their highest potential. Using a humanistic psychological perspective, his landmark book *Motivation and Personality* (1954) connected attributes in the environment to human activities based on the premise that physical, emotional, and social needs motivate behavior. This **hierarchy of needs** is explained visually in Figure 6.1. Fundamental physiological needs, physical comforts that support biological functions, such as breathing, eating, and resting, are depicted at the base of the pyramid. The next level up in this diagram are aspects of the environment that support safety and security, followed by sense of community or belonging, and then self-esteem. At the top of the pyramid resides *self-actualization* or highest potential in creative human endeavors. Later in his life, Maslow included a sixth level (above self-actualization), calling it a transcendence of self. "Transcendence refers to the very highest and most inclusive or holistic levels of human consciousness, behaving and relating, as ends rather than means, to oneself, to significant others, to human beings in general, to other species, to nature, and to the cosmos" (Maslow, 1971, p. 269). Cues in the environment that support transcendence may be found in spiritual or religious places, which assist people to contemplate the nature of their existence, facilitate connectedness, or feel access to a higher power. Features of meditation and prayer spaces may include darkness, silence, high ceilings, dramatic lighting, and symbols, among others.

Medical doctor and researcher Humphry Osmond was interested in how to improve patient settings, especially in group therapy sessions with people who suffered from alcoholism and schizophrenia. He coined the term "psychedelic"

TABLE 6.3

SUMMARY OF FOUNDATIONAL HUMAN-ENVIRONMENT THEORIES

Theory	Theorist (Year)	Use In Interior Design
Hierarchy of Needs	Abraham Maslow (1954)	Needs motivate behavior. Satisfy lower needs first. Used to develop an assessment checklist to evaluate how an environment meets human needs.
Socio-Architecture	Humphry Osmond (1959)	*Sociopetal* furniture arrangements encourage social interaction while *sociofugal* furniture arrangements discourage social interaction.
Place-Legibility and Wayfinding	Kevin Lynch (1960)	We create *mental maps* of our surroundings to navigate using a system of common elements: *paths, edges, districts, nodes*, and *landmarks*. Use all of these elements in a coherent *wayfinding* system which is legible by the end-users.
Proxemics	Edward T. Hall (1966) Robert Sommer (1969)	Habits, customs, and behaviors are reflected in dynamic *personal space zones*, and tendency to claim and defend our personal space (*territoriality*). Accommodate these tendencies in furniture placement that corresponds with the appropriate distances. Use boundaries and flexible furniture for end-users to adapt to their needs.
Prospect and Refuge	Jay Appleton (1975)	Aesthetic preferences in landscape result from need for survival. Provide areas for *refuge* to promote feelings of security and *prospect*, clear views outward fostering sense of opportunity.
A Pattern Language	Christopher Alexander (1977)	Use time-tested groups of qualities (*patterns*) to create ideal, meaningful environments for humans. Overlap them to create a poetic narrative or enhance richness of experience.
Affordances	James J. Gibson (1979) Don Norman (1988)	*Affordances* are qualities in an object or the environment that allow you to perform an action. Provide clear, perceptible cues in the built environment to inform appropriate behavior and use.
Biophilic Design	E.O. Wilson/Stephen Kellert (1984)	Our affinity towards natural elements is based on our brain's need for nature. Provide access to nature (real or simulated) in a variety of features, forms, processes, and relationships.
Third Place Theory	Ray Oldenburg (1991)	*Third places* are informal gathering places between first place (home) and second place (work) where people reflect, socialize, and reset. Provide comfortable, welcoming gathering spaces for impromptu or regular access.
Universal Design	Ron Mace (1997) Inclusive Design and Environmental Access (IDeA) Center (2005)	Design *products* and *environments* to be usable by all people, to the greatest extent possible, and without the need for adaptation or specialized design. Use a design *process* that enables and empowers a diverse population by improving human performance, health and wellness, and social participation.

Figure 6.1 Maslow's Hierarchy of Needs.

to describe the effects of drugs on human perception. He also coined the term "socio-architecture" to describe the way furniture can be arranged to support or discourage social interaction among people. **Sociofugal** furniture arrangements tend to discourage social interaction. They are used in airport and medical waiting areas, and in lecture halls. **Sociopetal** furniture arrangements tend to encourage social interaction used in environments such as dining, seminar classrooms, and meeting areas where conversation is the main activity. Figure 6.2 shows examples of both.

In 1960, an urban planner and researcher at MIT named Kevin Lynch asked 60 participants to draw maps (from memory) of the cities in which they lived. Such

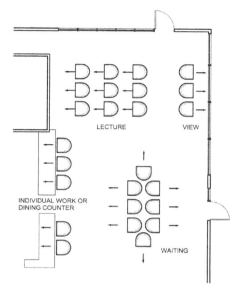

LECTURE   VIEW

INDIVIDUAL WORK OR
DINING COUNTER

WAITING

SOCIOFUGAL FURNITURE ARRANGEMENTS

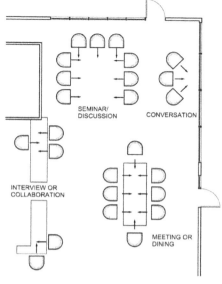

SEMINAR/
DISCUSSION   CONVERSATION

INTERVIEW OR
COLLABORATION

MEETING OR
DINING

SOCIOPETAL FURNITURE ARRANGEMENTS

Figure 6.2 Sociofugal and sociopetal furniture layouts.

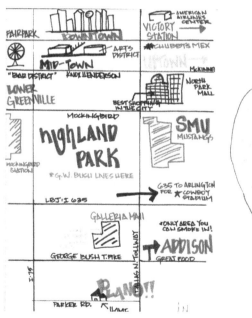

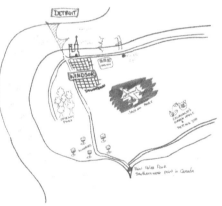

Figure 6.3 Two mental maps drawn by design students of their hometowns: one urban and one rural.

mental maps were not necessarily accurate, nor were they to-scale, but they represented how people imagined the spaces and features they used to navigate. Figure 6.3 shows two drawings by design students which represent their memory of navigating their home towns: one urban and the other more rural. Note the commonalities and differences in the two mental maps.

Lynch analyzed drawings like these for common elements, which emerged as *paths, edges, nodes, districts,* and *landmarks* (see Figure 6.3 for a graphic representation

of them). In his book *The Image of the City* (1960), he noted the system by which these conceptual navigational tools worked together to form a unified whole as **place legibility**.

- **Paths** are occupiable; identified as places that can be traversed as in a hallway or corridor, an aisle defined by furniture, or a swath of flooring material such as "rolling out a red carpet" or a runner.
- An **edge** is a non-occupiable boundary. In interior design, this could be a wall, a railing, a flooring

transition, a level change (as an elevated stage separate from the audience area), or a change in ceiling height.

- A **node** is a decision-making point. Usually, it is at the intersection of two paths with a directional quality of, "Here I am. Where should I go next?" An example would be an entry lobby, from which a visitor has the option of several destinations.
- A **district** is an area that someone can mentally go inside of, typically defined by a common function (food court) or type of occupant (staff area), but could also have unifying architectural detail such as ornate columns, high ceilings, hard surfaces, or similar lighting level or acoustic quality.
- A **landmark** is a distinct and unique external navigational tool that can be at any scale. A landmark can be a piece of artwork, a sign, or anything else that stands out as memorable. If the receptionist tells a visitor to "turn left at the red wall," the red wall would be the landmark.

Understanding the way that our brains read, internalize, and encode the environment, interior designers can consciously use these navigational tools, integrate them into a system of **wayfinding**. For example, to make people feel comfortable in a public space, provide clear paths of travel through flooring, and indicate change of area with a flooring change (edge). Enlarge intersecting hallways with a space (node) that has signage, decorative lighting fixtures, and colorful artwork (landmarks). Use architectural detail, higher ceilings, and brighter light level to differentiate public from private areas (districts). Most people rely on paths and landmarks mainly to navigate, but the use of districts and nodes make occupants feel more at ease and provide a greater comfort level. In the professional environment, wayfinding has become almost synonymous with signage. However, as you can see, signage (a type of landmark) is a small part of a comprehensive wayfinding package.

Cultural anthropologist Edward T. Hall observed interaction between members of different ethnic groups. His landmark book *The Hidden Dimension* (1966) offered a theory of **proxemics**. He identified nonverbal, body language as social norms, or learned cultural traits, yet also having a biological basis. Hall envisioned the distance people seemed to keep around themselves as an invisible, dynamic, personal space bubble that changed due to circumstances and relationship with the people around them.

The hypothesis behind the proxemic classification system is this: it is in the nature of animals, including man, to exhibit behavior which we call territoriality. In doing so, they use the senses to distinguish between one space or distance and another. The specific distance chosen depends on the transaction; the relationship of the interacting individuals, how they feel, and what they are doing. (Hall, 1966, p. 128)

For Western or American culture, he defined four distinct space zones: *intimate, personal, social,* and *public,* with a near and a far phase in each. See Figure 6.4 for dimensions.

We can use these distances as guidelines to inform our placement of furniture, especially in social and personal settings, so that occupants feel more comfortable. For example, to have co-workers sitting closer than four feet from each other (social zone) may violate their personal space bubble and make them feel uncomfortable. Alternatively, placing adjacent dining room seating further apart than 48 inches (personal zone) would probably make family members feel disconnected from each other, and therefore also uncomfortable.

"The theory of human habitation selection was first proposed in 1975 by an English geographer named Jay Appleton and seconded, more or less, by sociobiologist E.O. Wilson in his 1984 book, *Biophilia*" (Pollan, 2006, p. 49). Appleton sought to link our aesthetic preferences with our biological disposition to survive. He called for an ideal

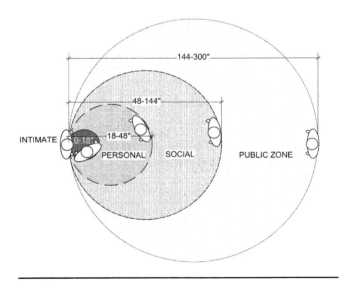

Figure 6.4 Hall's space zones: intimate, personal, social, and public, with dimension ranges (shown in inches).

environment to have both **prospect** (a clear view of opportunity and available resources) **and refuge** (a feeling of security or place to rest or hide). These can be actual spaces or can be represented through symbol or imagery. Artwork of landscapes can offer feelings of openness, and an overhang or canopy can create a sense of protection. **Biophilic design**, as expounded by Stephen Kellert and Elizabeth Calabrese, seeks to build on Appleton's and Wilson's theories to further satisfy our biological affinity for natural elements in the built environment. They call for the direct contact with nature (daylight, plants, weather, etc.) and indirect use of nature (images of natural elements, earth tones, organic patterns, etc.). For a full description of their theory and application see https://www.biophilic-design.com/.

In 1977, Christopher Alexander along with his team of researchers at University of California, Berkeley, set out to define and categorize a way of looking for human-environment problems and solutions in everyday life, in the plan of towns, buildings, and interiors. They published their findings in two related volumes, *A Timeless Way of Building* and *A Pattern Language*. They described entities called patterns, which are collections of qualities present in the environment that yield a meaningful or positive experience to the occupant. "Each pattern describes a problem which occurs over and over again in our environment and describes the core of the solution to that problem, in such a way that you can use this solution a million times over, without ever doing it the same way twice" (p. x). Alexander and his team defined 256 patterns, including #63 "connected play," #106 "positive outdoor space," and #246 "climbing plants." For a full list and explanation of the **pattern language**, and its goals for the design community visit https://www.patternlanguage.com/.

A principal theme of visual thinking or visual aesthetics is **Gestalt**. "Gestalt psychology originated as a theory of perception that included interrelationships between the form of the object and the processes of the perceiver" (Fagan & Shephard, 1970, p. 3). Gestalt emphasizes the tendency to view individual things as part of a whole, as illustrated by the principles of closure and figure-ground diagrams. According to Mallgrave (2011), "our perception of shapes comes through the application of form categories . . . understood in this way, visual perception is a kind of problem solving or a comparative distinguishing . . . much of which we perform unconsciously" (p. 93).

Cognitive psychologists James J. Gibson and Don Norman underscore the importance of visual perception of features in our environment which enable us to understand how to use them. They call these visual features **affordances**. A classic example of an affordance is the handle of a teapot that is the right shape and size for our hand to grasp, or a button that is the perfect size and shape to push with a finger (see Figure 6.5). An affordance can also be an object's height. A low wall or boulder may provide the ability to sit on it, while a tall wall affords privacy. An affordance of an object can also be the graphic instruction or signage that tells us how to use it, such as a red button to stop and green button to go. The important thing is that the affordances align with the actions to be performed rather than add to confusion. How many times have we approached a door with a handle and pulled on it only to find we have to push it open!

In 1991, sociologist Ray Oldenburg published *The Great Good Place*, which extolled the virtues of informal public gathering places as vital for society as well as for individual human well-being. Oldenburg (1991) contends ". . . daily life, in order to be relaxed and fulfilling, must find its balance in three realms of experience. One is domestic, a second is gainful or productive, and the third is inclusively sociable, offering both the basis of community and the celebration of it" (p. 14). Traditionally this **third place**, in between the first place (home) and second place (work or school), was a stand-alone café, pub, or community center. Today *third places* have been extended to include spaces for exercise and meditation, such as a gym or yoga studio. Developers and corporate clients, influenced by this theory, have added work-out areas, pools, and coffee bars to their corporate campuses as they seek to attract and retain their workers. They incorporate

Figure 6.5 Classic examples of affordances: visual features of an object that allow users to understand how the item is used, such as a button for pushing and a handle for grasping.

places for rest, relaxation, and informal conversation into other project types such as housing complexes, retail, and healthcare facilities.

One of the most powerful and enduring human-environment theories in recent history has been the theory of **Universal Design (UD)** by a team of researchers in North Carolina State University led by Ron Mace. Mace was an architect, product designer, and educator whose design philosophy challenged convention to provide a design foundation for a more usable world for everyone. At the Center for Universal Design, they coined the term *Universal Design* to describe the concept of designing all products and the built environment to be usable by everyone, regardless of their age, ability, or status in life. Their definition, "the design of products and environments to be usable by all people, to the greatest extent possible, and without the need for adaptation or specialized design" highlighted that physical design solutions be supportive, adaptable, accessible, and safe (NCSU, 1997). Emphasis was placed on flexibility of the environment as needs change over time, and on the prevention of injury or accidents. The seven principles for Universal Design are as follows (see Figure 6.7 for visual representation). A larger, more detailed version of this poster is available for download at https://www.ncsu.edu/ncsu/design/cud/pubs_p/docs/poster.pdf:

1. Equitable Use: Useful and marketable to diverse abilities
   - Provide the same means of use for all people
   - Provisions for safety, security, and privacy
   - Design appealing to all users
2. Flexibility in Use: Accommodates a wide range of preferences
   - Provide choice of methods in use
   - Accommodate left or right-handedness,
   - Facilitate accuracy,
   - Adapt to user's pace
3. Simple and Intuitive: Easy to understand regardless of language or experience level
   - Eliminate complexity
   - Be consistent with user's expectations
   - Accommodate diverse literacy/language
   - Provide prompts and feedback
4. Perceptible Information: Communicates information effectively using a variety of sensory techniques
   - Use pictorial, auditory, tactile, and other sensory modes to present information
   - Provide adequate contrast and legibility for people with sensory limitations
5. Tolerance for Error: Minimizes hazards and adverse consequence of accidental or unintended actions.
   - Arrange element to minimize possibility for errors
   - Provide warnings and fail-safe features
6. Low Physical Effort: Design can be used efficiently and comfortably and with minimum fatigue.
   - Allow user to maintain neutral body position and use reasonable operating forces
   - Minimize repetitive actions or sustained physical effort
7. Size and Space for Approach and Use: Appropriate size and space is provided for approach, reach, manipulation, and use regardless of user's body size, posture, or mobility.
   - Make all components easy to see and reach from standing or seated position.
   - Accommodate for variations in hand size and gripping ability.
   - Provide adequate space for use of assistive devices or personal assistance.

The definition of Universal Design was reinterpreted and amended by Inclusive Design and Environmental Access (IDeA) Center, University at Buffalo in 2005 to "a design process that enables and empowers a diverse population by improving human performance, health and wellness, and social participation" (Steinfeld & Maisel, 2012). The goals of this new characterization have been expanded to include the social, cultural, and emotional needs of end-users in a multidisciplinary approach.

Building on the foundational human factors theories, the power of Universal Design, and contributions of neuroscience, other theories are emerging from interior designers who do their own research. Interior designer Ingrid Fetell Lee founded *Aesthetics of Joy* (http://www.aestheticsofjoy.com/) after years of researching what brought people feelings of joy in their environment. Based on her studies she concluded that physical expressions of joy in the physical environment, such as confetti, bubbles, ice cream cones, and flowers, had common elements such as round shapes, a variety of color, and unexpectedness. She published her findings in *Joyful: The Surprising Power of Ordinary Things to Create Extraordinary Happiness* (2018). Watch her TED talk at https://youtu.be/A_u2WFTfbcg.

Interior designer Cynthia Leibrock, author of *Design Details for Health* (2011) champions innovative research and techniques for healthcare facilities, aging-in-place, making Universal Design seamless in both hospital and home interiors. Her Green Mountain Ranch in Colorado showcases over two hundred Universal Design products and details, and is available to visit for a hands-on learning experience at AgingBeautifully.org. Key features in her work include the use of scent for people with memory-impairments and dementia, and the use of **positive distractions** views of nature, artwork, water features, musical instruments, therapy animals, and many others. "A positive distraction has been defined as 'an environmental feature that elicits positive feelings and holds attention without taxing or stressing the individual, thereby blocking worrisome thoughts.' The term distraction itself refers to 'the direction of attention to a nontoxic event or stimulus in the immediate environment'" (Pati, 2010, p. 28).

In summary, biological, environmental psychology and social science theories, principles, and key terms discussed in this chapter should be considered when articulating interior design solutions during the design development phase. All project types should consider the physical and perceptive abilities of the occupants, culture, generational differences, and other human factors. Issues of privacy and crowding can be looked at through a variety

---

ACTIVITY 6.2
Applying Human Factors Theories to Your Project

Purpose: To help you articulate human-centered design solutions both in your project program and your project design solution.

Objective: Examine a particular room or space in your program that could be improved with regard to either quantitative or qualitative programmatic requirements. Define (or redefine) your needs using the terminology used in the theory. You may have to read some additional resources authored by the original theorist, or a scholarly source who interprets the theory.

Requirements: Use the following prompts to explore how your space intends to satisfy the following needs. Be as specific as possible in terms of supportive products, custom elements, lighting, window treatment, seating, work surfaces, signage, artwork, accessories, finishes, etc. How does your project seek to fulfill the following?

1. Hierarchy of needs:
   - Physiological
   - Safety
   - Belonging
   - Esteem
   - Self-actualization—how does your space optimize the abilities of the people using the space for its intended purpose? For studying, cooking, working . . .
   - Transcendence of self (typically found in a spiritual or religious setting)
2. Furniture placement
   - Sociopetal
   - Sociofugal
3. Wayfinding devices
   - Paths
   - Edges
   - Districts
   - Nodes
   - Landmarks

4. Proxemics—distances between fixed or moveable elements
5. Prospect and refuge
6. Patterns-groups of ideal qualities
7. Biophilic design—connection with nature or naturalistic elements
8. Third Place
9. Affordances
10. Positive distractions
11. How does your project intend to inspire joy?
12. Other. . .

How does your space satisfy the following needs? Be as specific as possible in terms of supportive ready-made or custom products, building elements, lighting, window treatments, seating, work surfaces, signage, artwork, accessories, finishes, colors, textures, and height or other dimension. You may have to do additional information gathering or consult some of the resources listed in this chapter to get specific details or products.

- Equitable Use
- Flexibility in Use
- Simple and Intuitive
- Perceptible Information
- Tolerance for Error
- Low Physical Effort
- Size and Space for Approach and Use

of theoretical lenses, as they are cultural and experiential constructs, and not just based on space allocation or density of people. Creating a sense of place, a meaningful narrative, and increasing comfort level of the end-user are essential to the field of interior design. The following activity will help you to integrate some of these theories into your current project.

ENSURING CODE COMPLIANCE, SAFETY, AND ACCESSIBILITY

Codes Research

The discussion about codes in this book is primarily to point you in an investigative direction or serve as a reminder that you need to apply what you have learned in a previous or concurrent codes class. There are many excellent books that offer detailed information about the history of codes; various technical aspects, including dimensioned clearances; and other guidelines that you will need in order to complete your project. We refer you to the many books written on the subject, especially *The Codes Guidebook for Interiors, 7th ed.* (2018) by Kennon and Harmon, and *Building Codes Illustrated, 6th ed.* (2018) by Ching and Winkel. In addition, we urge you to look beyond the textbooks to the Websites to access the code itself. You may need to consult multiple sources to get the information you need. It is strongly recommended that

you seek professional advice from an architect, or a codes consultant, familiar with your jurisdiction and project type. For a firsthand look at codes, go to the planning or building department in the project's jurisdiction to access their records department and speak with a codes official.

The overview of codes in this chapter emphasizes the importance of further research during the design development phase to ensure that your project meets current codes. To put the issue of codes in perspective, it has been said that designing a building to code represents the worst building you are allowed to get away with, legally. It is our job as designers to understand the historical reasons and intent behind the codes and to recognize what codes are: arbitrary minimums and maximums that have come to govern what is currently considered safe. Our building codes represent a consensus, an agreement by experts, about our hopes and fears regarding public safety and liability. It is an ever-changing body of knowledge that is altered by unexpected, natural, and man-made disasters and tragedies, such as hurricanes or bombs, or by changes in attitudes toward energy efficiency, land use, and population density. Table 6.4 helps show how codes should be applied to a typical project.

Your first task should be to find out the **Authority Having Jurisdiction (AHJ)** over the area in which your project is located. Each project must follow the codes that regulate the area the project occupies—such as *municipal codes* (those adopted by the local ordinances) and **zoning** designations regulating land use—as well as

---

TABLE 6.4

INCORPORATING CODES INTO THE DESIGN PROCESS

Code Area of Concern	What Should You Do?
Zoning/Land Use	• Determine AHJ (Authority Having Jurisdiction) of the project location. • Determine zoning restrictions and permitted uses in the project location. • Determine possible "overlay zones," such as planned communities, historic districts, or coastal regions. • Determine if project falls into areas of further restrictions or guidelines for example, a homeowners association (HOA).
Due Diligence	• Confirm ownership, and that property has a clear title: no liens or other legal obstruction. • Locate property boundaries, setbacks, easements, access points. • Document existing structures and site amenities; determine if they are permitted, code-compliant, or need to be updated to current code. • Seek out any existing documentation of the property such as a plot plan, lot description, "as-built" drawings, or previously permitted construction documents. Ask owner, designer or go to local public records office. • Determine height and floor area restrictions. • Determine if a survey by a licensed surveyor is required. • Determine access to and capacity of public utilities such as water, gas, and power.
Occupancy/Use	• Define occupancy classification(s) or use(s) of project. Calculate the area of each space. • Assign a function or an occupancy classification to each space. • Find out the occupant load factor (minimum number of square feet per occupant) for each space. • Calculate the occupant load (number of people) allowed by code for each space.
Fire and Life Safety	• Determine the fire-resistive construction type (Type I-V). • Determine the location and fire rating of fire-rated walls and partitions. • Determine flammability ratings required for finishes in each area.
Means of Egress	• Determine the number of exits from each space. • Determine placement of exits (minimum distance apart). • Determine door swing direction of exits (in direction of travel). • Calculate the exit width from each space (for large rooms). • Determine travel distances. • Avoid dead-end corridors. • Consider exit discharge and access to public way. • Locate illuminated exit signage and audible visual alarms
Accessibility	• Determine public accommodation or • Determine accessible routes, accessible parking spaces (quantity and location), entry, reception desk heights/toe kick, ramps, railing, flooring transitions, and restroom amenity locations. • Determine number of accessible restrooms. • Design requirements for accessible signage, content, and mounting.
Mechanical, Electrical and Plumbing	• Calculate the number of plumbing fixtures required. • Determine energy efficiency requirements of fixtures, appliances, heating and cooling systems, windows, etc. • Determine lighting requirements. Calculate lamp output, wattage, and light levels.
Additional Regulatory Agencies and Guidelines	• Determine if any uses require additional code requirements review by regulatory agencies such as DEH, OSHPD, DGS, DSA, etc. • Determine if any uses must follow additional guidelines or permits to operate such as a food establishment or commercial kitchen, a firehouse or police station, a public swimming pool, a salon, a school, daycare, or medical facility.

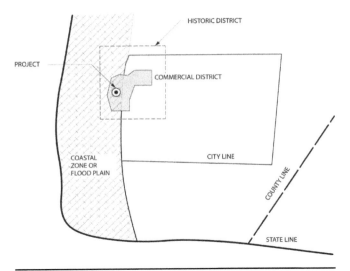

Figure 6.6 A project located within several overlapping zones or districts, each with different applicable codes and enforcing agencies.

the overlapping series of other zones the project happens to be in (see Figure 6.8). There are federal, state, and local (such as county, city, or town) building regulations, areas designated as historic districts or flood plains, as well as Homeowners Associations (HOAs) or Business Improvement Districts (BIDs) that have adopted CC&Rs (covenants, conditions, and restrictions) that may regulate exterior aesthetics, landscaping, water use, parking, and many other daily activities and amenities that will impact your design.

For projects that impact the public or that vary from what is currently accepted in the area (called a variance), there may be community board reviews or public hearings prior to a project being allowed. A designer must be aware of what is allowed in the jurisdiction, prior to the beginning of design. In the professional environment, it is essential to do a thorough codes review before performing any design work. A beautiful design for a restaurant will not be worth very much to a client if restaurants are not permitted in that location!

In addition, a conscientious designer researches the legal aspects of the project to limit her professional liability. This is called **due diligence** and often involves confirming who the owner is and whether there are any obstructions to performing design or construction work. Once again, interior designers may want to consult with an architect, or an attorney, when entering into a contract at the beginning of a project.

Occupancy Classifications

The second task in determining applicable codes involves looking at the use of the building and assigning the appropriate *occupancy classification(s)* to the project as a whole, as well as to the individual rooms and areas, as mentioned in Chapter 4. The *International Building Code (IBC)* currently categorizes occupancy in the following general categories:

A	Assembly
B	Business
E	Educational
F	Factory
H	Hazardous
I	Institutional
M	Mercantile
R	Residential
S	Storage
U	Utility

There are also subcategories within each of these general categories. For the specific definition of each of these categories and in-depth discussion, refer to the *International Building Code (IBC), Building Codes Illustrated 6th ed.* by Ching and Winkel (2018), or *The Codes Guidebook for Interiors 7th ed. (2018).*

Risk factors are the features or situations associated with a particular use that may be dangerous in an emergency such as fire. According to Kennon and Harmon (2018), "Risk factors consider the typical characteristics of the environment, the activity that will occur in the space, and the occupants using the space" (p. 55). The strictness of the codes for each classification is directly related to the danger posed by these factors.

What makes a theater (Assembly) more dangerous than an office (Business)? First, the sheer *number of people* concentrated into one space is dangerous. If there were a fire, there would be a high degree of crowding and panic as large numbers of people funnel through the exit doors. Second is *alertness* and *mobility* of the occupants. One of the most dangerous things someone can be doing during a fire is sleeping! Third, what is the occupant's potential *familiarity* with the space? This may be the first time someone has been to this particular theater, and the person may not know where the exits are located. And finally we consider the *spatial characteristics*, such as low light levels (difficulty seeing), high sound levels (occupants may not hear the fire alarm), and fixed seating (forcing evacuation through tight aisles) and *fuel load*, or the contents of the room that would contribute to the spread of fire—for example, the upholstered walls and seating and the hanging drapery.

The occupancy classification "Institutional" comprises subclassifications like Supervised Personal Care (Nursing Homes), Healthcare (Hospitals), Restrained (Prisons), and Daycare Facilities. Question: What do these occupancies have in common? A better question is what do the *occupants* of these spaces have in common? Answer: They all need assistance getting out of a burning building. Prisoners need to be let out, while hospital patients, the elderly, and young children may need to be carried out.

The writers of the code used risk factors when determining what the minimum safety features would be for each category. Codes officials use risk factors when determining the appropriate classification of a space. Interior designers also must evaluate the risk factors of each space to determine how they will classify the room in order to determine what codes to follow. To accurately designate occupancy classification, consider the type of activity occurring, the types of objects or finishes in the space, and the number of occupants who could be in the space. If you are unsure, "it is always a good idea to have a code official confirm your choice of occupancy" (Kennon & Harmon, 2018, p. 58).

Mixed Occupancy

In a mixed occupancy, two or more occupancies occur in the same building. Having more than one occupancy may require separation by fire-rated walls or you can have a non-separated mixed use, which would follow the stricter of the two classifications. Most of the commercial or institutional projects that you will be working on in school will be mixed use. A hotel may have a common lobby (Assembly), office areas (Business), and guest accommodations (Residential). Even a high school usually has an auditorium (Assembly), classrooms (Educational), and faculty offices (Business).

It is important to note that small areas occurring within an occupancy type may be an *accessory occupancy*, which is *an area less than 10 percent of the total* floor area, such as a 10 square foot storage closet opening into a 120 square foot office space (Business), or a 200 square foot office as part of a 2,500 square foot retail space (Mercantile). An

incidental use is a hazardous room or space that is always fire-separated but not considered a separate occupancy. These areas cannot exceed 10 percent of the total floor area, and are typically laundry, mechanical, or machine rooms.

Special Use

Areas defined as *special use* are those that require additional requirements, inspections, permits, certification, or plan review by the **Department of Environmental Health (DEH)**. This is usually required because the planned use affects the health and safety of the public on additional levels—because it provides services or treatments involving the human body such as food, hazardous materials, water, or biological waste. Additional regulations help prevent unsanitary conditions or any situation that may contribute to the spread of food- and body-related bacteria or disease. DEH rulings are the reason why restrooms in restaurants have signs reminding workers to wash their hands, why the flooring in restaurants has to have a sanitary cove base (for cleaning purposes), and why bars must have a three-compartment sink (one for high-temperature water, one for bleach, and one for rinsing). The following establishments or activities are considered special use:

- Automotive repair or car wash
- Body art, massage parlors, hair and nail salons
- Camps and other organized recreational facilities for youth
- Catering, mobile food trucks, and vending machines
- Commercial kitchens, restaurants, and other retail food facilities
- Public housing, shelters, and detention facilities
- Public swimming pools, bathhouses, and spas

Other state or federal government agencies may have additional requirements to be followed if you are designing healthcare facilities, schools or daycare centers. Many times state or federal guidelines will apply due to how the business is operated or registered, and whether the source of funding for the project comes from public or private entities.

Calculating Occupant Load

As previously discussed in Chapter 4, the minimum number of square feet required by code for each occupant to perform a certain use is called a *load factor*. In the IBC, the list of load factors is found in Table 1004.1.2 Maximum Floor Area Allowances Per Occupant. This information is transcribed in Table 6.5. Keep in mind that the information in this table may not apply to your project's jurisdiction, and it is subject to change over time. It is important that you verify which codes are applicable to your particular project.

To determine how many people can safely occupy a space, divide the total square feet by the load factor. This determines the **occupant load (OL)**. Written as an equation, it looks like this: Total SF/LF = OL. If a space has multiple uses, such as a multipurpose room, the occupant load for that space is determined by the use that indicates the largest concentration of people, often referred to as the *worst-case scenario*.

The occupant load is the number of people that can safely use the space, as determined by current code. It is an important number as it is used as the *basis for many subsequent design features that are required*. The occupant load is the number that helps determine total required number of exits, total exit width, and number of plumbing fixtures (toilets, lavatories, showers, and drinking fountains).

As you can see in Table 6.5, load factors are either *gross* or *net*. Gross square footage encompasses all the area within the walls, including shafts, closets, equipment, and built-ins. For example, a commercial kitchen has a load factor of 200 square feet *gross*. It makes sense that the cabinetry, appliances, and space for venting would be included in calculation of the square footage, because those items are essential to the function of the kitchen. In fact, it wouldn't be a kitchen without those things. On the other hand, an assembly space with tables and chairs (for eating and drinking) has a load factor of 15 square feet *net*. Net square footage allows you to deduct those items and base your square footage on the space that a person can move around in. See Figure 6.7 for a diagram of the two types of square footage discussed here: a commercial kitchen and a restaurant bar, dining and dance floor.

Means of Egress

There are three parts of a **means of egress** system in a building:

1. The *exit access* is anywhere in the building that is used for walking to or moving toward an exit.
2. The *exit* is the fire-rated element that separates the exit access from the exit discharge. This is most often

a door, but it can also be a fire-rated enclosure such as an exit stair or a horizontal exit passage.
3. The *exit discharge* is the area (either inside or outside the building) that is between the exit and the public way. The **public way** is an area open to the sky, usually a street or alley that is a minimum of 10 feet wide to allow for rescue vehicles to enter it.

The two factors that most typically determine whether a room or area must have at least two exits are occupant load and *travel distance*. Codes govern how long a distance is allowed before an exit is reached. The use of sprinkler systems greatly increases the permitted distance. Consult local codes for travel distance. A **dead-end corridor** is one in which someone would have to turn around and backtrack to reach an exit. If a person can keep walking continuously until reaching an exit, the corridor is not a dead end. The IBC usually limits the length of a dead-end corridor to 20 feet (or 50 feet in a building with an automatic sprinkler fire-suppression system).

Building codes and accessibility standards require that all means-of-egress doorways provide a minimum clearance of 32 inches, which is accomplished using a 36-inch-wide door. When two or more exits are required, at least two of the exits must be a minimum distance apart, which is at least one-half the longest diagonal distance within the building or space. This is referred to as the **half-diagonal rule**.

Accessibility

As interior designers, we must be aware of the Americans with Disabilities Act (ADA), which was signed into law in 1990. To protect the rights of individuals with disabilities, the ADA provides for equal accommodation and access to places of employment, public services, and businesses. The checklist of questions in Table 6.6 has been prepared to assist you in providing a plan that is accessible. Interior designers should be aware that the Department of Justice (DOJ) and the Department of Transportation (DOT) are responsible for enforcing Titles II and III of the ADA. Business owners are urged to comply to limit their *liability* (the chance that they will be sued for creating a space that is not accessible). This ADA checklist is designed to be used in full or in part, depending on the facility. For a downloadable pdf of the 2010 ADA standards visit https://www.ada.gov/regs2010/2010ADAStandards/2010ADAStandards.pdf.

TABLE 6.5

MAXIMUM FLOOR AREA ALLOWANCES PER OCCUPANT (AKA LOAD FACTORS)

Function of Space	Floor Area in Square Feet per Occupant
Accessory storage, mechanical equipment rooms	300 gross
Agricultural building	300 gross
Aircraft hangars	500 gross
Airport terminal	
Baggage claim	20 gross
Baggage handling	300 gross
Concourse	100 gross
Waiting areas	15 gross
Assembly	
Gaming floors (keno, slots, etc.)	11 gross
Exhibit gallery and museum	30 net
Assembly with fixed seats	Not Applicable (Number of fixed seats determines occupant load)
Assembly without fixed seats	
Standing only	5 net
Concentrated (chairs only)	7 net
Unconcentrated (tables and chairs)	15 net
Bowling centers	7 net
Business areas	100 gross
Courtrooms (other than fixed seating areas)	40 net
Daycare	35 net
Dormitories	50 gross
Educational	
Classroom area	20 net
Shops and other vocational rooms	50 net
Exercise room and locker rooms	50 gross
Fabrication and manufacturing areas (Hazardous)	200 gross
Industrial areas	100 gross
Institutional areas	
Inpatient treatment areas	240 gross
Outpatient areas	100 gross
Sleeping areas	120 gross
Kitchens, commercial	200 gross
Library	
Reading rooms	50 net
Stack area	100 gross
Mercantile (retail)	60 gross
Storage, stock, shipping areas	300 gross
Parking garages	200 gross
Residential	200 gross
Skating rinks, swimming pools	
Rink and pool	50 gross
Decks	15 gross
Stages and platforms	15 net
Warehouses	500 gross

Adapted from International Building Code. (2018). www.iccsafe.org.

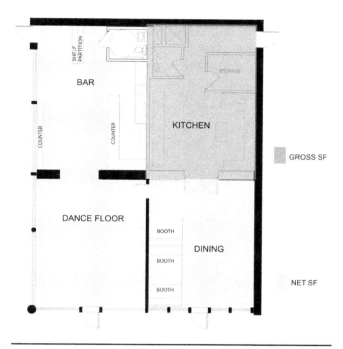

Figure 6.7 Diagram showing gross area versus net area in a restaurant project

Must all interior spaces comply with ADA Accessibility Guidelines (ADAAG)? Usually, any new construction would trigger the requirement for compliance with the guidelines. However, all facilities can be divided into two types:

- Places of **public accommodation**
- **Commercial facilities**

Places of *public accommodation* are businesses and facilities, such as a laundromat or a doctor's office, the public enters as a regular course of business. As you may expect, these businesses need to be accessible. *Commercial facilities*—offices or factories that the public does not access—do not necessarily have to comply. However, owners should be made aware that if an employee is physically impaired, the office may need to accommodate that person's needs.

Whom would you consult to determine whether your project needs to comply with ADA? In the professional environment, you may want to consult with a certified access specialist. At minimum become familiar with resources provided by United States Access Board (http://www.access-board.gov) and have a conversation about accessibility compliance with your client at the onset of a project.

If you are altering or adding to an existing building, you must comply "to the maximum extent feasible"

TABLE 6.6

REVIEWING YOUR DESIGN FOR ADA (ADAAG) COMPLIANCE

ADA Area of Concern	Does Your Design Comply?
Entrance/Route of travel	• Is there a route of travel that does not require stairs? • Is the route of travel stable, firm, and slip-resistant? • Is the width of the route the minimum distance required? • Can all of the object protruding into the circulation be detected by a person with a visual disability and a cane? • If there is a level change in the floor, is it accomplished using an accessible sloping ramp? • Are the doors, hinges, and hardware compliant? • Are the heights of all fixtures and amenities compliant?
Rooms and spaces	• Are all the aisles and pathways to goods and services accessible? • Have you shown the turning radius or area of a stationary wheelchair where appropriate? • Are the finish materials compliant? • Are the restroom layouts and fixture heights accessible? • Are the spaces for wheelchair seating distributed throughout? • Do counters and tables allow for height and knee clearances?
Wayfinding and signage	• Are there visual and audio alarms for emergency egress? Are there illuminated exit signs where appropriate? • Are signs compliant and mounted appropriately?
Other . . .	• Are you modifying an existing building? • Have you had a conversation with your client about access and compliance? • Consult a state certified access specialist to confirm your choices and to move forward confidently. • Have you considered Universal Design principles that go above and beyond ADA guidelines to accommodate the widest variety of people?

unless you have a specialist determine the alteration is technically infeasible. "If the modification or additional scope needed to meet the ADA requirements are not 'readily achievable' (meaning not without difficulty or considerable expense) or is determined to be an 'undue burden' (meaning disproportionate to the financial situation of the owner or project), the regulations often allow for exceptions to strict compliance" (Kennon & Harmon, 2018, p. 48).

According to CASp Manual (2016), the ADA contains a list of 21 examples of modifications that may be *readily achievable*:

1. Installing ramps;
2. Making curb cuts in sidewalks and entrances;
3. Repositioning shelves;
4. Rearranging tables, chairs, vending machines, display racks, and other furniture;
5. Repositioning telephones;
6. Adding raised markings on elevator control buttons;
7. Installing flashing alarm lights;
8. Widening doors;
9. Installing offset hinges to widen doorways;
10. Eliminating a turnstile or providing an alternative accessible path;
11. Installing accessible door hardware;
12. Installing grab bars in toilet stalls;
13. Rearranging toilet partitions to increase maneuvering space;
14. Insulating lavatory pipes under sinks to prevent burns;
15. Installing a raised toilet seat;
16. Installing a full-length bathroom mirror;
17. Repositioning the paper towel dispenser in a bathroom;
18. Creating designated accessible parking spaces;
19. Installing an accessible paper cup dispenser at an existing inaccessible water fountain;
20. Removing high pile, low density carpeting;
21. Installing vehicle hand controls.

(CASp, 2016, p. 7)

Since your project is a school project, the Council of Interior Design Accreditation (CIDA) expects that you will produce a project that respects all humans and meets the minimum requirements set forth in the ADA.

Designated historic buildings, and some religious institutions may be exempt from complying with the ADA Accessibility Guidelines. For a building to be considered *historic*, it must be "listed (or eligible to be listed) in the *National Register of Historic Places*, or designated as historic by a specific state or local authority" (Kennon & Harmon, 2018, p. 493). Historical significance may be based on physical aspects of its design, materials, form, style, or workmanship, or the building may have been associated with important events, activities, or persons. The National Register of Historic Places can be accessed on the Internet at http://www.cr.nps.gov/nr/listing.htm. Federal buildings (GSA, DOD, and USPS) must comply with ABA Accessibility Guidelines. Federally funded housing (HUD) must comply with Uniform Federal Accessibility Standards (UFAS). For more information visit www.access-board.gov.

INTEGRATING BUILDING SYSTEMS

What Are Building Systems?

Understanding how a building is put together is essential to helping you design spaces that can be more efficient (in terms of cost) and more easily maintained and repaired. **Building systems** can be visualized as various systems in a living organism: structural (skeletal system), heating/plumbing (circulatory system of the heart and blood vessels), ventilation (pulmonary or lungs), electrical/security (the brain and nervous system), cladding (skin), etc. Mechanical engineer and facilities manager for the Salk Institute of Biological Studies in La Jolla, California, Tim Ball, says, "taking care of a building is like taking care of a living creature. It breathes in fresh air, takes in clean water, receives deliveries of goods and services, circulates and distributes the air, water, goods and services, and expels waste" (T. Ball, personal communication, August 25, 2018). When space planning, we must be sensitive to placement of entry points for arrivals of people and goods, and removal of trash.

Structural systems include the foundation and framing. Foundation types include shallow (slab-on-grade, crawl space, and basement) and deep foundations (driven, friction piles, and cast-in-drilled-hole or caissons). Conventional framing includes the use of wood, steel, concrete, and unit masonry (block or brick). Newer or innovative methods of construction such as rammed earth, straw bale construction and use of recycled or up-cycled products as building materials are being developed all the time. Enclosure systems include exterior finish systems, non-structural or non-load-bearing **curtain walls**, and **opening protectives** (doors, windows, and skylights). Wall thickness, ceiling heights, and relative thickness of floor, ceiling, and roof structure, and location of openings in walls and roofs will show up on a design development building section, which will be discussed in Chapter 7.

While you may not always have a choice over what your building shell consists of, you should understand the possibilities and constraints of each framing system. For example masonry walls (brick and block) limit size and location of openings for windows and doors. In a two-way structural steel system you can have unlimited exterior glazing or very large doors, but a regular series of a grid of columns (bays) to consider. Figure 6.8 illustrates some common structural framing systems: A. One-way steel truss on steel columns, B. Load-bearing exterior wall with interior columns with pier footings, C. Stud-framed walls on slab foundation, D. Two-way steel framing on deep cast pile footings.

Mechanical/Electrical/Plumbing Systems (MEPs) include Heating Ventilation and Air Conditioning (HVAC), plumbing supply system (piped water and natural gas), sanitary system or drain/waste/vent (DWV),

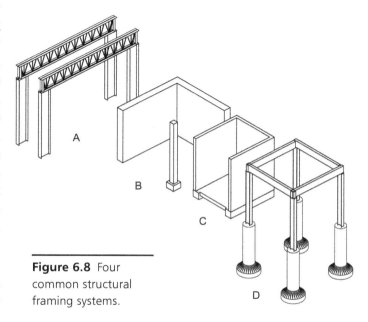

Figure 6.8 Four common structural framing systems.

security and communication systems, fire protection systems (detection, alarm, and suppression), and conveying systems (horizontal and vertical circulation) such as moving walkways, lifts, stairs, escalators, and elevators. Within the building shell there are such a number of systems that need to be integrated in the ceiling, such as lighting, fire protection, acoustics and security/communication, that often you will need to consult specialists. The sizing and specification of these systems will come in the construction documents phase. For now, you should just know, for example, that elevators need an adjoining mechanical room, either next to, below, or above. Or if your building is going to be heated and cooled by an all-air system, you will need to provide space in the plenum for ducting, and locate supply diffusers and return registers in the appropriate locations. Or that you will need to show illuminated exit signage at means of egress exit locations. Examples of design development reflected ceiling plans will be shown in Chapter 7. We also have to be aware that over time, systems need to be accessed by people who will clean, repair, and replace worn out elements.

According to architect Paul Johnson (personal communication, 2009), six basic questions need to be considered in the selection of any building system:

1. What will give the required functional performance?
2. What will give the desired aesthetic result?
3. What is possible legally? (Zoning, Code, ADA, CCRs)
4. What is best for the environment? (Green architecture)
5. Can it be built? (Constructability)
6. What is most economical?
    Life–Cycle Cost Analysis:
    Initial Investment (including loan costs)
    Installation costs
    Maintenance and upkeep costs
    Energy consumption
    Replacement costs

Incorporating Sustainability: Passive Measures and Active Systems

The first step to incorporating sustainability is to use what you learned from doing a site analysis discussed in the previous chapter. A passive measure in sustainability means that your building does not need to rely on energy to maintain the temperature, and other aspects of indoor air quality such as relative humidity, good acoustics, and light level for human comfort. This concept is symbolized by the "south-facing cave" which stays warm in winter and cool in summer without use of special equipment. Note how your building or interior spaces relate to compass directions of north, south, east and west. In schematics you may have planned your spaces around the sun path. Now in design development you can take advantage of the natural light to supplement or replace artificial lighting (daylighting), and prevailing breezes for natural ventilation (see Figure 6.11). Consider the *thermal mass* of your building shell, its resistance to heat transfer, or ability to retain heat. Consider the size, placement, and operation of windows, skylights, and wind scoops to facilitate cross ventilation, stack effect, and displacement ventilation.

Current sustainability concepts such as *Living Building Challenge* and *Earthship Biotecture* (https://www.earthshipglobal.com/) view the entire project as an ecosystem, or autonomous constructions. While not all projects can be "off the grid," all projects can be designed to minimize their reliance on conventionally produced electricity and fossil fuels. Can your building be self-sufficient in terms of energy production and use? Can you recapture gray water from lavatories to irrigate flower boxes? Can you capture rainwater to supplement water supply? Many of these systems will show up when you cut a section through your building, which will be explored in research-based presentation techniques in the next chapter.

Selecting Interior Features
Furniture, Fixtures, and Equipment

Furniture, Fixtures, and Equipment (FF&E) are the objects in a space that help assist with the function of the space. Architects (and builders) tend to differentiate (1) items that are installed to become part of the building from (2) items that are not permanently attached. The two tend to come from different budgets. To architects, "FF&E" stands for *Furniture, Furnishings, and Equipment*: freestanding elements that are purchased separately, under separate contract by the owner and/or purchasing agency. Fixtures such as toilets and lavatories would fall under the base building budget and would be purchased by the contractor for installation by the contractor.

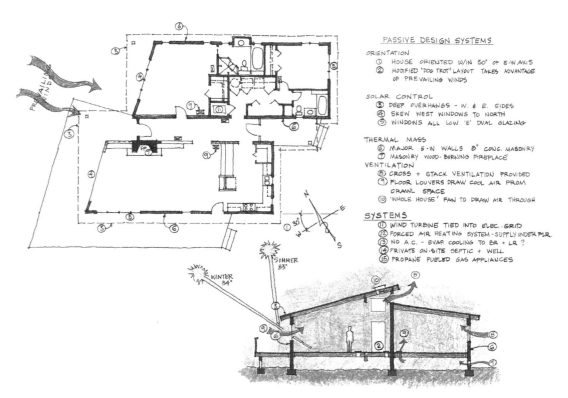

PASSIVE DESIGN SYSTEMS

ORIENTATION
① HOUSE ORIENTED W/IN 50° OF E-W AXIS
② MODIFIED "DOG TROT" LAYOUT TAKES ADVANTAGE OF PREVAILING WINDS

SOLAR CONTROL
③ DEEP OVERHANGS - W. & E. SIDES
④ SKEW WEST WINDOWS TO NORTH
⑤ WINDOWS ALL LOW 'E' DUAL GLAZING

THERMAL MASS
⑥ MAJOR E-W WALLS 8" CONC. MASONRY
⑦ MASONRY WOOD-BURNING FIREPLACE

VENTILATION
⑧ CROSS + STACK VENTILATION PROVIDED
⑨ FLOOR LOUVERS DRAW COOL AIR FROM CRAWL SPACE
⑩ 'WHOLE HOUSE' FAN TO DRAW AIR THROUGH

SYSTEMS
⑪ WIND TURBINE TIED INTO ELEC. GRID
⑫ FORCED AIR HEATING SYSTEM - SUPPLY UNDER FLR.
⑬ NO A.C. - EVAP COOLING TO BR + LR ?
⑭ PRIVATE ON-SITE SEPTIC + WELL
⑮ PROPANE FUELED GAS APPLIANCES

Figure 6.9
Diagrammatic building section showing natural ventilation and daylighting.

As an interior designer, you might not make that distinction. The information you collect about the elements that go into the interior space, the "FF&E," could be defined as *Furniture, Fixtures, and Equipment*. Fixtures are part of the total package of what you select and, later, specify. It is important, though, to remember which budget they do come out of and who is responsible for purchasing the item during the contract administration phase.

Most large commercial furniture companies continually produce high quality research to support their system furnishing's design features. Look on their websites for **white papers**, concise, authoritative reports proposing solutions to a complex, or current, issue, such as ergonomics, privacy, co-working, collaboration, engagement, or work styles. These reports provide interior designers with persuasive arguments for guiding and defending their furniture selections.

Online product sourcing company Sweets™ allows you to search for manufacturer's literature alphabetically by manufacturer and product information using the Construction Specifications Institute (CSI) format. Visit https://sweets.construction.com/ to browse, search, and select products from catalogs, and download CAD blocks or Building Information Management (BIM) objects to import directly into your digital drawing file. Companies

such as *3Form* (www.3-form.com) provide information about the technical details of using their products for wall partitions, doors, countertops, railings, light fixtures, and signage. Call on product representatives and vendors to help you provide evidence that their product is right for the job in terms of durability and flammability ratings. Browse design magazines and books to get the latest trends and information about the newest products. In addition to talking to people and looking up information in books and magazines, go to showrooms and physically sit in the chairs that you will be selecting for your project! Chapter 8 discusses mock-up and usability testing if you are designing custom furniture or you want to see how a combination of elements works in a room.

Applying Color Theory

Color theory consists of basic constructs such as *hue*, *saturation* or intensity, and *value*, as well as physiological and psychological effects of color. In addition, color theory also addresses the compositional effects of colors, relationship and apparent effects of colors when placed next to each other. As interior designers, we are interested in all of these theories in order to create a research-based color scheme for our project.

Traditionally, interior designers were taught standard color harmonies and cautioned that: 1) floors should be relatively low in value and saturation so they would hide soil and provide an optically firm base, 2) walls should be rather light and neutral in hue to provide a value gradation from floor to ceiling and to avoid clashes with colors of paintings and furnishings, and 3) ceilings should be very light to give a sense of spaciousness and reflect lighting well. (Zelanski & Fisher, 2003, p.167)

However, once you are aware of the "rules" of color, you can break them, based on your own insights or further research. According to professional color consultant and collage artist Anja Schoenbeck (personal communication, October 15, 2008), there are three main areas of research that you will want to focus on during design development.

1. Understand (and be able to communicate with your client) how your color choices affect peoples' perception of the size of the room(s). The technical and theoretical aspects of color, such as adding white (to make a *tint*) or black (to produce a *shade*), or adjusting the *intensity* of the *hue*, will help you to create a palette to enhance the spatial characteristics. You should also thoroughly research such theoretical aspects as *harmony, proportion,* and *contrast.*
2. Understand the physics of light and the biological or physiological impact of color on the human eye, so that you can apply the color to produce the effect you desire. The appearance of color depends on the presence of natural light and the quality of artificial light.
3. Understand the *symbolic* meanings of color: the cultural perceptions associated with color that may affect your users emotionally. In Chinese culture, for example, the color white is associated with death or mourning while red is associated with success and marriage. Research psychological impact, both hidden and obvious, before you present a color palette.

Schoenbeck continues, "Interior designers must comprehend the bigger picture and understand that all aspects are inevitably linked. The thing about color is that a designer's personal preference may be completely irrelevant to the circumstance." Color choice must be complementary to architecture, materials, style, function, and concept. If the client suggests particular colors, analyze whether those color wishes are appropriate. Do they suit the structure, style, function, etc.?

Going past the materials lab, I saw a 12" x 12" piece of carpet that was a hideous red/violet color. I said to myself, 'How could anyone possibly use this on the floor?' I brought it with me to class to show the students how bilious this color was. I threw the carpet sample down in the middle of the classroom floor and we all looked. Well, it was beautiful. It was the right amount of color in the right location, a jewel tone in a large field of gray. It was somehow transformed, and my perception was changed. It was then that I realized there is no such thing as a *bad* color. It all has to do with location, proportion, and context. (A. Schoenbeck, personal communication, October 15, 2008)

If you have not already done so during the programming phase, compile some research studies or information from peer-reviewed sources to help gain an understanding of the color perceptions of your end-users, both from a biological and cultural perspective. As we age, our eyes undergo changes, such as the yellowing of the cornea, so the way we perceive color changes as we age. There are many studies having to do with the calming effect of color, how some colors increase heart rate or metabolism, or cause people to feel hungry. Studies on animals reveal that dogs see a more limited color spectrum than humans. Take some time to thoroughly understand the impact of color before proceeding to the selection of your palette.

Developing a Palette of Materials

During design development, it is essential that you clearly indicate the design intentions, the major goals of the project, and the design details—without getting too caught up in construction details. As Ballast (2013) explains it, "the design intent is the approach the designer and owner decide to take to satisfy the program requirements and specific need arising from these requirements" (pp. 21–23). He goes on to say that it "includes the overall appearance . . . balanced against practical considerations such as codes, cost and material limitations, the design intent is the basic starting point for developing and reviewing a detail." The emphasis on design intent during design development makes sure that the details contribute to the design concept as well as "resolve problems of connection or transition."

You have already determined performance criteria for the materials in your program; then, during the schematic design phase, you have selected a preliminary material palette. Now it is time to refine your selections and educate yourself about the installation, maintenance, and sustainable aspects of the materials. Consult textbooks that are devoted to the properties of interior finishes such as *Interior Design Materials and Specifications* (2013) by Lisa Godsey and *Specifying Interiors 3rd Edition* (2017) by Maryrose McGowan. Now would also be an excellent time to incorporate color theory in your color selections, and to realize how color and texture interact with each other to bring your design together. Finally determine the flammability ratings for each material, to make sure they do not conflict with the code requirements of the space you are considering using them in.

Overall, the design development material palette should represent a system that responds to the functional requirements of the flooring, walls, ceilings and built-in elements, while supporting the design concept. It should consist of individual selections that are in keeping with the budget and maintenance schedule. Use and abuse considerations in an institutional environment are vastly different from a home environment. In a school or hospital, for example, materials must resist much more foot traffic, soils such as blood or urine, daily cleaning routines using harsh chemicals such as bleach, impact from carts or skateboards, and the effect of end-users who do not necessarily want to be there, such as graffiti or vandalism. Safety is a number one consideration of all materials. Select tempered or shatterproof glass, slip resistant flooring; minimize trip hazards, and sharp corners or edges.

In a finish plan, discussed in Chapter 7, you will apply these finishes with your overall goal to enhance wayfinding, as discussed earlier in this chapter. Here are some reminders of how to use the elements of wayfinding to tell a story through your materials:

- Use swaths of color or texture or pattern to indicate travel access or direction.
- Use changes of material in walls, floor and ceiling, changes in ceiling height to differentiate areas or create perceptible boundaries.
- Create a common color palette with accents to distinguish areas, and/or use of a detail, a pattern or texture to identify and unify an area or district.
- Inset a logo, decorative pattern or "area rug" to identify a lobby or decision-making point; create a volumetric shape such as a cube or dome to heighten awareness at nodes.
- Provide highly visible, distinctive signage, artwork, a decorative light fixture, water feature, planter, wall of accent color. Create other sensory landmarks using pleasing and memorable scents, sounds, and textures.

There is an important distinction between material *selection* and *specification*. Material selection is a recommendation you make in order to determine whether the client will accept the general idea of a material, such as soft, resilient or hard flooring, or even more specifically, a patterned carpet tile, a wood-look vinyl plank or white polished granite. This is one step before **specification**, which "describes the quality of material and their construction or installation, information that cannot be communicated graphically" (McGowan, 2006, p. 32). In the design development phase, you are usually *selecting* the material. Material selection involves getting and showing samples (loose or mounted on a board) of the actual materials to elicit the client's approval, as described in the next chapter. Designers can also provide preliminary pricing, technical information such as durability and flammability ratings, as well as indicate how and where the material will be used in a variety of drawing types, discussed in the next chapter. It is not until contract document phase, that you would include written specifications.

Conclusion

Every aspect of your project during the design development phase can be informed, enhanced, improved, and transformed through information. From navigating through your space plan to the way the spaces are ventilated, sound is controlled, light is manipulated, or a door is opened, your design solution must respond to human factors, conform to codes, and be economically viable. True innovation comes from an intense observation, analysis of the problems to be solved, followed by an ability to absorb and utilize information from a variety of sources. A research-based design is completed using evidence in order to take a risk and propose something new.

What motivates each decision during this phase? From the color of a wall treatment to the placement of each piece of furniture, you should always have a reason why you made that decision. The strongest design solution comes from an informed position. Go back to the written program and add details about what you have discovered through this design development phase. This will help guide you in a research-based design presentation, explored in the next chapter.

References

Alexander, C. (1977). *A pattern language.* New York: Oxford University Press.

Ballast, D. K. (2013). *Interior design reference manual: Everything you need to know to pass the NCIDQ exam, 6th edition.* Belmont, CA: Professional Publications.

CASp (2016). Retrieved January 4, 2019, from https://www.documents.dgs.ca.gov/dsa/casp/CASp_Manual.pdf#page7)

Ching, F. D. K. and Winkel, S. R. (2018). *Building codes illustrated: A guide to understanding the 2018 International Building Code, Sixth edition.* Hoboken, New Jersey: Wiley.

Fagan, J. and Shepherd, I. L. (1970). *Gestalt therapy now: Theory, techniques, applications.* New York: Harper & Row Publishers.

Godsey, L. (2017). *Interior Design Materials and Specifications, 3rd ed.* NY: Bloombury Publishing.

Goldhagen, S. W. (2017). *Welcome to your world: How the built environment shapes our lives.* New York: HarperCollins Publishers.

Hall, E. T. (1966). *The hidden dimension.* New York: Doubleday.

International Building Code. (2018). Retrieved from www.codes.iccsafe.org.

Kennon, K. E. and Harmon, S. K. (2018). *The codes guidebook for interiors, 7th ed.* New York: Wiley.

Lynch, K. (1960). *The image of the city.* Cambridge, MA: MIT Press.

Mallgrave, H. F. (2011). *The architect's brain: Neuroscience, creativity, and architecture.* West Sussex: Wiley-Blackwell.

Maslow, A. H. (1971). *The farther reaches of human nature.* New York: Viking Press.

McGowan, M. (2006). *Specifying interiors: A guide to construction and FF & E for residential and commercial interiors projects.* Hoboken, NJ: John Wiley & Sons.

North Carolina State University. (1997). *The principles of universal design* (version 2.0). Raleigh: The Center for Universal Design. Retrieved January 6, 2019, from https://projects.ncsu.edu/ncsu/design/cud/about_ud/udprinciples.htm.

Oldenburg, R. (1991). *The great good place: Cafe?s, coffee shops, community centers, beauty parlors, general stores, bars, hangouts, and how they get you through the day.* New York: Paragon House.

Pallasmaa, J. (2005). *The eyes of the skin: Architecture and the senses.* Great Britain: Wiley-Academy, a division of John Wiley & Sons Ltd.

Pati, D. (March, 2010) "Positive Distractions" *Healthcare Design.* 10(3), 28–34. Retrieved December 20, 2018, from https://www.healthcaredesignmagazine.com/trends/architecture/positive-distractions/.

Pollan, M. (2008). *A place of my own: The architecture of daydreams.* New York: Penguin Books Ltd.

Steinfeld, E. and Maisel, J. (2012). *What is universal design?* IDeA Center for Inclusive Design and Environmental Access, University at Buffalo, retrieved from http://udeworld.com/goalsofud.html.

Sternberg, E. M. (2009). *Healing spaces: The science of place and well-being.* Cambridge, MA: Harvard University Press.

United States Access Board (2010). ADA Standards. Retrieved January 6, 2018, from https://www.access-board.gov/guidelines-and-standards.

Zelanski, P. and Fisher, M. P. (2003). *Color,* 4th ed. Upper Saddle River: Prentice Hall Inc., A Division of Pearson Education.

RESEARCH-BASED PRESENTATIONS 7

The river is moving.

The blackbird must be flying.

— WALLACE STEVENS *Thirteen Ways of Looking at a Blackbird* (stanza XII)

CHAPTER OBJECTIVES

When you complete this chapter you will be able to:

- Engage your anticipated audience with a compelling, comprehensive, research-based design development presentation.
- Present your interior design solution using a combination of conventional deliverables, innovative elements, and dynamic formats.
- Storyboard your presentation to communicate the research, program, concept, and design process.
- Employ time-saving tips and time management tools to meet deadlines, for both individual and group projects.

Congratulations! Preparing your design presentation means, first, that you have made a selection from among the many ideas you generated during schematics and, next, that you have embarked on the articulation of a single scheme using the input of multiple resources during the design development phase. Now the focus has shifted to the *representation* and *communication* of your design to your intended audience. This process can be viewed as a separate design endeavor, calling on excellence in drawing craft, graphic design principles, and composition skills.

Effectively presenting your design involves stepping back to identify (1) your audience, (2) the central message or key elements of your design, and (3) how to make the story of your design process clear, meaningful, and engaging. It also involves taking the time and effort to craft your presentation to minimize errors or sloppiness. Careful attention to detail is an ideal attribute for anyone headed into the design profession. Exceptional,

KEY TERMS

Demonstration	Perspective view
Design jury	Process work
Floor plan	Prototype
Gantt chart	Reflected ceiling plan (RCP)
Grade	
Information visualization	Scale model
	Section perspective
Interior elevations	Site plan
Meeting minutes	Storyboard
Mock-up	Thumbnail sketches
Orthographic drawing	

or well-thought-out, interior designs may be obscured by poor presentation, particularly when viewers have difficulty understanding the visuals, or are distracted by poorly mounted elements or inadvertent typos. Conversely, average or ordinary design solutions may be presented extremely well, gleaning accolades from all involved.

UNDERSTANDING YOUR AUDIENCE

In the design studio in school, we have a process that helps prepare students to present in a professional environment or studio critique. A panel of design professionals referred to as a **design jury** assembled by your instructor to watch your presentation, ask questions, and offer feedback. Derived from the French *Ecole de Beaux Arts* and German *Bauhaus* tradition, this ritual seeks to transfer wisdom from expert to novice, almost as a rite of passage. Figure 7.1a shows a jury consisting of an architect, an engineer, a codes official, and an interior designer.

Many schools employ a formal presentation format in which students present individually, in a private or semi-private setting. Other schools have an open forum where student work is pinned up gallery style for a more public display. Some instructors will call on community members to act as real-life clients, or end-users, as in an experiential-learning or service-learning project, which seeks to have student projects benefit the local community. Regardless of your school's presentation style, you will likely present your design solutions with a verbal explanation that you have prepared in advance, and then field questions from the participating jury members. Sometimes your project will inspire discussion amongst the jury members which may also prove to be insightful. Figure 7.1b shows a student presenting to a client and end-users (a local rabbi and members of his congregation) for a redesign of a religious center.

The jury review can be difficult for some students who may have anxiety about public speaking or dread receiving negative remarks about their work. But the process is highly informative and helpful if you view it as an opportunity to get valuable information from industry professionals volunteering their time to give back to the future of the profession. If the feedback is critical, it is a good idea to listen without becoming defensive, and then thank that juror for their input. When faced with a question you did not expect or prepare for, you can let them know that it is "a good question," that you had not considered, but will seek answers to in the future.

Your fellow classmates, your instructor, as well as other visitors who drop in unexpectedly should each be able to understand *what* you did and *why* you did it, and feel they learned something after your presentation has concluded. This may seem like a daunting task, but due to the fact that *you* collected the information, developed the program of spaces, analyzed the applicability to your site, and creatively worked on a solution, you are the only person who can do it!

According to educator and cognitive psychologist Roger Carl Schank, knowledge is made up of stories. Schank (1990) stated "in order to learn or understand something, our minds attempt to process everything we see and hear by comparison to what we have already experienced. From this reminding we gain new insights about the world around us" (p. 19). As people listen to you explain your project, they connect and compare what you are telling them with their own prior knowledge. Therefore, the big message or central point of your presentation must not only be clear but also relatable.

For an industry professional, your presentation should show that you understand current practice, statistics, facts, and trends. Use any of these as your starting point, building on convention to create something truly innovative. They will naturally know how to read a floor plan or a building section, particularly if you have a proper line weight hierarchy, follow convention in scale, and label everything.

A client or end-user may need assistance in understanding a floor plan, an elevation, or building section. You may need to show your design project using more

Figure 7.1a Typical panel of jurors consisting of design professionals.

Figure 7.1b Student presenting to a design jury of a client and end-users.

interactive or universally understandable expressive devices such as perspective views, virtual model walk-through, or three-dimensional objects they can touch, hold, and look through. Figure 7.2 shows two students presenting to clients using a combination of handouts, boards, a PowerPoint slide show, and a scale model. You need to connect their understanding of the current space, their business work flow, or problems they have expressed, to the needs you have identified during the programming process, and the solutions you are proposing. If you have interviewed members of the jury as part of your research, you will want to let them know they have been heard, and that conversations with them have influenced your design ideas. It is a good idea to quote them during your presentation, using words taken directly from your interview transcript or an informal interaction you have had with them that was particularly memorable.

A design educator will want you to showcase what you learned from books, research studies, and peer-reviewed articles on the subject. They will also want to know about the data collection methods you employed, your analysis of the original data, your concept development process work, and how you translated all of it into your design solution.

When you are presenting, keep in mind the importance of nonverbal communication, such as hand gestures, facial expressions, and posture. Your body language tells your audience how you are responding to their feedback. Remain open and comfortable with comments. Consider the project a success if it sparks a dialog among the jurors. Volunteer to be a part of that exchange of ideas and be

open to the opportunity when it arrives. As the saying goes, "You want people to keep correcting you. When they have stopped, then you know they may have given up on you."

Although you are presenting your project to hear and accept criticism, there are some basic things you can and should expect from your jurors (Tate, 1987):

- Respect
- Common courtesy
- Honesty
- Willingness to answer your questions and clarify comments when asked

At the same time, as a person who has set aside time to offer help to you, there are certain things a jury member will expect from you (Tate, 1987):

- Readiness for criticism
- Clear explanation of your ideas
- Preparation to talk as well as listen
- Professionalism

In addition, jurors will expect you to have a firm grasp of professional terminology, ample vocal projection, and a high level of enthusiasm for your project. If this is your capstone project, defending your thesis to a jury is an opportunity for continuing professional relationships with jurors. It could be a great networking tool for you as you transition into the professional world. In addition to professors and other academics, your panel is likely made up of professionals who are always looking for talent. Thank them for any and all feedback. It is appropriate to send a handwritten note or at least an email to all jurors, thanking them for their time and the value of their feedback. Even if they disagreed with some of your ideas, they are there to help you learn, and ultimately, to become a better designer.

It is a good idea to imagine who your ideal design jury would be. Can you involve community leaders, government officials, or benefactors who could potentially fund your project? Can you ask community members or potential end-users to comment on usability and appeal of your project? What kind of feedback are you looking for, and who would be able to provide this information? Most instructors invite fellow design professionals and other colleagues to serve on the design jury, but sometimes students can suggest or recruit their own jury members. Activity 7.1 allows you to take a moment to brainstorm and imagine your dream team—the ideal group of people to view your presentation.

Figure 7.2 Students presenting to a design jury of a clients and end-users using a combination of handouts, boards, a PowerPoint slide show, and a scale model.

ACTIVITY 7.1
Selecting Your Ideal Design Jury or "Dream Team"

Purpose: To assemble an ideal panel to view your presentation and give you valuable feedback.

First, identify someone from each of the following groups: design professionals, qualified experts, design educators, client, end-users, community leaders, or benefactors. With permission from your instructor, reach out to each potential jury member and invite them to your final presentation. Give your instructor the contact information for each potential juror, and keep your instructor updated on the status of your inquiry. If it is your responsibility to make sure your jury members show up for your review, send them a friendly reminder a few days before your big day to confirm that they'll be attending. Once the presentation is over, send each jury member a written thank you note to express your appreciation.

In the spaces below, list the name, contact information, and other notes for each potential jury member:

1. Design Professional:_____

    Name of Person: _____

    Organization/Company: _____

Address:_____

Phone:_____

Email:_____

Date of Invitation:_____ Status of Invitation:_____

Area of Expertise:_____

Notes:_____

2. Qualified Expert: _____

    Name of Person: _____

    Organization/Company:_____

Address:_____

Phone:_____

Email:_____

Date of Invitation:_____ Status of Invitation:_____

Area of Expertise:_____

Notes:_____

3. Design Educator/Faculty Member

    Name of Person: _____

    Organization/Company:_____

Address:_____

Phone:_____

Email:_____

Date of Invitation:_____ Status of Invitation:_____

Area of Expertise:_____

Notes:_____

4. Client Representative: _____

   Name of Person: _____

   Organization/Company:_____

Address:_____

Phone:_____

Email:_____

Date of Invitation:_____ Status of Invitation:_____

Area of Expertise:_____

Notes:_____

5. Actual or Potential End-User: _____

   Name of Person: _____

   Organization/Company:_____

Address:_____

Phone:_____

Email:_____

Date of Invitation:_____ Status of Invitation:_____

Area of Expertise:_____

Notes:_____

6. Community Leader or Benefactor: _____

   Name of Person: _____

   Organization/Company:_____

Address:_____

Phone:_____

Email:_____

Date of Invitation:_____ Status of Invitation:_____

Area of Expertise:_____

Notes:_____

DESIGN DEVELOPMENT PRESENTATION COMPONENTS

The presentation itself is a graphic design project, separate from your interior design solution. You may start by acknowledging meaningful influences to your project development including people you talked to, lectures you attended, journal articles you read, or facilities you toured. Note observations which yielded sudden insight, or quotes from colleagues which helped clarify a concept or led to a novel solution.

As discussed in Chapter 1, you triangulated your data through reading, observations, and asking questions—and you can enter this triangle from any point. Similarly, in presenting the story of your design process, you can start with any of these points. What best suits your project and your audience? Clients might want to see the original space first in order to familiarize themselves with existing conditions. They want to hear that you've listened to their wants and how you arrived at a design concept derived from your intense study of their problems. They may look at the craft of your presentation to make assumptions about you, as a designer, your attention to detail and the care you took in selecting the materials, cutting them precisely, and aligning the elements when laying out the boards. Professional designers might want to hear about how you used tools and processes they are familiar with to solve the problem. They might be sensitive to conventions and when and how you broke them. They will also want to make sure your decisions are evidence-based, code compliant, and technically feasible.

You must be able to communicate your ideas to an audience verbally as well as visually. Your presentation must be well rehearsed and contain substantial references to your research, as you will be defending your conclusions and will need to draw upon that research to support your ideas. "Own" your ideas but, at the same time, be willing to discuss your ideas and communicate openly without getting defensive. The quality and substance of your research should give you the confidence you need to present your ideas to a room of critics. In fact, you should be so familiar with your program (what you designed) and design concept (how you designed it) that you can state it clearly and concisely without referencing your notes or any other "cheat sheet." Some people call this the *elevator speech*. If you had 30 seconds in an elevator to tell a stranger about your project what would you say?

Arrive early. Your presentation begins the moment you walk through the door, so take care of the messy stuff before you get there or at least before your audience gets there. Always dress appropriately and professionally. Be careful with clothing that can distract, such as dangly jewelry or loud patterns. You do not want your attire competing with or distracting from the work you have produced. During your presentation, stand up straight, face your audience, make eye contact, and speak clearly. Nothing can substitute for adequate preparation, so organize your thoughts and practice, practice, practice!

Drawings and documents produced during the design development phase are intended to continue to communicate the design to the client, giving them enough information to understand all of the elements and details to make informed decisions, but designers should be careful not to go too far, in case they still need to make changes. Your goal is also to highlight and emphasize the *innovation* that exists in your project. The idea that your project adds to the existing body of knowledge of interior design will be particularly essential in a thesis or capstone project. Perhaps your project takes existing objects or spaces and uses them in a new way. Or perhaps you have detailed a piece of furniture that has never existed before. Whatever the innovative elements or principles in your project, they will be strongest and most successful if they emerge from the research that you have done.

The purpose of the design development presentation phase has these closely related parts. Develop presentation materials which seek to

- Express your design using a variety of techniques, including boards, PowerPoint, virtual and physical models, mock-ups, and handouts in order to communicate, to the best of your ability, the feeling of the interior space.
- Communicate with the client, industry professionals, and other stakeholders during the design development phase visually in a stand-alone format which can speak for itself without you around to explain it. In other words, label everything!
- Accurately depict design features, the material, colors, and textures—and all of the furnishings, fixtures, lighting, and architectural elements—that make up your solution in order to elicit educated decisions from viewers. This requires the use of

clear line weights and industry-standard scaled drawings rendered to show design intent, and samples of the actual materials.

- Clearly portray a comprehensive solution yet recognize that some aspects of the project may require further modifications. Inspire the viewer to share your vision yet encourage the exchange of opinions and preferences. Tell a story; make it memorable.
- Gain acceptance of all aspects of the design, and approval from client to move on to *contract documents* (specifications and dimensioned construction drawings and details which communicate to builders).

In a professional environment, design development presentations would be used for preliminary pricing (or to procure a *soft bid* from a contractor). Ultimately, an interior designer wants the client to indicate their approval and "sign off" on the design development drawings so that she can proceed to construction documents. Construction documents are the detailed, dimensioned, scaled drawings with notations and specifications that communicate to the contractor how the project is to be constructed, the precise location and size of each element, and the exact material and color to be purchased and installed.

Conventional Drawings

The role of the scaled **orthographic drawings**: floor plan, reflected ceiling plan, building section, elevations, is to express the design in conventional drawing techniques. In the design development phase, it is essential that you achieve a clear level of graphic resolution in your drawings. The layers of information that you add depend on what you are trying to communicate to the final jury: to your instructor, to your fellow classmates, to your acting client, or to the end-users. With the proper use of hierarchy of line weights; appropriate size of text; readable font; subtle use of color to indicate materials, circulation, or program; and an attention to detail, the drawing can look "rich"—that is, containing and communicating a variety of information while being completely legible.

In a research-based presentation, these orthographic and rendered drawings also serve to indicate and underscore all of the information you have gathered. Your final presentation boards and all of the components on

them should be enticing to the viewer. Ultimately, when clients look at your drawings, you want them to say, "Yes! I want my space to look exactly like that!"

The following is a list of each drawing and a checklist of research-based items that should be included in each one.

Site Plan

On the design development **site plan** show:

- Some surrounding context: streets, buildings, trees, and paths, including some ancillary structures that would be important for people arriving to your project such as bus stops. Label surrounding businesses or features you learned about during your site analysis: attractive amenities such as coffee shops or parks as well as potential sources of noise or odor which influenced your space plan or other design decisions.
- Access to site and entry sequence for those arriving by car, shuttle, bike, or walking, and accessible route for people using mobility assistive devices. Show street name, driveway curb cut, parking, sidewalks, ramps, fences, and gates.
- Draw the building roof or outline, but do not show interior floor plan; this is a bird's eye view.
- Red arrows indicate main and secondary entrance(s). Label entry points, especially if there are more than one, such as public, visitor, patient, staff, private, deliveries, and so forth.
- Outdoor amenities, such as courtyards, balconies, roof gardens, landscaping, sunshade devices or awnings, play equipment, outdoor seating, water features, planters, kiosks, free-standing signage, lighting elements, etc.
- Compass direction or north symbol to remind you to talk about the sun path and prevailing breezes.

Optional elements to include:

- Scale (if applicable), usually in **engineering scales**—1:20, 1:50, 1:100
- Property lines, setbacks, easements
- Adjacent buildings, business or man-made features, such as a tower, parking lot ,or historic landmark. Include business locations that would give information about competition or complementary uses in the vicinity to inform your client that you

Figure 7.3 A clear site plan which includes surrounding context including local businesses and other community amenities, as well as scale and north symbol.

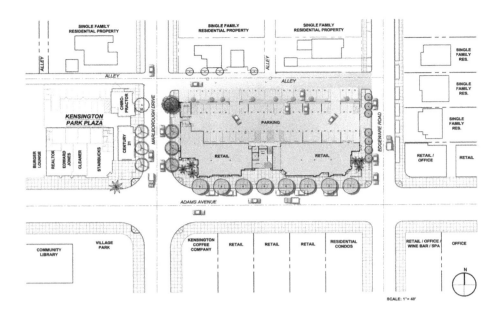

Time-Saving Tip for Site Plans

To save time, use a satellite image as a background to provide context for your site plan. You can paste an image into CAD, scale it, and then trace over the structures in CAD. Or export your CAD-generated site plan into photo editing software, turn down the opacity of the satellite image, and use as a background graphic to get a sense of the rich texture of the surrounding neighborhood.

---

have researched the neighborhood thoroughly for relevant possible conflicts or supportive amenities.

• Adjacent natural features, such as parks, shorelines, large trees, and other points of interest that might indicate a focal point or view. You can label the drawings with arrows from your project pointing to the direction of the view. This is particularly important if you are presenting to the owner of the home or facility and want to show that you considered views in your space planning.

If your project included architectural additions, increasing the enclosed interior space, you may want to differentiate between what was existing and changes you made. In a professional environment this is always required if you are to submit it for approval for permits. Oftentimes an architect will do this drawing. But interior designers may be called on to provide this service, especially if they are applying interior design principles to livable exteriors, such as outdoor kitchens, patios, or healing gardens. If some areas have multiple or flexible uses, show a layout of one of the uses and label the area with other possible uses.

Figure 7.3 provides an example of a typical site plan.

Floor Plan or Furniture Plan

According to Grillo (1960), "a plan is, in reality, a horizontal section" (p. 194). It is cut four feet above the floor. Use your **floor plan** to highlight all the information you gathered about the building shell. Show the thickness of structural walls and non-load bearing partitions, and the regular grid of columns in bold line weights or filled in or *poched*. But the plan represents more than just physical elements.

A design development plan indicates the relationship of rooms to one another and the flow of one material or pattern into another, as well as how the rooms are broken up in concentrated areas of activity through furniture placement. "We can now understand that when we refer to a plan as a structure, it means not only its expression of purely physical construction, but the equilibrium of the areas it defines, submitted to the many forces which control human living. We can, in the same manner, speak of the structure of a painting or of a piece of music. We can speak of a *strong* plan and a *weak* plan" (Grillo, p. 197). Because we walk around on a horizontal plane, the plan is the first place we look for circulation patterns. A design development furniture plan using a good graphic line weight hierarchy and subtle wash of color to indicate flooring, with a dropped shadow technique is shown in Figure 7.4.

Checklist of what to show on a design development furniture plan:

❏ Label all rooms and key features
❏ Show the thickness of structural walls and non-load bearing partitions, and the regular grid of columns in bold line weights or filled in (poched).
❏ Show all built-in elements, such as countertops, low walls, and fixed and non-fixed Furniture Fixtures & Equipment (FF&E), using a medium line weight. Show the functional use of the rooms, your understanding of human factors, as well as how the layout supports your design concept.

❏ Indicate different flooring transitions using a thin line. Indicate materials using wash of color and/or very thin hatch pattern. Do not over render to obscure space plan. May use hand rendering or Photoshop or combination of both. May use shadow technique to give a three-dimensional quality to flat floor plan.
❏ Showcase your understanding of codes, including means of egress, minimum corridor width and exit doors (swinging in direction of travel). Show accessible areas with dashed turning radius, or dashed stationary wheelchair.

Building Section

Building sections are important drawings which cut a building lengthwise or in the short direction, a cross section. It is used by interior designers to communicate the relationship of the building envelope to interior spaces, as well as relative heights of interior spaces. If you have a balcony, a pool, or atrium, it is advisable to cut your building through that feature or space to maximize the communicative power of the building section. In a design development section, you do not have to show the detail of the construction of the wall, nor the layers of materials that are used to create the exterior finishes or interior of the wall assembly. Typically, in a section, you will show the relative thickness of the walls, roof, and floor, and a very bold line where the building meets the top of the

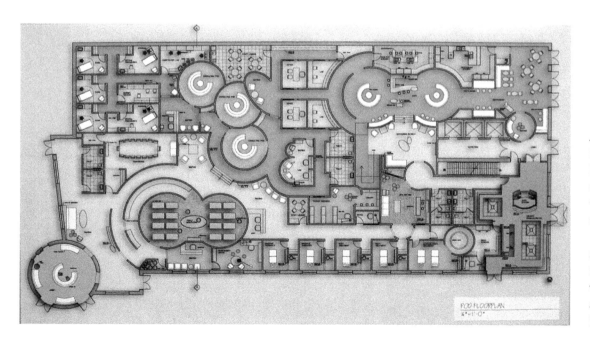

Figure 7.4
Furniture plan of a 10,000 square foot fertility clinic drawn at 1/8 inch = 1 foot with a good graphic hierarchy of line weights, shadow, and subtle flooring indication.

Time-Saving Tip for Rendering Floor Plans

Turn off all layers in your CAD document. Turn on one layer at a time to isolate only those objects that you want to put on each Photoshop layer. Plot, print, or export each of these as its own pdf file. Go to Plot, choose dwgtopdf.pd3. Choose monochrome maximum quality, 1/8 inch scale. Open the individual pdf files in Photoshop. Select all, copy, and paste the contents of each file so that you end up with one file. Organize the layers in the order shown in Figure 7.5.

Now you can independently edit the layers. Use paint bucket to fill a background color on material transitions layer. Do not forget to provide a line that acts as a material transition at the door threshold, and then paint bucket within the door swing. You don't want the door swing to read as an object! Once you have an area of color, use the magic wand tool to select, then cut and paste on a new layer. You can then adjust the opacity and color to achieve exactly the background color of that finish without effecting any other object or layer.

Poche your walls with the paint bucket tool. Adjust the opacity of the hatch patterns, layer and color until they resemble grout lines. You can leave the FF&E clear, use paint bucket tool to fill with white, or you can color individual pieces to match the actual materials, or "color code" the furniture for each area. You can now apply the "drop shadow" layer style on this layer to create a subtle yet powerful three-dimensional effect.

Text now floats above the floor plan and can be erased without disturbing the base plan. You don't have to worry about filling in or around the individual letters. If you wish, you can save the turned on and off layers as "layer states" in CAD to make it easier to export next time.

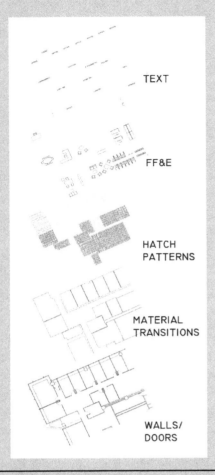

Figure 7.5 Layers exported to photo editing software from CAD document.

ground, or **grade**. The following is checklist of what to show in a building section:

- ❏ Accurately show the structure of the building shell where the section cut occurs using bold lines, or poche to show what is being cut through. Show how the building meets the ground (or foundation), exterior walls, windows, skylights, door openings, overhangs, thickness of floor and ceiling assemblies, and roof structure.
- ❏ Show interior ceiling heights using dropped ceilings, horizontal structural elements such as

trusses and beams, stairs, elevators, and other vertical circulation structures.
- ❏ Relative thicknesses of walls to indicate resistance to heat (thermal mass) or sound transfer, glass, etc.
- ❏ Show the interior elevations that would be viewed past the section cut using a thin line weight.
- ❏ Show ceiling mounted elements such as accent light fixtures and furniture, and human figures as entourage using a medium line weight.
- ❏ Show passive sustainable systems, such as natural ventilation or daylighting.

Section Perspective

Using the computer to produce virtual models has led to less traditional drawings, such as plan perspectives, or has made some innovative conventional drawings easier to produce, such as the **section perspective**, an orthographic section drawn to scale, which includes a vanishing point so that all of the spaces beyond the section cut appear in perspective view, similar to looking in to a dollhouse. For an example, see Figure 7.6.

Computer software offers ease in locating the angle of the perfect isometric or axonometric view, so that we can highlight the most dynamic view before printing or plotting. The computer also allows a "surgical" precision, meaning we can cut away or remove a wall and rotate the camera view to exactly the angle needed to highlight important aspects of the design.

Interior and Exterior Elevations

Unlike building sections, **interior elevations** end at the intersection of perpendicular walls, or the edge of a wall, creating a front view of the wall. They are used to show key accent walls such as feature or display walls, destination walls, built-ins, artwork, interactive storage, and signage. Typically drawn from 1/4 inch = 1 foot for large areas, 1/2 inch = 1 foot for kitchens and baths and up to 3/4 inch =1 foot for more detail, scale your interior elevation to fit the presentation format, the amount of detail you want to show, and how far away your audience will be seated, so that they can see the drawing clearly. Also

- Render to show texture/color/pattern of all materials. Show baseboard or other trim, handrail, wainscot, etc.
- Use entourage to indicate scale and use.
- Provide notes indicating important dimensions or features not visible in a rendering.

- Use rendering devices, shadows, and line weights to help give depth to a flat drawing as shown in Figure 7.7.

Interior Perspective View

An interior **perspective view** should show sufficient floor, walls, and ceiling to give an overall three-dimensional impression of how the interior will look and feel (see Figure 7.9). It is a good idea to position the viewer (or the camera view) in a place where the widest view of the room is possible, especially highlighting decision-making points. The standard vanishing point should be at eye level of a typical viewer. If the end-user is at standing height, that may be between 5 and 6 feet above the finished floor. However, if the end-user is a child or seated in a wheelchair, you may have to adjust the height to more accurately match the perspective of the viewer. The author once drew a kitchen design from the cat's viewpoint because the client wanted to make sure the new design was welcoming to all members of the family!

- Show how placement of walls, furnishings, and changes in flooring material shows paths and edges for wayfinding. Show signage and other way-finding devices (paths, edges, nodes, landmarks . . .).
- Show how all features, including signage legibility, transaction counters, changes in level, material transitions, handrails, and door hardware meet or exceed accessibility requirements, and align with the principles of Universal Design.
- Use ceiling height changes, lighting level and architectural detail such as soffits to differentiate areas, as well as indicate your understanding of room acoustics. Show lighting: ambient, task, and accent.

Figure 7.6 Section perspective cut from a virtual model.

Figure 7.7 Interior elevation of wine bar display wall and built-in booth seating with entourage, partially rendered.

Time-Saving Tip for Creating Exterior Elevations

Many times, an interior design presentation needs to include an exterior elevation. Interior designer Gerald Bouvia III recommends this quick way to get an existing exterior elevation drawn in CAD, re-designed, and rendered for presentation. First take a good digital photo of the front of the building, typically from across the street so you can get a straight-on shot. Then paste the digital photo into CAD. Scale up the drawing based on one element you have measured of the actual building such as a door width or a window sill height. You can always estimate if you did not have an opportunity to measure anything. Then trace over the building in your CAD program. If there are multiple elements of the same thing, just copy and paste. If the building is symmetrical, just draw half and mirror. Then print out your elevation, put a piece of trace paper over it, and do a quick sketch of your design changes. You can scan that drawing back in and draw over it, and lightly render for a professional look. See Figure 7.8 for the steps involved.

Figure 7.8 Four steps to quickly generate a building's exterior elevation design by interior designer Gerald Bouvia III.

Figure 7.9 Interior perspective of dog wash showing flooring, wall treatment and ceiling features as wayfinding devices, as well as appropriate entourage.

- Show color/texture of materials and how they support your concept.
- Use entourage to show scale and function of space. How different would Figure 7.9 be without use of a dog in the bath area and retail dog products on the shelves?

Reflected Ceiling Plan or Lighting Plan

A **reflected ceiling plan (RCP)** is another opportunity to showcase how your concept influences the flow of space, without the worries of slip resistance, tripping hazards, or other downsides of level changes that occur on the floor plan. NCIDQ tests on basic lighting concepts such as ambient, task, and accent lighting, but you can also show your research-based design skills by integrating building systems components such as HVAC supply diffusers and returns, fire detectors, alarms and sprinklers, and emergency exit lighting. If the room depends on sound system speakers or security devices such as cameras, these can also be shown on the reflected ceiling plan.

- Show changes in ceiling height using shades of gray (with a legend), or numerical ceiling height placed in an oval (architectural convention).
- Show lighting design basics (ambient light, task, and accent), show fixtures using standard symbols, and daylighting features. Optional to include circuits and switching.
- Show architectural ceiling elements such as skylights, soffits, beams, skylights, etc.
- Show ceiling materials to show your understanding of acoustics, including suspended acoustical grids and other specialty ceilings.

Details, Process Work, and Information Visualization

If you have designed custom furniture or other features such as built-in storage, reception desk, light fixture or signage, you may want to show a *section detail* through that item how it is attached to the wall or floor or suspended from the ceiling.

For additional visuals, consider simple but substantial images such as "before" photos and plans of the existing conditions (before you made changes)—they are always useful to establish the underlying reasons or urgency for your design intervention. Use **process work**, such as diagrams and preliminary sketches in your design presentation, to show the early stages, emergence and evolution of your design ideas, and how they were shaped by feedback during the schematic design phase. Employ collaged imagery to communicate abstract programmatic and design concepts.

Between the initial data collection (raw data of observation and measurement) and the final presentation is a process of selecting, sorting, editing, summarizing, and arranging. It is your job to make sure that the images and text combinations you use clearly and accurately support what you have found and communicate your design intent. Tufte (1997) urges designers to create visual explanations employing strategies which ensure "the proper arrangement in space and time of images, words, and numbers—for presenting information about motion, process, mechanism, cause and effect" (p. 9). This is referred to as **information visualization**. In Figure 7.10, three photos seek to communicate a complex set of programmatic ideas behind a playground design: the idea of a balance of safety versus danger in playground design.

Figure 7.10 Manipulated imagery to communicate complex abstract programmatic concepts such as safety in a playground.

The interior designer starts off her presentation with these three photos to pose the question, "are we conceptually placing children in an overprotective bubble?"

In his book *Information Visualization: Perception for Design* (2013) Colin Ware states, "visualization has become an external artifact supporting decision making" (p. 2). In both science and design we rely on symbols and graphics to communicate our big ideas. According to Tufte (2006), "in modern scientific research . . . 25% of published materials are graphs, table, diagrams, and images; the other 75% are words" (p. 83). Combining words, numbers, and images creates a "bond between verbal and nonverbal evidence" (Tufte, 2006, p. 83).

We can use color to *label, measure, represent,* or *decorate* (Tufte, 1990, p. 81). You can color code a floor plan by program area; you can differentiate ceiling heights on a reflected ceiling plan using shades of gray; you can show water features as a pale blue throughout your drawings; and/or you can also selectively use vibrant color to attract attention to the focal point of the room, like photo-realistically rendering the brick, wood mantel, and fire in a fireplace.

When it comes to presentation techniques, do your best to push the boundaries of conventional drawings. Produce composite images that cross the border between computer and hand-drawn, blurring the boundary between man and machine. Keep asking yourself, "Is there another way to represent this idea?" You can use different media such as watercolor painting, chalk on textured paper, or a layered collage of found objects from the project site. Entertain the idea of a "full-scale" drawing or a drawing so large you feel like you could inhabit it.

Scale Models, Mock-Ups, Prototypes, and Demonstrations

Scale models in the interior design process can range in materials, level of craft, detail, and focus. A typical model used for design presentation is a *study model,* which would be roughly constructed and act as a three-dimensional extension of a diagram or sketch, or a *finish model,* which would include furnishings, and indicate finishes of the walls and floor. Criss B. Mills (2011) *Designing with Models: A Studio Guide to Architectural Process Models* 3rd edition, explores the rich variety that exists in architectural approach to model making. He sees "interior models" as a form of design development model typically constructed at 1/4 inch = 1 foot or 1/2 inch = 1 foot as useful for visually "'walking through" the space, observing it in three dimensions, many ideas can be generated" (p. 18). Most often, interior models can show the effect of daylight through windows or other openings, explore artificial lighting effects through colors and patterns, and simulate the interior finishes and textures to evoke a visceral response in the viewer. Figure 7.11 shows a finish model that does all of the above.

According to Lee, Wickens, Liu, and Ng Boyle (2017), a **mock-up** is a very crude approximation of the final product or space, often made in foam core or cardboard. It is often used to help understand functionality and task analysis in human factors engineering. In interior design, mock-ups are frequently used in furniture and product design as an effective and inexpensive design tool to conduct in-house testing and preliminary evaluation of usability. Unlike a prototype, which will be discussed

Figure 7.11 Three views of a student's scale model to study filtering daylight to reduce damage to artwork while still providing the benefits of natural light to museum occupants.

shortly, a mock-up usually comes relatively early in the design process and is not usually presented to the client. Photos of it, or results of the testing, may be shared as shown in Figure 7.21 at the end of this chapter.

Prototypes

If budget and time permit, after preliminary issues have been identified through testing of mock-ups, the next step might be to create a **prototype** of a product or space.

Unlike a mock-up, which can be made from foam or cardboard with glue guns and pushpins for assembly, prototypes frequently have more of the look and feel of the final product but do not yet have full functionality. Similar to a mock-up, a prototype will give users and designers something to react to and use in testing design criteria (Lee et al., 2017).

In Figure 7.12, interior design student Christopher Little purchased four picture frames from a craft store to create a prototype of patient room signage for the

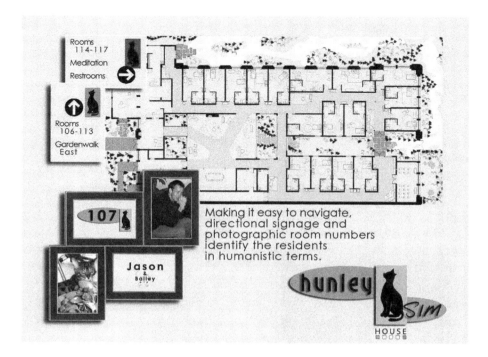

Figure 7.12 Prototype of personalized signage system crafted from four picture frames adds to the wayfinding package of a design presentation for a hospice.

Figure 7.13 Interactive, gallery-style presentation of design ideas for student dorms to university staff as part of a service learning project.

design of a hospice. His research had shown that viewing photos of patients (and their pets) deepened a sense of empathy in caregivers and visitors. He speculated that it could also help with room identity and wayfinding. He created an easy, safe, and inexpensive way to incorporate personalization which appealed to staff during his design presentation.

Figure 7.13 shows an interactive, gallery-style presentation of design ideas as part of a community-based, service learning project. Student interior designers decided that university staff, including in-house contractors, maintenance workers, and housing placement managers would be more inclined to respond to a hands-on presentation of new design ideas for campus dormitories. Students built a display that urged university staff to vote on their favorite drawings, view scale models, play with full-scale mock-ups, and touch prototypes.

A **demonstration** adds the fourth dimension of time. You may have a presentation idea that requires putting something together or deconstructing something in front of your viewers. This adds to intrigue and entertainment value. Consider dimming the lights, adding music, and the value of watching something unfold or be put away. Consider using animation with your voice narrating over it or video to express any aspect of your project that can be transformed, or how it is expected to change over time. In the next chapter we will further discuss interactive tools and how to elicit feedback from your audience through the use of feedback sheets, rubrics, and assessment recording devices.

Putting It All Together

The design development phase ends with a presentation to a client or a jury. Your project should be presented so that it indicates all of the information and research that has gone into the process: information collected through your literature review, interviews, surveys, observation, and case studies—as well as your analysis of the information during your design process, including your written thesis, program, site analysis, statistics, and diagrams. Your project would not be complete if your presentation did not address codes, sustainability, and other guidelines that you have spent many hours researching.

All your hard work and research should be represented in your final presentation: the research, the program, and the design. How can you showcase your thinking process and express how much you have learned over the course of this studio project? Should you create a PowerPoint to commence your verbal discussion, set the stage, and provide a background of research? When the lights are out and the audience is focused on the images on the screen, what are the key points that you want to express about your program, your site, the information you gathered, and the preliminary sketches? You are preparing the audience to see your final rendering. How else can you present this series of experiences? In a handout or a brochure?

Presentation techniques should be researched and planned (as a design project in and of itself). Constantly refine them and look for ways to innovate, in search of the perfect way to educate your final jury about your thesis, your program, and your design solution—and your contribution to the body of knowledge of interior design.

STORYBOARDING YOUR PRESENTATION

Juxtaposition of Drawings

When two images are placed next to each other, it is human nature to compare them. Viewers go back and forth trying to see what is similar about the two images or how they are different. It is important to be clear about how the drawings are related to each other (if they are at all). What do you think is the relationship of the two spaces depicted in the two perspectives in Figure 7.14?

ACTIVITY 7.2
Determining Key Points and Central Message

Purpose: To help focus visual and verbal components of the presentation.

Reflect on your experience during the programming, schematics, and design development phase up to this point. Use the following questions to guide you in determining key points and central message of your presentation:

1. What was the starting point of your project or your original research question(s)?

   _____

2. What statistic or fact about your subject do you think is most compelling?

   _____
   _____
   _____

3. What was a key quote from something you read? Cite the source.

   _____
   _____
   _____

4. What was an interesting point made during an interview? Who said it?

   _____
   _____
   _____

5. What was an "aha" moment during your project journey?

   _____
   _____
   _____

6. Write down a way you can involve your audience in your presentation:

   _____

7. Write down the central message of your presentation:

   _____
   _____
   _____
   _____

SANCTUARY PERSPECTIVE

THERAPY OFFICE PERSPECTIVE

Figure 7.14 Juxtaposition of two perspectives—how are they related?

In the United States and other Western countries, in addition to reading from left to right, we tend to view the page from top to bottom. Contrary to this, however, is the architectural convention that floor plans be placed below reflected ceiling plans, and that first-floor plans be placed below mezzanine or second-floor plans. Architects read from bottom to top as the first-floor plan is usually placed below the second-floor plan, aligning the two floors via the vertical circulation (stairs, elevators).

When you are planning your final presentation, it is imperative to review and understand the fundamentals of graphic design. A good habit to get into is to **storyboard** your final presentation boards. Typically, the act of *storyboarding* is a term associated with planning a sequence of shots for a television show or movie but can also be applied to the layout of a book or magazine spread. Similarly, you can begin by sketching a series of boxes to represent drawings that you would like to see placed next to each other along with notes about direction (pace and emphasis) and accompanying discourse. Storyboarding helps you to arrange the drawings in the sequence in which you plan to address them in your verbal presentation. Which drawing should be talked about first? Storyboarding also helps you to determine hierarchy. How large should each drawing be? Which ones should be emphasized? The most important drawing could be the largest. It could also be strategically placed first, or it could be in the center of the board which is also a way to show how central that drawing is to your project.

Start with a Thumbnail

Thumbnail sketches are small sketches that can literally be as small as your thumbnail, or as big as a couple of inches in width and/or height. Think of the kind of drawing that might be seen on a cocktail napkin. Thumbnails are intended to capture the basic ideas for page composition, like header placement, column structure, and text alignment, without allowing the temptation to focus on small details too early in the process. They can be quickly sketched, allowing rapid idea iteration. Don't like the one that just took 30 seconds to draw? Start another one right beside it. To keep them general, it's best to start with rather small sketches. Then slowly size them up as more details need to be worked out.

Figure 7.15 was a tiny exploratory sketch generated by a student when she was asked to think about the series of boards for her final presentation. Her thesis project was an innovative design that would be used as a dance studio during the day and convert to a nightclub in the evening. She was interested in conveying the sense of music, movement, and rhythm that united the two uses. She began to explore the idea that the boards would be oriented vertically to correspond to upright figures, and that they could be cut with in an undulating edge to represent dancing. Notice the use of white boxes and black boxes to represent a variation of day scenes and night scenes, which reflected her innovative program of day and night use, and how the uneven placement further indicates the sense of motion. Then, she imagined that the drawings of the night scenes could act as connections, extending past the edges of the individual boards, to link the presentation together. After she drew the series of boards, she said they reminded her of puzzle pieces—an excellent way of looking at an interior design presentation!

Figure 7.16a also shows a series of sketches by an interior design student. This project was a conversion of a former firehouse to an art gallery with a live/work loft above. The background color of the boards recall the reddish brown color of the structural brick walls, which are to be revealed and enhanced, as well as the consistently placed, layering of elements on top of these textured walls,

Figure 7.15 Interior design student thumbnail sketch of presentation boards for a dance studio and night club.

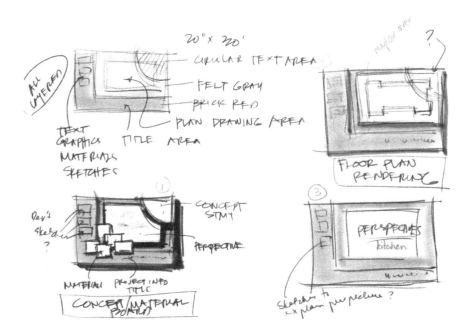

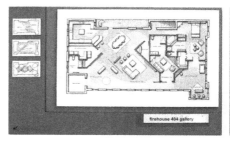

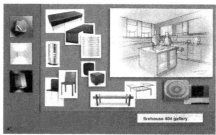

Figure 7.16b Final presentation boards for the firehouse residence project.

which reflected his design concept. This storyboarding activity helped the student to see he could consolidate all of his drawings, concept statement, and material samples onto three boards, as seen in Figure 7.16b.

Figure 7.17 shows a layout technique that goes beyond hand sketching. For students who want an accurately scaled storyboard, the computer is a great tool. In this example, the precision of the drawing allowed for a more detailed layout. Interior design student used the computer to block out her final presentation of a women's museum focused on presenting the accomplishments of women through the past, present, and future.

Her design concept consisted of a contrast of circular shapes that were traditionally symbols of femininity with a sense of revelation and an overall rectilinear progression to represent achievement. All of the drawings are proportionally to-scale and labeled for clarity. The bold labels represent emphasis, a reminder to her to spend more time presenting these drawings in her verbal presentation. The numbers represent the order in which she plans on discussing each drawing, starting in the middle and moving outward in a fairly unpredictable counterclockwise direction, furthering her idea of unexpectedness, fluidity, and grace.

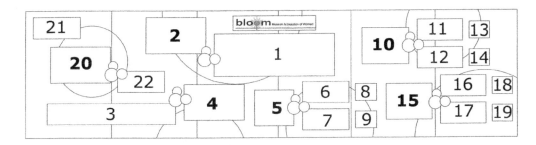

Figure 7.17 Digital storyboard technique using proportionally to-scale boxes for each drawing to create a layout on six vertical presentation boards. Drawings are numbered and labeled for sequence during verbal presentation. Bold numbers indicate emphasis.

1. Furniture Plan
2. Lobby Perspective
3. Gallery Elevation
4. Gallery Perspective
5. Women of the Past Perspective
6. Women of the Past North Wall Elevation
7. Women of the Past South Wall Elevation
8. Women of the Past Section B
9. Women of the Past Section C
10. Women of the Present Perspective
11. Women of the Present North Wall Elevation
12. Women of the Present South Wall Elevation
13. Women of the Present Section B
14. Women of the Present Section C
15. Women of the Future Perspective
16. Women of the Future North Wall Elevation
17. Women of the Future South Wall Elevation
18. Women of the Future Section B
19. Women of the Future Section C
20. Gift Shop Perspective
21. Gift Shop North Wall Elevation
22. Gift Shop South Wall Elevation

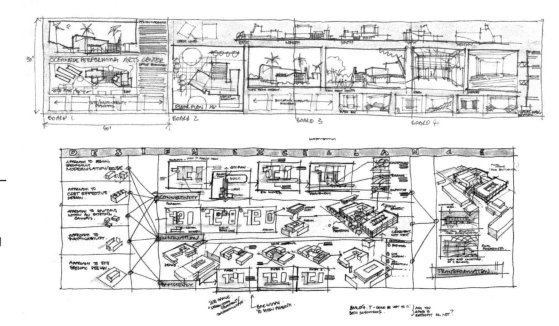

Figure 7.18 Architect Gary Leivers plans out his presentation to clients using thumbnail sketches to represent each drawing, supplemented with dimensions and other notes to himself.

Figure 7.18 shows a layout technique by a professional architect who regularly storyboards his design presentations to clients. He uses thumbnail sketches of each drawing to create a composite miniature version of what the end product might look like, along with notes to himself about dimensions of boards and how to achieve the desired outcome of the presentation.

ACTIVITY 7.3
Telling Your Story Graphically

Purpose: To graphically compose a storyboard of elements arranged in a way that helps you tell the unique story of your project.

How can you compose a presentation unique to your project? How can your project boards "speak" to your jury before you even open your mouth? Reflect on your answers to questions in Activity 7.2 and then brainstorm ideas using the prompts below.

What is your design concept in five words or fewer?

_____

Brainstorm: which images show your design concept graphically?

_____
_____
_____

Which program area(s) are essential to show? List three here:

1. _____
2. _____
3. _____

What project features need to be showcased? List three here:

1. _____
2. _____
3. _____

Which drawings will show the above listed rooms and features best?

_____
_____
_____

What drawings (or other project components) are you most proud of?

_____
_____
_____

Now, generate thumbnails of possible final board compositions. Use these sketches to explore whether your boards are better presented vertically or horizontally, or whether certain shapes or materials should be carried through on all boards. When you have explored multiple options, storyboard one or two of them. On 11 x 17 paper, compose storyboards or scale mock-ups for your final presentation boards. Use color and text as necessary to show the following:

- Drawings
- Relative sizes of drawings
- Drawing placement
- Rendering style (hand-drawn versus digital) to be used
- Board format (horizontal versus vertical)
- Location of title block
- Board colors or material to be used
- Mounting technique to be used
- Any other information that would communicate your final presentation goals

TIME MANAGEMENT TOOLS

Do you enjoy making lists? If you do, you are not alone. And you are more likely to achieve your goals. Emmy award-winning television producer Paula Rizzo extols the virtues of list-making in her book, *Listful Thinking: Using Lists to Be More Productive, Successful and Less Stressed.* In an interview for *Forbes* magazine she stated, "writing something down really solidifies the goal and makes it more attainable. A study at Dominican University of California found once you put pen to paper on a goal— you are 33 percent more likely to actually achieve it. Not only do you become more motivated but you are reminded of your goal and become more accountable, too" (Johnson, 2015). Rizzo continues talking about her process, "every night before I leave my desk I run through every single thing I need to do the following day and I'm very specific and deliberate about what I write down. That way when I get into work in the morning I have a roadmap of intentions set for the day."

As an interior designer, you are probably visually oriented, so a graphic way to list your to-do items is to create a storyboard, pin it up at your work area, and check off the items (or use a highlighter) as you complete them.

PROJECT MANAGEMENT: A WAY TO ORGANIZE YOUR TASKS

For group projects and for more detailed checklists, it is recommended to try a project management tool called a **Gantt chart**. These charts consist of a list of tasks, organized by design phases, in a column on the left-hand side, with an expanded calendar to the right, typically created in an Excel spreadsheet (or similar) program. You can see a modified Gantt chart created by a student to plan out her thesis design quarter in Figure 7.19. She picks a start time and end time to each task and notes some tasks may be done simultaneously such as "finalize floor plan" and "order material samples," whereas other tasks must be executed consecutively. She can render perspective views only after she has received her samples so that she can match colors in the rendering to the actual samples.

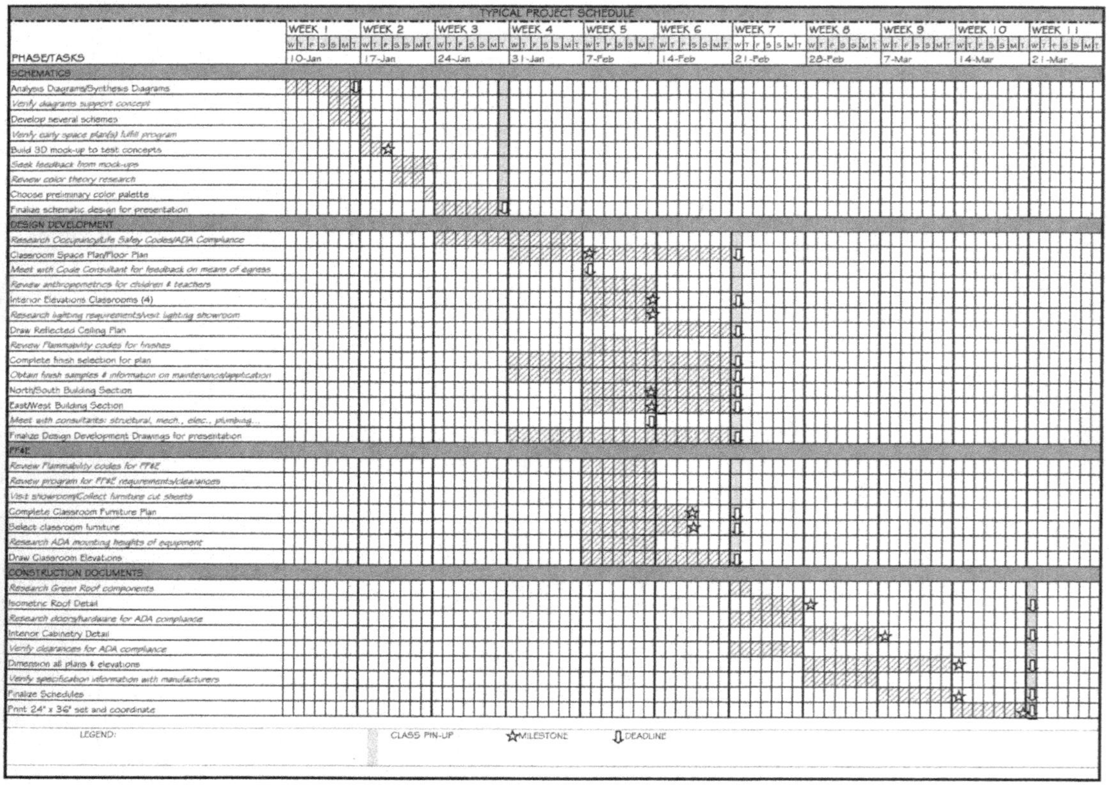

Figure 7.19
Modified Gantt chart used by a student as a project management tool.

In this example, internal milestones (personally imposed goals) are symbolized by a star, and externally set deadlines (or due dates) with an arrow. On any given day during the 11 weeks of the quarter, the student can see what tasks she should be working on and can adjust her schedule to accommodate changes along the way. If multiple people are working on the project with her, the tasks can be color-coded for each person. In Figure 7.19, the student has planned to use the three days before the diagrams are due (at the end of the first week) to "verify diagrams support concept." In the middle of the second week she has set herself a personal milestone: to build a model. She'll spend the days following this milestone getting feedback on the models, as well as doing research on color theory—two tasks that can be done concurrently. The Gantt chart does not reflect the actual hours to be spent on the project; you would record those on a time log or time sheet. Rather, it gives you a visual representation of the project schedule that you and your instructor have agreed on. It will help your instructor see that you have set reasonable amounts of time for each task and are being mindful of deadlines.

STUDENT PRESENTATION EXAMPLES

Example 1: "The Shelf Help" Universal Design Product Presentation

A group of interior design students documented their research-based design for a product they called "The Shelf Help" in an information booklet. In it they documented (1) the history of the refrigerator, (2) statistics from American Association of Retired Persons (AARP) about aging-in-place seniors needing assistance with Basic Activities of Daily Living (BADL), (3) results of a survey they conducted of refrigerator use by their classmates, (4) an in-depth interview with a 29-year-old woman who uses a wheelchair, (5) drawings of the proposed product, and (6) the results of testing a cardboard prototype they built of the product.

On a page titled "Where It All Begin" they wrote about their interview experience. "We asked, if she could change any three things about her space what would they be? The

first thing she wanted to change was her refrigerator. . . . Simply reaching for a snack was something that she needed assistance doing. This interview was the genesis of our design process and how we identified the problem to which we wanted to find a solution."

They noted the limitations of the current design and how the theory of Universal Design helped them formulate a solution. But they wanted to see how universal was the problem? So they set out to conduct a survey called "What's In Your Fridge?" which asked students to take pictures of their own appliance interior and respond to survey questions. "We found that everyone experienced functionality and organizational issues. Not being able to easily find things and ultimately wasting food because it was forgotten or hidden."

After analyzing the photos and survey data, they arrived at three overall programmatic concepts: organization, accessibility, and functionality. The students drew an information graphic to summarize their findings in a fun, light-hearted way that would be particularly attractive to all ages, shown in Figure 7.20.

Then they looked for concept inspiration. "We were inspired by several items that already possess the qualities that we wanted to add to our product. The sock drawer separator, . . . *caboodle* or stackable art bin . . . [and] pull-down shelving system for upper

Regular Shelf   Shelf-Help

Figure 7.20 Light-hearted information graphic by interior design students showing the thinking behind their refrigerator improvement.

Figure 7.21 Full-scale mock-up and demonstration graphic of "The Shelf Help" with handle and insert options.

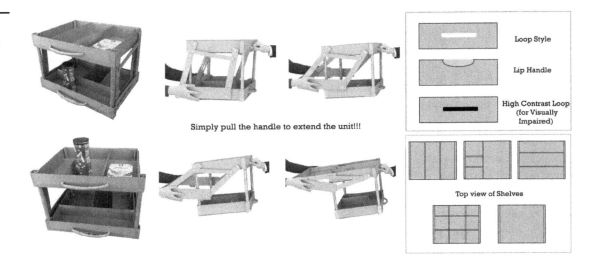

Simply pull the handle to extend the unit!!!

Loop Style

Lip Handle

High Contrast Loop (for Visually Impaired)

Top view of Shelves

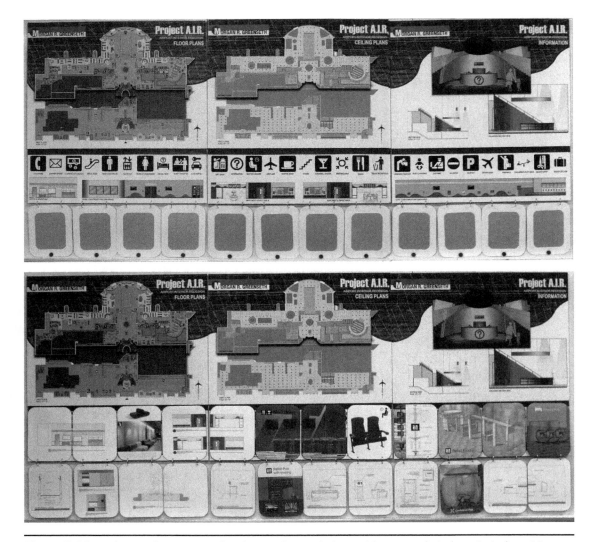

Figure 7.22 An innovative presentation for an airport design: with a row of airplane "windows" in the closed position (at top of photo); in flipped up position to reveal detailed drawings and held by a magnetic strip (bottom of photo).

Figure 7.23 Morgan Greenseth flipped up each detailed drawing in a choreographed manner to present her airport design to a design jury.

cabinets that makes reaching items that are higher up easier to access." Combining the attributes or affordances of these existing products led to the design prototype in Figure 7.21.

Example 2: "Project A.I.R." Thesis Project Presentation

Morgan Greenseth's "Project A.I.R." pulled from research on stressful environments and made use of the inefficient "downtime" that people experience while waiting at an airport by providing Universal Design features and amenities not often seen in typical airports. She showed her 100,000 square foot facility floor plan and reflected ceiling plan at 1/16 inch = 1 foot scale along the top of the presentation boards with details (at various larger scales) below. In order to focus attention, Morgan revealed one detail at a time similar to Vanna White on "Wheel of Fortune." Each board component was held in place by a strategically placed magnet, and a hidden magnetic strip.

Example 3: "Morph" Hospitality Project Presentation

Interior designer, Gerald Bouvia explains, "My senior project was a little restaurant called 'Morph.' The main concept I wanted to convey was that it changed four times a year. I created a modular furniture system that staff can easily move around and place per season. In the final presentation I showcased the four configurations within existing column bays." As you can see in Figure 7.24, Gerald used a consistent digital layout on each board which "embraced the white space," as he said. He used a limited palette of colors to create a harmonious look throughout the six boards. The first two boards established the exterior, kitchen, bar layout, lighting, and the custom pull-out hostess stand, all elements that would be consistent throughout the year. Each of the remaining four boards showed the differences per season: dining arrangement, color change technology, and fabric chair runner. The key, he said, is "whatever you do to one drawing, you do to all of the drawings. Make it consistent."

**Figure 7.24a and
7.24b** Graphically cohesive
set of six boards which
showcase innovation
in a student's capstone
hospitality project called
"Morph" designed to easily
transform by restaurant
staff for each season.

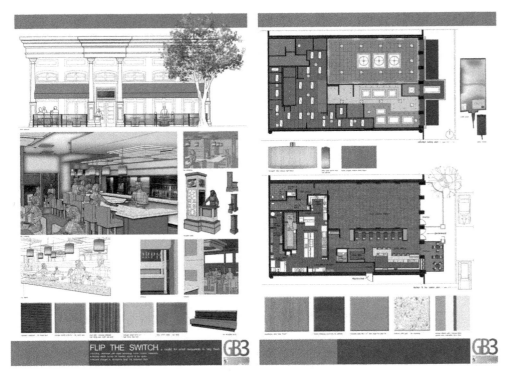

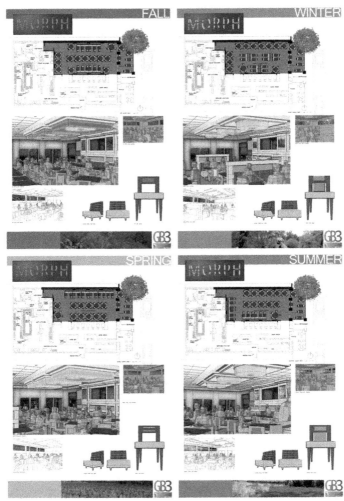

FEEDBACK TOOLS AND TIPS

Your first line of defense in preparation for a successful presentation is practice. Practice in front of other designers, as well as non-designers so that you know that your words can be understood by a variety of audience members. Interior designer Gerald Bouvia III advises interior design students to use your presentation boards as your "cue cards" for the presentation, and not to read from additional note cards. He urges designers to face the audience, make eye contact, and occasionally turn to the boards for clues about what to speak about next. The best testing ground for your presentation is in the classroom or studio environment. Your peers are a rich source of feedback. You should encourage others in your peer group to be critical and give honest feedback, not just compliment your work. Use Activity 7.4 and 7.5 to get some written feedback from your interior design colleagues.

ACTIVITY 7.4
Garnering Peer Review

Purpose: To elicit useful feedback from classmates at a preliminary or practice presentation.

Have each student conduct their presentation using all of the visuals completed as part of design development while other students in the class watch the presentation and provide feedback by writing answers to the following questions. Answers will be shared anonymously with the presenter at the conclusion of their presentation.

Questions with regard to presentation content:

What seems to be the main focus of this presentation?

_____

_____

How did the designer incorporate research into the design?

_____

_____

Describe three positive attributes of the design presenter should consider showcasing or emphasizing. What stood out as most memorable or interesting? What surprised you?

_____

_____

If the presenter had more time, what would you recommend be corrected, clarified, expanded upon, or more detailed?

_____

_____

Is there anything you would recommend minimizing or removing from the presentation?

_____

_____

Any helpful comments about body language, word use, energy level, or intonation? Additional comments?

ACTIVITY 7.5
Cultivating Gallery-Style Review Feedback

Purpose: To assess if the presentation boards function as stand-alone communication devices.

In addition to the questions posed in Activity 7.4, the following questions can be asked about a poster-style presentation or to judge whether the presentation boards can be sent to a client or design jury without the designer conducting an accompanying verbal presentation. This can be done as an in-class pin-up scenario, or presentation boards can be hung along a semi-public hallway for a school-wide audience. Presentation boards can also be posted digitally (on a screen or online) to receive the following survey comments:

What is your overall impression of the presentation boards? Are they clear, professional, and appealing?

_____

_____

What is the program? _____

What is the concept? _____

Who is the client? _____

Who are the end-user(s)? _____

What evidence was used to inform the program, concept and/or design decisions? _____

_____

What else did you learn from viewing these presentation materials?

_____

_____

What questions do you still have for the designer? _____

_____

_____

_____

During your design presentation, at minimum, it is a good idea to have a trusted classmate take notes, as you will likely not remember everything that was communicated in the process. In a professional environment, you would want to designate a colleague to take **meeting minutes**, recording the comments made during the meeting so that there is an objective record of the proceedings. You can also ask permission to audio record the presentation session, and set up a personal recording device such as an app your phone—*Voice Record Pro* is free and highly recommended by the author.

If you finish presenting, and no one has a question or comment for you right away, there may be an awkward silence. To reduce the chance of this happening, one trick is to leave some things unsaid during the presentation so that you can anticipate some initial questions they will ask. You will have answers ready for them and seem very prepared and knowledgeable. Another trick is to end your presentation with a question, such as "does anyone have any questions for me?" or "what are your thoughts on this proposal?" You could even have specific questions prepared for them, just in case no one steps up immediately to comment on your project. Activity 7.6 asks you to prepare a list of questions (or build on the ones provided) you would like your design jury to answer for you. You can distribute the questionnaire to the jury members at the start of your presentation, if it is approved by your studio instructor.

ACTIVITY 7.6
Getting the Most from Your Design Jury

Purpose: To provide your design jury with a list of questions that will give you the written feedback you are seeking.

Sometimes the stress of presentations will make it difficult for you to absorb all of the valuable information being shared. Take a moment to reflect on what you would like your reviewers to focus on and what kind of feedback you would like. Make a list of open-ended or rating's scale or a checklist of items that people can check off. Leave room and indicate where you would like them to leave additional comments. Consider some of these kinds of questions, and then write a list of your own:

1. What aspects of the project design process meet or exceed your expectations of an entry-level interior designer?

    Programming/PreDesign task documentation
    - Literature review
    - Conducting experiential or original research
    - Client interview/surveys
    - Understanding space functions and work flow
    - End-user(s) profile
    - Communicating needs
    - Stating the problems to solve

    Schematics solution exploration
    - Concept imagery and written statement
    - Process work: diagrams, sketches, study models
    - Illustrated flexibility in thinking and creative problem solving

    Design development articulation
    - Space-planning
    - Wayfinding/signage
    - Code compliance/means of egress/accessibility
    - Integration of building systems/structure
    - Lighting
    - Acoustics
    - Furniture selection
    - Finish selection
    - Use of accessories/artwork
    - Details
2. What aspects of the project warrant further consideration or improvement?
3. Consider the following list and check all of the areas in which the presentation met your expectations of an entry-level interior designer.
    - Professional appearance/attire
    - Verbal presentation skills/use of terminology
    - Craft of physical presentation/CAD, rendering, etc.
    - Use of evidence to support design decisions
    - Social responsibility/sustainability
    - Other _____

Conclusion

The juried design presentation is, once again, about gathering information—this time from a group of qualified individuals who are taking time to learn about your project and offer you further information. As interior designer and educator Allen Tate stated in the classic volume *The Making of Interiors: An Introduction* (1987), "Jury is difficult for some students, but the occasion is also highly informative. Here the student's work is given full attention by well-informed, professional designers. Give them your full attention, take notes if you wish. . . . Criticism of another student's work allow you to be more objective—not only in hearing the comment, but in its possible application to your own project" (p. 77). If you view the presentation as another information-gathering process, you will find the experience more rewarding.

References

Grillo, P. J. (1960). *What is design?* Chicago: Paul Theobald.

Johnson, E. (December 15, 2015). The life-changing magic of list-making. *Forbes Magazine*. Retrieved January 14, 2019, from https://www.forbes.com/sites /emmajohnson/2015/12/17/the-life-changing-magic -of-list-making/#31baf7ae76b9.

Lee, J. D., Wickens, C. D., Liu, Y. and Ng Boyle, L. (2017). *Designing for people: An introduction to human factors engineering*, 3rd ed. Charleston, SC: CreateSpace.

Mills, C. B. (2011). *Designing with models: A studio guide to architectural process models*, 3rd ed. Hoboken, NJ: John Wiley & Sons.

Rizzo, P. (2014). *Listful thinking: Using lists to be more productive, successful and less stressed*. New York: Start Midnight, LLC.

Schank, R. C. (1990). *Tell me a story: Narrative and intelligence*. Evanston, IL: Northwestern University Press.

Tate, A. (1987). *The making of interiors: An introduction*. New York: Harper & Row, Publishers.

Tufte, E. R. (2006). *Beautiful evidence*. Cheshire, CT: Graphics Press, LLC.

Tufte, E. R. (1997). *Visual explanations: Images and quantities, evidence and narrative*. Cheshire, CT: Graphics Press, LLC.

Tufte, E. R. (1990). *Envisioning information*. Cheshire, CT: Graphics Press, LLC.

Ware, C. (2013). *Information visualization: Perception for design*. Waltham, MA: Elsevier, Inc.

DESIGN AS A CIRCULAR PROCESS 8

It was evening all afternoon.

It was snowing

And it was going to snow.

The blackbird sat

In the cedar-limbs.

> — WALLACE STEVENS *Thirteen Ways of Looking at a Blackbird* (stanza XIII)

CHAPTER OBJECTIVES

When you complete this chapter you will be able to:

- Employ feedback tools to assist you in getting the most out of the design presentation and juried review process.
- Apply rubrics, assessment charts, and checklists to help evaluate your design solution.
- Understand the role of research during the contract documents and contract administration phases.
- Be familiar with ways to measure the success of the built environment to inform future projects.
- Prepare your work for portfolio or publication and explore ways to contribute to the body of knowledge of the interior design profession.

You have prepared an attractive, highly informative presentation for your design jury, instructors, and fellow classmates. Does this mean your project is complete? Not necessarily! In the academic environment, the studio critique provides yet another opportunity for information gathering. This chapter will explore checklists and other assessment tools to help you evaluate the success of your design solution. In the professional environment, research is incorporated into details and specifications, as well as ongoing monitoring during construction. Further testing and evaluation can continue long after the project is completed and occupied. We will discuss the cutting-edge

KEY TERMS

Abstract	Mixed methods
Assessment	Portfolio
Conference poster session	Post-Occupancy Evaluation (POE)
Continuing Education Unit (CEU)	Request for Information (RFI)
Environmental stressors	Rubric
Heuristic	Safety Risk Assessment (SRA)
Hypothesis	Shop drawings
International Interior Design Association (IIDA)	Usability test
	Value Engineering (VE)

ways that design researchers are collaborating with neuroscientists and others to measure, record, and track human-environment interaction to inform future designs. The chapter ends with a comprehensive matrix of key points in this textbook to help close the loop between research and design.

EVALUATING YOUR DESIGN SOLUTION

To many students, getting a good grade is a primary goal. They view getting a numerical or letter grade as essentially the same thing as being assessed. This is not necessarily true. In an interior design studio, **assessment** is the process of making a judgment about meeting an industry or professional standard, usually conducted by seasoned designers. When assessing creativity in a studio project, it is about whether the student exceeded expectations in terms of the way a problem is solved. Your instructor or design jury can assess the qualities of an artifact you have produced, such as a drawing, a model, or other project deliverable required to complete the assignment. Or they can assess your design process, evidence of design thinking that carries through the making of multiple artifacts, showing the evolution of the design over time. Feedback from an assessment may be correcting an incorrect assumption you have made about the nature of materials or the mis-application of a building code. Your design critics may also remind you to consider errors of omission such as a missing exit door or accessible clearance in a critical location.

Assessment may involve a measurement such as earning points or being assigned a grade. Or it may be more of a two-way communication tool that informs both student and instructor about the learning that is taking place. Seen in this way, assessment tools may be more of a motivational means, in which you mark your own progress, or use performance criteria (as in a rubric or checklist) to set your own goals. In this case, all assessment tools can be potential means of *self-assessment* used to answer the following questions.

- What does my instructor think is most important about this project?
- What would a client or end-user need to see or hear?
- How would a professional designer approach this problem?
- What are additional design criteria I should consider?

There are different types of assessments. *Formative assessments* are used to point out strengths and weaknesses along the process of design. These types of assessments may be informal, intermittent, and carry lower stakes, since they are part of a larger task. Examples are conversations you have with your studio instructor as part of a "desk crit" (short for desk critique) or midterm reviews. These are contrasted with a *summative assessment* which would be a more formal, and typically more stressful, final presentation. A summative assessment could also be evaluation of a portfolio piece intended to show mastery of skills needed to advance to the next level or gain entry-level employment. In a design studio, which is a problem-based learning environment, instructors typically perform a *divergent assessment*, which acknowledges multiple possible solutions or a wide range of interpretations.

In contrast, a *convergent assessment* looks for a correct answer. This could be a calculation, recall of a fact, or anything else on a traditional multiple-choice test or exam.

According to Cherry (2018) "grading could be considered a component of assessment, i.e., a formal, summative, final and product-oriented judgment of overall quality of worth of a student's performance or achievement in a particular educational activity . . . a comparative standard of measurement and sets up a competitive relationship." In contrast, a typical "assessment measures student growth and progress on an individual basis, emphasizing informal, formative, process-oriented reflective feedback and communication between student and teacher." It is important to understand and recognize the difference, so that you will not be frustrated or annoyed with outcomes—you can view the results as they are intended and not get defensive or unduly upset.

Figure 8.1 is an example of a typical interior design studio project evaluation **rubric**, to view as a guide to prioritize the many facets to your project. See if your project meets the minimum in each area of concern. Or perhaps you have exceeded the minimum in terms of how much attention you have given to that criterion. For example, perhaps your project has adequately addressed human factors but is not fully code compliant. Maybe your understanding and representation of the building systems (load-bearing structural walls and columns) is apparent, but your design concept is not evident in the space plan of the new walls or layout of furnishings. What does it mean to meet the minimum requirements? What needs to be improved to complete this phase of project development?

Heuristic Evaluations

A **heuristic** has been defined as a "mental shortcut that allows people to solve problems and make judgments quickly and efficiently" also referred to as "rule-of-thumb strategies" (Cherry, 2018). In a *heuristic evaluation*, you consider the characteristics of your design and determine whether the design meets the previously set criteria and requirements. This process gradually reduces the number of design solutions available to meet the set criteria and requirements. A heuristic evaluation does not yet involve your client or end-users; you're still working closely with the designers and consultants as the experts. Often, it is a matter of distributing a simple checklist (such as the one shown in Figure 8.2) to multiple persons, because

RUBRIC FOR GRADING FINAL PRESENTATION

Ratings:	5	4	3	2	1
Clarity of Visual Presentation	Drawings and graphics are outstanding, perfectly clear and show innovation	Shows a depth of skill and personal commitment beyond average	Graphics support thesis and drawings are adequate	Project meets minimum standards but shows lack of skill in composition	Shows lack of understanding or visual communication skills
Craftsmanship/ Skill	Beautifully and patiently executed: it is as good as hard work could possibly make it	Work is excellent.	Adequate, Average, minor evidence of carelessness	Below average craftsmanship. Project lacks professionalism	Poor craftsmanship. Crooked or wrinkled mounting; typos or spelling errors
Concept and Design	Displays strong personal vision which is supported by research. Adds to knowledge in interior design profession.	Work was based on research and problem was solved in creative, logical way.	Idea was carried through adequately.	Shows little evidence of illustrating incorporation of research or innovation.	Shows no evidence of original thought or creativity.
Space Planning/ Code Compliance	Building codes are seamlessly incorporated and enhance space plan	Codes issues are addressed in design solution	Project complies with building codes, but not fully addressed in presentation	Minor Evidence of code violations	Project ignores or violates building codes
Finishes	Selected creative, environmentally responsible materials. Incorporated color theory into color selection.	Selected creative, appropriate colors and materials, well represented on boards	Selected appropriate materials, adequately represented on boards	Not enough attention to materials selection	No materials presented.
Overall professional consistency	Professional level skills in verbal presentation and use of technology. Professional dress and professional level conduct throughout presentation	Well paced and well thought out verbal presentation, used design terms appropriately	Communicated project adequately and in a manner consistent with school requirements	Needs improvement on verbal presentation skills and conduct	Presentation lacked skills necessary to communicate the project

Figure 8.1 Example of a rubric for assessing (and assigning grade level) to aspects of the interior design studio project final presentation.

Item #	Functionality Review Checklist	Rating + (5) ---->(1) -	Comments
1.1	Do the following aspects of the home office meet the program requirements?	O O O O O	
1.2	Worksurface area?	O O O O O	
1.3	Worksurface color/material/texture?	O O O O O	
1.4	Worksurface height?	O O O O O	
1.5	Worksurface adjustability?	O O O O O	
1.6	Undercabinet storage for files and office supplies?	O O O O O	
1.7	Upper-cabinet and wall-mounted storage accessibility and usefulness?	O O O O O	
1.8	Does the design foster effective interpersonal communication?	O O O O O	
1.9	Does the design have good ambient lighting?	O O O O O	
1.10	Does the work area have good task lighting?	O O O O O	
1.11	Does the design offer a sense of privacy?	O O O O O	
1.12	Does the area have good acoustics?	O O O O O	
1.13	Does the design allow user to perform tasks efficiently?	O O O O O	
1.14	Does the design offer a place for display of personal items or artifacts?	O O O O O	
	Aesthetic Review Checklist		
2.1	Is there a sense of visual continuity with surroundings?	O O O O O	
2.2	Is there an overall design concept?	O O O O O	
2.3	Are the colors and materials in keeping with an overall design concept?	O O O O O	
2.4	Do the colors, materials and artwork enhance the work environment?	O O O O O	
	Other Concerns Review Checklist		
3.1	Does the office design meet budget constraints?	O O O O O	
3.2	Is the office design able to be constructed within the allotted time frame?	O O O O O	
3.3	Does the office design address durability?	O O O O O	
3.4	Does the design use recycled or repurposed items?	O O O O O	
3.5	Does the design specify items which are energy efficient/sustainable?	O O O O O	
3.6	Is the office design easy to clean or maintain?	O O O O O	

Figure 8.2 Heuristic evaluation—a checklist of Universal Design criteria for a home office.

obtaining evaluations from more than one source greatly increases the chance of uncovering more potential problems with the design solution. Heuristic evaluations shorten decision-making time and allow people to function without constantly stopping to think about their next course of action (Newell, Shaw, & Simon,1967).

You have made hundreds if not thousands of decisions in the course of designing your interior design project, from space planning to material selections. At each stage,

even if you are unaware, heuristics play important roles in both problem solving and decision making. According to Cherry (2018) members of the design jury may critique your work using a *representative* heuristic that "involves making a decision by comparing the present situation to the most representative mental prototype." One distinction between a novice and an expert designer is the sheer number of different instances of design solutions they have encountered, tried, and implemented—much higher than someone who is just starting out. This gives a seasoned designer much more evidence on which to base the decision to design something a certain way. However, over time, these "rules of thumb" practices may get too solidified, causing the designer to continually produce the same, or similar, designs over and over. Designers may become biased to think the way they do things is the "correct," or only, way.

So, while best practices are good to learn, designers should also be cognitively flexible, and open to new ideas as new information becomes available. A designer new to the profession does not have the preconceived notions of the way things *should* be and is more likely to focus on the way things *could* be. This is a benefit of being a newcomer to the profession; seeing problems and solutions from a fresh perspective.

According to Interaction Design Foundation (n.d.):

- Heuristics can help the evaluators focus their attention on certain issues.
- Heuristic evaluation does not carry the ethical and practical issues/problems associated with inspection methods involving real users.
- Evaluating designs using a set of heuristics can help identify usability problems with individual elements and how they impact the overall user experience.
- Generating your own heuristics is an important skill to have.

(Retrieved from https://www.interaction-design.org /literature/topics/heuristic-evaluation)

An interdisciplinary team of researchers from the fields of industrial design, engineering, and psychology at designheuristics.com have come up with a list of "The 77 Design Heuristics" to help designers generate novel solutions. They have flash cards for purchase to help encourage a playful use of these principles.

Two theories discussed in Chapter 6, Alexander's "Pattern Language" and Gibson's "Affordances," are both examples of design heuristics, as they both refer to ideal circumstances or situations without specifying explicit solutions. In the design process, "the designer mediates between the design project at hand, a lifetime of lived experiences, knowledge of existing solutions (i.e., precedents) . . . a designer's repertoire, or a personal source of generative metaphors . . . an experienced designer also carries with them a conceptual repertoire—similar to a curated collection, yet largely buried in memory as tacit knowledge—which they are able to apply to new design problems" (Gray, et al., 2016, p. 5). Gray et al. (2016) propose that "a designer builds dynamic links between disciplinary canon (containing both precedents and intermediate-level knowledge of strategies) and their own conceptual repertoire. Over time, the heuristics become incorporated into the designer's individual repertoire" (p. 6).

Usability Testing

As discussed in the previous chapter, *mock-ups* are usually very rough foam core or cardboard approximations of the design frequently used in furniture and product design as an effective and inexpensive design tool. Sometimes mock-ups are more extensive and realistic, such as in the example of selecting the colors for the new museum galleries at the Oklahoma City Museum of Art. After reviewing the art to be hung in each gallery, the design team made initial paint selections. Mobile "walls" were constructed to approximate the gallery conditions. The designers painted these walls and the conservators hung the art on the various walls, to test for appropriate color selection in each gallery. Once the paint and artwork "mock-ups" were complete, the curator and the design team critically evaluated the selections. It was a valuable process. The team found that once the anticipated lighting was applied, the initial color selections were too light, and did not enhance the artwork. Designers refined the color selections, working with lighting consultants as well, to determine final wall paint color.

If budget and time permit, after preliminary issues have been identified through heuristics and the evaluation and testing of mock-ups, the next step might be to create a *prototype* that would have more of the look and feel of the finished product but may not yet have full functionality. Mock-ups and prototypes are commonly used to conduct **usability tests**, also called *pilot tests*, which evaluate whether a design or space is easy to use or "user friendly." While a heuristic evaluation identifies problems and narrows down the potential design solutions, *usability testing* evaluates those design solutions as they involve interaction with a user (Lee et al., 2017).

In school, you are mainly getting feedback from instructors, their colleagues, professional designers and experts, as well as fellow classmates. But increasingly it is

ACTIVITY 8.1
Creating an Assessment Checklist

Purpose: To generate a list of design criteria for others to evaluate your project.

Carefully review the checklist in Figure 8.2. Then consider your own program, concept, and user requirements. Write a list of questions that you would like evaluators to consider when reviewing your project. Use the following template, which includes a ratings scale for each question and column for evaluator's comments.

TABLE 8.1

TEMPLATE FOR CREATING AN ASSESSMENT CHECKLIST

#	Functionality Review Checklist	Ratings scale + (5). → (1) –	Comments
1		○ ○ ○ ○ ○	
2		○ ○ ○ ○ ○	
3		○ ○ ○ ○ ○	
4		○ ○ ○ ○ ○	
5		○ ○ ○ ○ ○	
Aesthetic Review Checklist			
1		○ ○ ○ ○ ○	
2		○ ○ ○ ○ ○	
3		○ ○ ○ ○ ○	
4		○ ○ ○ ○ ○	
Other Concerns Review Checklist			
1		○ ○ ○ ○ ○	
2		○ ○ ○ ○ ○	
3		○ ○ ○ ○ ○	

important to get feedback from those who are going to use the space or who would have commissioned you to design the space. It is important to recognize these are not necessarily the same person. In some cases, a person will hire you to design their own house. In that instance the client is also the end-user. However, on most other types of projects, such as commercial, retail, hospitality, institutional (schools, healthcare, religious facilities, to name a few), the organization who hires you, such as a board of directors or owner, is not necessarily going to be using the space. Or, if they do, they may not be the only person using the space.

A research-based designer will advise the client that both actual end-users (people who are currently working in or using the space) and potential end-users (other occupants such as visitors, maintenance crew, children,

guests, future employees, and so forth) are a valuable source of information and should always be considered in the design process. Think of all of the possible kinds of people using a space. For example, when designing a café, one might consider the baristas, the maintenance crew, and the various kinds of customers—regulars, tourists, families, students, as well as people with physical limitations.

To prepare the usability test, first you must clearly establish what "usability" is in this situation and identify the *task scenario*, or representative tasks to help you establish whether the criteria for usability have been accomplished. You must also have a clear definition of when a task has been completed. You will then prepare a test schedule, or *agenda*, which will serve as the script that all parties involved will follow. Finally, you will need to identify and arrange a location and time for the usability test to take place, then identify representative users and invite them to attend. It is usually better to schedule "too much time" for the testing process rather than "just enough," as having extra time leaves more time between sessions for you or your team to take notes and discuss issues.

The following is a list of supplies you will need to conduct the usability test:

1. Videotaping equipment or camera, and release or consent forms if applicable
2. A test schedule or formal script, so that all participants involved have equal experiences
3. A pre-evaluation questionnaire or other means of checking that your participants match the required profile of your end-user
4. Your task scenario or list of tasks, together with clear criteria for measuring whether they have been successfully completed
5. Logging sheets on which to record timing, events, participant actions, concerns, and comments (see Table 8.2 for example)
6. A post-evaluation questionnaire to measure user satisfaction and understanding and to glean any additional information that participants may want to provide

7. Compensation, an appropriate "thank you" gift, or a thank you card for each of your user representatives

Unless your usability test is very simple and informal, run a test scenario to ensure that the process runs smoothly. This test doesn't require real users, just a means of running through the tasks with any available person. In all other respects, the test run should be as close to realistic as possible. During the test, make sure your participants are put at ease. Also, unless absolutely necessary, do not prompt your participants during the test as it might influence the results. Finally, record the events in as much detail as possible, as well as proposing inferences as to why events occurred as they did. Your notes do not have to contain a solution to the issue or problem, because you and your team will be generating options after the testing is complete. Rather than focusing on solutions, focus on gathering information to inform the design process later. Figure 8.3 is an example of a photo you might take to record your observations of an end-user participating in the task scenario.

A common mistake is to conduct the usability testing with insufficient time—or willingness—to make improvements and implement recommendations. This lack of time is often due to budgetary constraints. If it is unlikely that changes can be made, the testing is a waste

TABLE 8.2

LOGGING SHEET FOR USABILITY TESTING WITH ANNOTATION LEGEND

USABILITY TEST FORM			
Product or Space Description:			
Observer:			
Date/Time:			
Task	User Experience Code	Observer Comments/Insights	Severity Code
	TC NC R Q C F		0 1 2 3 4
	TC NC R Q C F		
	TC NC R Q C F		
	TC NC R Q C F		
	TC NC R Q C F		

Legend:	TC = Task Completed	0=None
	NC= Not Completed	1=Low
	Q=Question asked by user	2=Medium
	C=Comment made by user	3=High
	F=Frustration noted	4=Severe

Figure 8.3 Photo of end-user in a re-designed kitchen assessing usability of implemented design solutions.

of time and money. Another common error may be due to the designer inadvertently influencing the testing results, a nod to the Hawthorne Effect discussed in Chapter 6, which is the propensity for people to change their behavior when they know they are being studied. As the observer you want to avoid influencing what is being observed. Instead, just watch, listen, be attentive, be patient, and objectively record what you observe. Maintain an attitude of professional neutrality and avoid using remarks like "good" or "well done," which imply that the person, not the system, is being tested. Avoid finishing participants' sentences for them or verbalizing what you think is on their minds. Testers often provide users with too much information, making recommendations along the way.

Being a participant in a usability test for a space or product can be a fun learning experience. At some point in your career, you may be called upon to be a representative user yourself.

APPLYING RESEARCH TO CONTRACT DOCUMENTS PHASE

During the contract documents phase, interior designers seek the expertise of consultants, and trade professionals, to complete detailed construction drawings and written specifications. Consultants you may find on a typical project team are listed in Chapter 6. There may be a

civil engineer, structural engineer, mechanical engineer, electrical engineer, licensed plumber, acoustical or sound engineer, architect, landscape architect, general contractor, project manager, and subcontractors who specialize in installations, such as framer, drywall installer, finish carpenter, painter, mason, electrician, and plumber. These team members can give insight into the nuts and bolts of what needs to be included in your details and specifications. As noted in Chapter 6 you may also include people who have a focused area of expertise such as a lighting designer, furniture designer, industry trade professional, manufacturer representative, or product vendor.

Timothy Smith, a lighting designer from the Smithsonian Institution in Washington, DC, tells a story about the consequences of documenting your design in isolation and waiting too long to speak with an expert about the issue at hand. Specializing in museum exhibits, he shares the following:

> Professional experts, such as a lighting designer, are often not consulted or interviewed until the last minute, but they should be involved in the project from the beginning. The lighting designer is the educator of the lighting criteria since so few people are experts. Not consulting the experts results in mistakes. In the case of lighting design in museum exhibits, mistakes can result in shadows that make work illegible, or in complex nooks and spaces that are not lit. Unfortunately this kind of mistake isn't realized until installation and it is much more complicated and expensive for the lighting designer to fix the problem at that point. (Timothy Smith, personal communication, June 2008)

One way in which consultants and experts are directly involved in the contract documents phase of interior design is through **value engineering (VE)**. According to the U.S. Department of Agriculture, "value engineering (VE) is a systematic, functional, and creative analysis of a construction requirement to achieve the best functional combination of cost, reliability, and performance, over the life-cycle of products, systems, equipment, facilities, services, and supplies" (U.S. Department of Agriculture, 2008).

The VE process for interior design will involve the entire design team, including the designer(s), the client, the contractor, and other experts such as the project manager, architect(s), and engineer(s) if relevant. The team works together to review the project costs and to identify ways to get the most value for the available budget. For example, in a public building the original design might have called for terrazzo tiles installed in various patterns on each floor of the building. After the budget is reviewed and the ratio of value to cost is evaluated, the design might be value-engineered so that the terrazzo is used on only the first floor and vinyl tiles, installed in similar patterns, are used on all subsequent floors. This solution allows the translation of the original design concept from expensive to more affordable materials as the design moves from more public spaces to more private ones.

VE usually begins in the first half of contract documents and often includes the following phases:

1. *Information Phase*—The team gathers information about the program requirements, project design, background, constraints, and projected construction costs. The team identifies high-cost areas.
2. *Speculative/Creative Phase*—The team identifies alternatives for accomplishing the functional and creative design intent.
3. *Evaluation/Analytical Phase*—The team evaluates the alternatives from the Speculative/Creative Phase to determine those with the greatest potential for cost savings and project enhancement.
4. *Development/Recommendation Phase*—The team researches the alternatives and ideas selected in the Evaluation/Analytical Phase and prepares descriptions, sketches, and life cycle cost estimates to support VE recommendations and proposals.
5. *Report Phase*—The team presents VE recommendations to the client and other team members in a verbal presentation and written document. (U.S. Department of Agriculture, 2008)

Your consultants should be involved in this process, as they can help you to research and identify the design solutions that will best solve the problem of cost and provide alternate affordable solutions. At this point, your level of research is what allows you to hold on to your creative ideas and intent through the cutting process. The more options you have to present at a VE meeting, the more likely you are to have some control over the outcome, rather than letting the contractor or another person make the decisions for you.

For example, in one hospital emergency department, the design team was told through the VE process that the organic and playful design pattern they planned for the rubber flooring was too complex and expensive, and that the contractor was recommending that the design team remove the pattern and simply choose one color of flooring and install it without the pattern. The designers knew that the pattern, which involved using different colors of rubber in different areas, was essential to the wayfinding process. Also, it created a more human scale and a less institutional feel in what is otherwise a potentially intimidating space.

The design team decided to follow up by researching who was doing the installation and finding out the real reason for the high cost. Their research revealed that the contractor for the hospital was a small operation and it was the contractor's lack of tools and technology to precisely cut and install such an intricate pattern that was driving up the cost. In the end the designers recommended a simplification, rather than an elimination of the design, which turned out to be satisfactory for all parties involved. Had the designers not done their own investigation into the problem, they wouldn't have been able to suggest this better option.

USING RESEARCH DURING CONTRACT ADMINISTRATION PHASE

The interior designer can also be contracted to perform services during the *contract administration phase*. If a project came in over budget, it is common for the design to be implemented in phases. In this way, the entire design can be realized, but over time allowing the client to accrue funds in between the phased implementation. Phased implementation divides up the master plan into discreet smaller projects that are related and ultimately unified in design intent and consideration.

During this phase, while a building is under construction, interior designers may review **shop drawings**. These are submittals of drawings, samples, and product literature in response to the specifications written by designers. Shop drawings show the interpretation of the design by the builder or installer. For example, a stone fabricator may produce a drawing that shows the seam locations, and the edge detail, along with a material sample to confirm approval before cutting and installing a countertop. A shop drawing sometimes seeks to substitute another product in place of what has been called out. It is up to the designer to decide if the product submitted meets program requirements and is a suitable equal for what was specified. Research into the product is essential at this point.

An interior designer may also conduct site visits to observe progress during construction, issue *purchase orders*, to formally place an order with a vendor or supplier and respond to **Request for Information (RFIs)** and *change orders* if clarifications need to be made to the contractor or design modifications need to be made. Designers may also help receive deliveries and install furnishings, artwork and signage (commonly referred to as "move-in" or an "install"). Interior designers may also instruct building occupants how to use the newly installed furnishings, communication devices or environmental control systems in the new facility.

Post-Occupancy Evaluations

Research methods can continue beyond the traditional end to the phases of design into the life cycle of the use of the built environment, after the project is occupied, to cull data in to inform future projects of similar scope, function, or end-user population. Designers can conduct **post-occupancy evaluations (POEs)** or collect data while the building is in use for years after the project is occupied. A *post-occupancy evaluation (POE)* is performed after the client and/or users move into and have begun using the space. The evaluation allows the designer to gather information on occupants' satisfaction or focus on particular

aspects of the design that may have been more innovative, experimental, or untested. It gives the designer a chance to educate him- or herself for future projects—identifying successes and uncovering unanticipated problems to avoid in the future.

There are various ways to conduct a POE. It can be as simple as an informal conversation, a distributed questionnaire to survey end-users, or a checklist of items to guide observation. Sometimes, to be more objective, experts are called in as a third party to conduct a more formal, or rigorous, POE, using special equipment such as sensors, or other special equipment to measure air quality, temperature, energy efficiency, and other physical aspects of the building itself. It is also common to conduct POEs in order to test the occupants' understanding or use of complex building systems, sustainable features, as well as how the built environment affects productivity, work flow, or overall health and well-being of the occupants. Depending on the scale of the evaluation, a public presentation might be made at conferences to share with other design professionals or results of the POE will be posted on websites devoted to showcasing or recognizing evidence-based design projects.

Many of these organizations were discussed in Chapter 1.

The Center for Health Design provides a free evaluation and data collection toolkit called **Safety Risk Assessment (SRA)**, which can be used by a designer or client agency to collect data from an existing location. This data can be used to generate "insights in outcomes," as shown in Figure 8.4, which provide evidence to inform the next

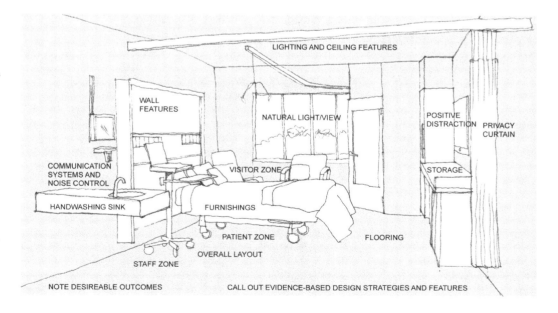

Figure 8.4 Adapted from an online interactive graphic that informs people about evidence-based design strategies for an Intensive Care Unit (ICU), from https://www.healthdesign.org/insights-solutions/design-insights-strategies-tool/intensive-care-unit-patient-room.

iteration of the project, or future projects. For example, in the design of an intensive care unit (ICU) "there are six components of consideration: infection control, patient handling, medication safety, falls, behavioral health, and security." More can be found at www.healthdesign.org /sra/about/toolkit.

Annotations that accompany an evidence-based design strategy for an ICU cite studies and other peer-reviewed sources for reasons why use of an element, such as a privacy curtain, directly benefits end-users. Desirable outcomes such as reduced risk of contamination, reduced patient stress, improved patient satisfaction, noise reduction, enhanced visual privacy, and improved air quality can be achieved through implementing a non-institutional looking, low VOC-emission fabric that is easily washable (ICU Outcomes Strategies, p. 36, retrieved from https:// www.healthdesign.org/sites/default/files/donghia/ICU _Outcomes_Strategies.pdf).

What More Can Be Measured?

Society for Neuroscience (2018) asks you to

> Think about what happens in your body and mind when you speak in front of a crowd—your brain state is very different from when you are asleep. Perhaps you notice changes in your breathing, heart rate, or stomach. Maybe your thoughts are racing or panicked. Or maybe you are energized and excited to perform for your audience. These are examples of the complex brain state called arousal. (p. 9)

Arousal is important for normal everyday activity such as working, or for emergency situations such as avoiding

danger. The level of arousal varies across a spectrum from low to high. However, environmental factors can raise the brain state of arousal through high levels of sensory input or *stimuli*, such as noise (auditory) and clutter (visual), creating an unwarranted, negative side of arousal commonly known as *stress*. How can we identify these **environmental stressors** and use evidence-based interior design strategies to mitigate or eliminate them? As discussed in Chapter 6, understanding and creating healing environments often involves measuring physiologic responses of occupants to different environments.

Nowadays we have so many portable physical activity monitoring devices and corresponding apps on our phones, shown in Figure 8.7. We can map our route taken, distance traveled, number of steps walked, heart rate, and even how much sunlight we received. And we can track these individual data points over time to see trends or patterns. We can also cross reference these bits of information with physical attributes of the environment, such as light levels, noise levels, and colors, to determine how the environment positively or negatively affects our physical health and emotional well-being.

We can also measure other aspects of how the physical environment impacts the occupants. For example, light monitor sensors, and corresponding apps, let you know the light levels of your surroundings. You can use this information to conduct controlled experiments to see how light levels correspond with end-users' heart rate—a simple physiological response to measure stress. We can also track eye movement to see what a person is looking at or what attracts their attention. We can also measure psychological responses through satisfaction surveys or self-reports of anxiety level, extent of enjoyment, and

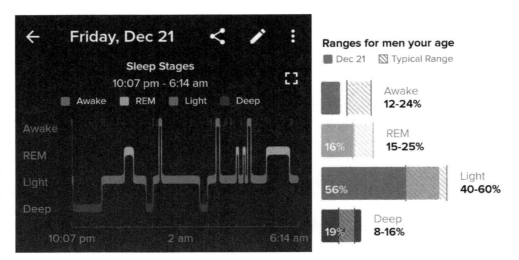

Figure 8.5 Screenshot of sample data and benchmarks for monitoring sleep stages through an app and device developed by *Fitbit*.

appreciation of aesthetic qualities of an environment. Individually, these measurements may not tell us anything; however, when we relate these findings with observation of behavior and other sociological responses to an environment, we can also measure focus, attention or ability to concentrate, and we can turn our attention to creating environments for people with attention deficit disorders (ADD or ADHD) or those on a highly sensitive sensory spectrum, such as those with Autism.

Dr. Satchinanda Panda has explored the use of these individual devices, a custom app designed for his study, as well as self-reports from volunteers through the Internet to collect data from people from around the world. In his myCircadianClock study, Dr. Panda is looking at the intersection of circadian rhythm (sleep, wake, and exposure to daylight) and food intake to see the combined impact on metabolism, weight, and overall health. On the website, the stated goal is to "create an unprecedented database of daily behaviors and health status from people. . . . Studying real-world data will help researchers better understand the complex relationships between sleep, diet, and healthy living. It will also provide insight into how smartphones can enable new types of clinical research." See Figure 8.8 for an information graphic about the study.

As Berger (2003) states, "the opportunities for genuine research are everywhere. Every town or city is full of public records that sit neglected, environmental conditions that no one is monitoring, businesses and families whose histories have never been explored" (p. 76). Every community has buildings that sit empty waiting for the right socially responsible use; institutions that have been operating for decades that need a fresh perspective in how

Figure 8.6 Graphic advertising new app to record personal data about food, sleep, and physical activity for a scientific research study by Dr. Panda at the Salk Institute for biological Studies in La Jolla, California, retrieved from mycircadianclock.org.

to operate or become more sustainable; and community members looking to improve their living, learning, working, and entertainment environments. Interior designers can conduct **mixed methods** forms of research using quantitative measures, qualitative (rich description), and semi-experimental methods to see how aspects of the physical environments such as scents, furniture layouts, and other attributes affect productivity (a complex behavioral response by measuring completeness of a task), mood (using a self-reported survey or personal journaling techniques to measure a general state of mind or emotional disposition), or well-being (physiological data to measure physical health, observation to record behavior, and self-ratings to measure mental health).

There are infinite ways to incorporate quantitative and qualitative data gathering methods into your design process. According to Society for Neuroscience's *Brain Facts* (2018), electroencephalography (EEG) technology used to record electrical activity of the human brain in response to a variety of stimuli and activities can be paired with functional Magnetic Resonance Imaging (fMRI), a technology that uses magnetic fields to detect activity in the brain by monitoring blood flow. "fMRI provides an indirect view of neuron activity, but magnetoencephalography (MEG) detects actual electrical currents coursing through groups of neurons. Studies using electrical recordings from inside the human brain can be paired with fMRI to tell us more about the brain activity patterns of the default mode network and how brain regions coordinate their activity during tasks that utilize the functions of this network" (pp. 64–65). These studies help identify which brain regions "are involved in emotion, personality, introspection, and memory" in order to ultimately understand "how brain function drives behaviors in humans. . . [and] uncover many principles of learning and memory" (p. 108). The Society for Neuroscience (SfN) concludes, "As new techniques and technologies emerge, scientists will add them to their repertoire of techniques that can deepen our understanding of the brain and suggest new ways to help people whose lives are affected by brain disorders (pp. 110–111). Interior designers can add to the conversation by proposing ways to use this information and co-direct studies which collect this kind of information. Neuroscientists can partner with interior designers as both professions continually seek the answer to the questions: what more can we measure, and what does it mean?

Gray and Malins (2016) call for a creative research paradigm: "The development of technology has led us to a point where we are inundated with instruments and devices that allow us to sense, experience, collect, store, analyse and communicate far more information than ever before. The vast range of 'tools' for investigation has expanded the range of existing research methodologies and methods and made possible new ones" (p. 94). They urge designers to use creativity in order to perceive new kinds of information, in a cycle of reflection and action, in order to move knowledge forward in the arts and design professions.

DOCUMENTING AND ARCHIVING YOUR WORK

Documenting your research-based design process is essential to continuing the circular nature of interior design. At some point, another designer might want to reference any aspect of the collection of information you have compiled to inform his or her own research-based design. From the beginning of your research, document everything! Keep a record of the author, date, and title of publication of each important information source. You can use computer application tools such as Zotero to help you collect, organize, and cite your research sources. Note the date, location, and participants at each interview, or on your casual notes during observations and on your formal writing. Get into a habit of putting your name and date on all sketches, drawings, and presentation materials. Scan all process work, including sketches, diagrams, and trace paper work, at a high resolution (300–600 pixels per inch, or ppi) even if you're not sure it will be valuable. If the image on the paper had some kind of input toward the development of your design, keep it. You might be surprised how important that information is for cohesively presenting your ideas, connecting the information with the design solution. Professional designers looking to recruit new talent repeatedly comment that while the polished portfolio pieces are nice, they are more interested in understanding how a potential employee thinks and solves problems. These skills are more evident in your process work.

Photograph your presentation boards and all other presentation components, such as models and material selections, in high resolution, using a tripod to help display your work and obtain well-presented images. You might also have someone photograph you during your presentation to show how you interact with potential clients. Print out digital work at a minimum of 300

dots per inch, or dpi, for incorporating work into your academic **portfolio**. The portfolio will become a living archive of your work, showcasing your design process and your graphic communication skills. Berger (2003) states, "every written or graphic presentation of work, every oral presentation or performance can be, and should be, prepared with aesthetic consideration" (p. 80). His advice: you need to know that "quality means rethinking, reworking, and polishing" (p. 90).

There are multiple ways to document and archive your capstone project or thesis work. The most common are the bound *thesis book* and the *project binder*. Frequently, students use velo binding or spiral binding to create their bound book. Both are common binding techniques offered at many print shops. Another option is to simply use a three-ring binder, creating a cover page and carefully organizing the sections. However, because you will want to keep a record of your thesis or capstone project for a long time, book binding is strongly recommended. It is more durable, compact, and professional looking than other methods. It can also be duplicated easily, which is important if your school requires that you submit a copy for the library archives. Institutions often have specific requirements for the documentation and archiving process, so you should check with your instructor before deciding how to proceed.

Berger doesn't believe there is a single model for portfolio that suits everyone. Sometimes deciding what to showcase can be a learning process itself. Frame what is important to you and what you see as major milestones in your growth as an interior designer. You could make a collection of audio or video recordings of your presentations as a montage of speaking skills to put on a website. Or show the evolution of your skills chronologically as one project morphs into another using digital modeling software. Or perhaps you take an early project and redesign it years later with a new understanding of code compliance or Universal Design principles. You could also showcase your ability to gather original data, from early simple observational studies to more advanced multidimensional data collection methods.

Sharing Your Work with a Wider Audience

How does your research-based design contribute to, expand, or inform the broad profession of interior design? According to Berger (2003), every final draft you complete should be done for an "outside audience" (p. 99). One way of transitioning from your studio project presentation to a wider audience is to create and submit your work to be shown as part of a **conference poster session**. According to Alley (2013), "The purpose of scientific posters is to present work to an audience who is walking through a hallway or exhibit. At a conference, the presenter usually stands next to the poster, thus allowing for passers-by to engage in one-on-one discussions with the presenter. In a hallway, posters are stand-alone presentations for passers-by." His website, craftofscientificposters.com, offers free templates for you to easily create your own scientific poster. The site also shows examples and offers advice. To be effective, the author reminds us, the poster first has to attract someone who is standing or walking by who may have limited time or be distracted. The title should be catchy or memorable. Use upper and lower case in place of all caps since it will be easier to read. Make sure the audience recognizes the subject and purpose within a few moments of seeing the poster. Differentiate areas on the poster to make them fun to read. Rely on photographs, drawings, and graphs with captions, bullet points, or short sentence text descriptions rather than long blocks of text that can be intimidating or dissuade someone from reading. Figure 8.9 shows a conference poster showcasing a study called "Situated Studio: Cultivating Social

Responsibility in Interior Design Education." The catchy title is meant to spark interest in the subject matter, and the corresponding graphics of engaged design students, process work and colored graphs convey the subject material in a clear, compelling manner.

If you would like to go one step further, consider writing an **abstract** for a conference paper presentation or to submit to a peer-reviewed periodical for publication. Good examples of academic platforms for publishing are the *Journal of Interior Design* (JID), which is sponsored by Interior Design Educators Council (IDEC). IDEC hosts annual regional and international conferences which accept student submittals. Past conference proceedings and future conference themes can be found at idec.org.

If you look again at Chapter 1, you will see that you have now come full circle—all of the organizations, websites, and other information sources you have consulted are now places you can seek out to publish your newly minted research-based project. Each of these organizations offers membership opportunities to engage with their members and keep up-to-date on current topics and trends. You can enter design competitions and apply for research grants. In addition, look around at local colleges and universities that have design programs may also have a lecture series, or their own form of conferences, that offer opportunities for you to present your work. At first, you can sign up to

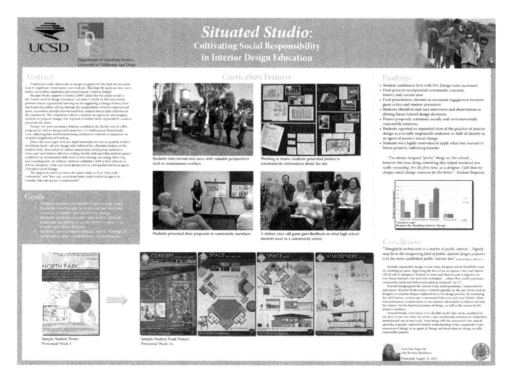

Figure 8.7 Conference poster designed by the author presented to educators at the University of California, San Diego.

attend. When you feel confident your research fits their venue, you can submit your work.

What Kind of Researcher Are You?

The question is, what kind of research-based *designer* are you? Do you use evidence to gain the respect and confidence of your client, using reliable information and process that produces human-centered designs? Do you use peer-reviewed scholarship, or conduct your own scientific inquiry to cultivate a reflective practice? Do you continually learn, becoming an expert in one area or another, while being open to new ideas that may come from unexpected sources? Do you look for research opportunities, exhibitions, writing venues, public forums to speak about the power of design and expand awareness of the importance of the built environment, in whatever specialty area you choose? Do you seek out community partnerships, grant proposals, enter competitions, and see every project as a possibility to collect data and to learn more? As Berger (2003) advises, "do something well and build from there" (p. 152).

In a recent online interview, Jane Fulton Suri (2019), IDEO partner emeritus and executive design director, reflects on the evolution of empathy in design during her 30-year career at IDEO and why bringing curiosity into your work takes courage. She says, "Design thinking is human thinking . . . being human and adaptive and responsive to the environment is continually changing . . . naturally evolving." She had identified three research threads which are traditionally studies separately but she now sees as coming together: "(1) physical and cognitive ergonomics; focus on fit between our abilities and limitations and the world around us, (2) anthropology and material culture considering the meaning of artifacts rituals and behaviors, and (3) workplace design which focuses on engagement and co-creation."

According to Hamilton (2003), there are four levels of commitment and methods in design research:

- *Level 1 practitioners* make a careful effort to base their design decisions on available evidence. By staying current with literature in the field, they attempt to follow the evolving research related to the physical setting. They interpret the meaning of the evidence as it relates to their projects, and they make judgments about the best design for specific circumstances.

- *Level 2 practitioners* take the next important step. Based on readings, they *hypothesize* (a **hypothesis** is a tentative prediction of the relationship of two or more variables) the expected outcomes of their design decisions and subsequently measure and evaluate the results. These designers must understand the research, interpret the implications, and build a chain of logic connecting the design decision to a measurable outcome, reducing arbitrary decisions. The potential for bias in gathering and reporting results means they must resist the temptation to report success and downplay failure.

- *Level 3 practitioners* follow the literature, hypothesize intended outcomes of design, and measure results—and then go further by reporting their results publicly. Writing or speaking about results moves information beyond the firm or client team. These practitioners are taking a chance, as it subjects their research methods and results to scrutiny from others who may or may not agree with the findings. Level 3 practitioners should seek advanced education to enable greater rigor in the research process.

- *Level 4 practitioners* are scholar–practitioners who perform the same tasks: following the literature, hypothesizing outcomes of design decisions, measuring results, and reporting their findings. These designers go further by publishing their findings in peer-reviewed journals or collaborating with other academics. They subject their work to the highest level of rigorous review.

According to Hamilton, there are also "level-zero practitioners." These designers may ignore research in the design of their projects, or might take isolated comments from an article, make a personal interpretation that fits their design bias, and claim that the subsequent design is evidence-based. A level-zero practitioner likely has not read the original research and might misinterpret important principles.

What kind of researcher are you? What kind of researcher do you want to be? Whether you are a student or a professional, opportunities to impact the direction of the interior design field increase with the depth of your research-based practice. If you strive to make design decisions that are inspired by the best-known evidence in the field, you will benefit yourself as a professional as well as benefiting the people who will experience the spaces you design.

DESIGN AS A CIRCULAR PROCESS

Although this book is written with an academic audience in mind, there is really no difference between the information communicated here and the tools you will use every day in your professional experience. We all know people who are perpetual students, never seeming to move beyond the walls of their schools. For your own future, take on the heart not of a perpetual student but of a habitual learner as you make your transition into the interior design profession.

Essential to an interior designer's success is the process of constant self-education and evaluation, through all kinds of research and information-gathering. In fact, once you pass your professional exams, such as the NCIDQ (National Council for Interior Design Qualification) or LEED (Leadership in Energy and Environmental Design) or join our various professional organizations, such as **International Interior Design Association (IIDA)**, you will be required to complete a certain number of **Continuing Education Units (CEUs)** each year. There is an expectation that design professionals keep current on subject areas addressed in this textbook: codes, building systems, sustainability, accessibility, advancements in technology, psychological and behavioral theory, and other human factors. Designers can also stay current on improved research methods and tools which help with data collection, analysis, and application.

Conclusion

Table 8.3 is an overview of key points covered throughout the book and how the chapters all fit together. In this table, the underlying idea of each chapter is identified, with reference to a particular figure, table, or activity that you may want to review. Use this table as a quick reference to make sure you understand each point fully. Although these seem to be presented in a step-by-step manner, like design itself, each topic is fluid and flexible in its relationship to you. It is up to you to determine how research will inspire your program as well as your design process.

References

Alley, M. (2013). *The craft of scientific presentations*, 2nd ed. New York: Springer-Verlag.

Alley, M. (n.d.) Creating a poster. *Scientific Posters*, retrieved January 31, 2019, from https://www.craftofscientificposters.com/design.html.

Berger, R. (2003). *An ethic of excellence: Building a culture of craftsmanship with students*. Portsmouth, NH: Heinemann.

Cherry, K. (November 13, 2018). Heuristics and cognitive biases. *Verywell Mind*, retrieved January 27, 2019, from https://www.verywellmind.com/what-is-a-heuristic-2795235.

Gray, C. and Malins, J. (2016). *Visualizing research: a guide to the research process in art and design*. New York: Routledge.

Gray, C. M., Seifert, C. M., Yilmaz, S., Daly, S. R. and Gonzalez, R. (2016). *What is the content of design thinking? Design heuristics as conceptual repertoire*. IOWA State University: Industrial Design Publications.

Hamilton, K. (November 2003). The four levels of evidence-based design practice. *Healthcare Design* 3(9): 18–26.

Interaction Design Foundation (n.d.), https://www.interaction-design.org. Retrieved August 2019.

Lee, J. D., Wickens, C. D., Liu, Y., and Ng Boyle, L. (2017). *Designing for people*: *An introduction to human factors engineering,* 3rd ed. Charleston, SC: CreateSpace.

Newell, A., Shaw, J. C., and Simon, H. A. (1967). The process of creative thinking. In H. Gruber (Ed.), *Contemporary approaches to creative thinking*. New York: Atherton.

Panda, S. myCircadianClock. Retrieved August 2019.

Society for Neuroscience (2018). *Brain Facts: A primer on the brain and nervous systems*, 8th edition. Washington, DC, retrieved August, 18, 2018, from www.BrainFacts.org.

Suri, J. F. and Howard, S. G. (2019). *The art of the insight: Learnings from 30 years of curiosity and empathy*. IDEO U, retrieved January 24, 2019, from https://www.facebook.com/ideouonline/videos/2120612904687755/.

TABLE 8.3

VISUAL MATRIX OF KEY POINTS OF RESEARCH-BASED PROGRAMMING FOR INTERIOR DESIGN

Chapter	Key Point #1	Key Point #2	Key Point #3
1	Research as an everyday experience	Human-centered design terminology and resources	Develop a research question
2	Develop a research plan Figure 2.2	Collect your own data Figure 2.5	Building and context information Figure 2.10
3	Programming process matrix Table 3.1	Understand programmatic concepts. Figure 3.1	Diagrams for analysis Figure 3.2
4	The role of the design concept Figure 4.3	Methods for determining space allocation Figure 4.9	Components of the project program Table 4.5
5	Design concepts types Table 5.1	Diagrams for synthesis Figure 5.6	Generate multiple schematic design diagrams Figure 5.18
6	Consult experts Tables 6.1 & 6.2	Link human factors theories to your design solution Table 6.3	Incorporate building systems, codes and accessibility Table 6.4
7	Understand your audience Figure 7.1b	Rendering tips for project components Figure 7.9	Storyboard your presentation Figure 7.16a
8	Feedback tools Activities 7.4 and 7.5	Assess your work Table 8.1	Prepare your work for a wider audience Figure 8.7

Appendix A
PROGRAM EXAMPLE

HUMANITY:

HELP CENTER FOR THE HOMELESS

Center for the Homeless

The project logo consists of the overlay of three symbols: the eye, the earth, and an ancient Greek symbol for strength. www.symbols.com

One recurring theme throughout the research process was that people who become homeless often feel invisible therefore the overarching design concept is twofold: (1) *"Making visible the invisible"* to the general public, and (2) *"Being seen and making connections"* for the population the facility serves.

A lotus floating on a clear pool, symbolizing reflection and awareness, underlies this design concept combining reflective, translucent, and transparent materials punctuated with areas of softer textures and interactive features to promote visibility, inclusion, and engagement. Using a palette of cool neutrals with accents of teal, blues, and purples along with circular elements, intertwining patterns and filtered natural light, it seeks to evoke a sense of cleanliness and connection, and to spark hope.

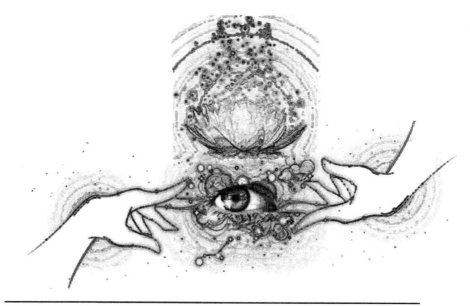

Figure 1 Design concept imagery/collage.

Student: Kathleen Quiroz
Date: February 22, 2019

PROJECT PROPOSAL

PROJECT GOALS AND MISSION STATEMENT

The mission of Humanity Help Center for the Homeless is to encourage and empower people who have become homeless through access to food, healthcare, legal services, and bathing and laundry facilities. The center's mission is to operate with support, care and inclusion, to build on each individual's unique abilities and inner strength, putting them on a path to healing and renewal, while fostering a sense of community.

According to the 2017 US Census there are roughly 554,000 homeless men, women, and children without shelter on any given night. A recent survey conducted in the city of San Diego counted 8,576 homeless in one night, one-third of these people were children and 11 percent military veterans.

Based on a combination of findings from past studies and original field research, the 20,000 SF center will offer services and programs to the homeless population local to the project site. Services on ground floor will include:

- Food-To-Go Care Packages
- Personal Storage/Lockers
- Self-Serve Laundry Facilities
- Shower Facilities
- Clothing Exchange/Attire for Employment

Other services that the research indicates is needed recommended for future growth of this project (to be expanded to second floor or future addition).

- Housing Resources
- Legal Services Consultation
- Education Outreach: Employment, Self-Defense, Parenting, Money Management
- Mental Health Evaluation and Referral
- Private and Group Counseling
- Basic Medical Care/Urgent Care
- Dental Treatment
- Veterinary Care
- Hair Salon

FIELD RESEARCH RESULTS

In a participant survey conducted February 10, 2019, at 1:30 p.m., I interviewed 23 homeless people at the park using a standardized questionnaire. Fourteen men (including two veterans) and nine women (who had with them a total of four children) agreed to participate. Of the sample population, four had children with them and five had dogs. After qualifying questions and a brief warm-up, participants were asked to pick their top five choices from 17 potential services to be offered at the resource center. Services selected by ten or more participants were incorporated into the project goals and program areas. See Figure 2 for table of responses.

After the survey, "Food Bank" was changed to "Food to Go" as this seemed to be more important and relevant to the population who lack access to can openers or cooking facilities.

The survey process yielded several great suggestions of services I had not previously considered, such as self-defense classes.

Homeless Resource Center Survey

Services	1	2	3	4	5	6	7	8	9	10	11	12	13	14	15	16	17	18	19	20	21	22	23	24	25	Totals
Art Studio			1									1		1												3
Clothing for Interviews/Clothing	1		1		1			1				1		1	1	1	1	1			1	1				12
Dental Service	1	1		1		1		1		1	1	1		1		1					1	1				12
Drop-in Child Care	1							1						1							1					4
Food Bank/Food to Go						1		1	1	1		1	1	1	1	1	1	1	1	1	1	1	1			16
Game Night				1			1							1												3
Group Therapy Sessions				1		1					1								1				1			5
Job Training			1	1		1	1		1		1	1	1													8
Medical Clinic	1	1		1			1		1	1		1	1		1	1	1	1		1	1	1	1			16
Money Management			1		1		1				1							1				1				6
Nutrition Counseling																										0
Rehab Counseling						1									1											2
Self Defense								1		1	1			1	1		1			1						7
Technology Training		1					1				1		1										1			5
Therapy	1		1	1	1	1	1		1						1			1	1							10
Veterinary Services		1						1											1	1		1				5
Youth Center														1					1							2
Given	Computer Lab, Housing Counselors, Job Placement, Laundry, Lockers, Meeting Space, Phones/Messaging, Showers, Soup Kitchen/Cafe, Toiletries																									
Suggestions	Place to leave documents (IDs, etc.), PO Box, Diapers, Feminine care, Reading glasses, Backpacks, Bike Storage, Socks, Self Defense classes, Water, Parenting classes, Tarps, Umbrella																									
Notes	Clothing for Interviews was changed to just clothing, and Self Defense was added after interviewing several individuals																									

Men 14
Women 9
Children 4
Vets 2
Dogs 5

Figure 2 Matrix showing survey results indicating the top five services voiced by participants: Food-to-go, medical clinic, dental services, clothing for interviews, mental health/therapy. n=23.

SITE ANALYSIS

Located at the north end of a small park in North Park, San Diego, the original 8,000 SF structure, the former home of North Park Senior Community Center and San Diego Police substation, will be expanded and transformed into Humanity Help Center for the Homeless.

The site is located at 2719 Howard Avenue; San Diego, CA—it is on the north end of North Park Community Park. Cross streets are Idaho and Oregon. See Figure 3.

According to Zillow.com, the neighborhood is populated by:

- Median age: 34
- Average household size: 2
- Median income: $48,716; Average income: $67,059
- Ethnic make-up: predominantly White and Hispanic, some African American and Asian, with some "other"
- Homes are mostly rented in the area
- Most people drive to work, or work from home, but 23 percent take public transportation.

The site is currently being used for the SDPD North Park Storefront Office in a section of the building on the west end. The rest of the building is not in use.

The existing building is approximately 8,000 SF and has room to extend on the west, south, and east sides, as well as vertically. A local landmark and historically significant water tower is located across the street to the north, as well as an indoor soccer center. The view of these buildings and water tower are currently seen from one of the main entrances. Neither are particularly nice to look at, which reinforces the idea of wanting to relocate the main entrances as well as re-orient the main facing side of the building to the west.

The park itself is located within a residential neighborhood, and is just one block south of El Cajon Blvd., and a few blocks from 30th Street. The neighborhood for the most part is quiet and picturesque with craftsman-style homes and apartments that each have their own character border the park. Restaurants and services are located on El Cajon, which makes the site convenient for people that want to get a bite to eat. There are bus stops along El Cajon Blvd., as well as a few blocks over on 30th street. The site is surrounded by many beautiful old-growth trees that offer shade and a connection to nature. There is ample parking all around the community park. On the south end of the park, there is a recreation center that offers after school programs and a children's playground. There is also a middle/high school there as well. On a site visit conducted on February 6, 2019, at 1 p.m., I noted a lot of activity by a variety of people—families, picnicking, dog walking, as well as many homeless people currently using the park. There is a restroom near the children's playground where many homeless were gathered. I also noted that the children from the middle/high school use the grass and park for physical education (i.e. running, soccer, etc.). The park overall has a very upbeat energy. It is active and used by many different types of people: children and their parents, school children, recreation center patrons, people from the local neighborhood, homeless, meeting space (AA meetings every week day at noon).

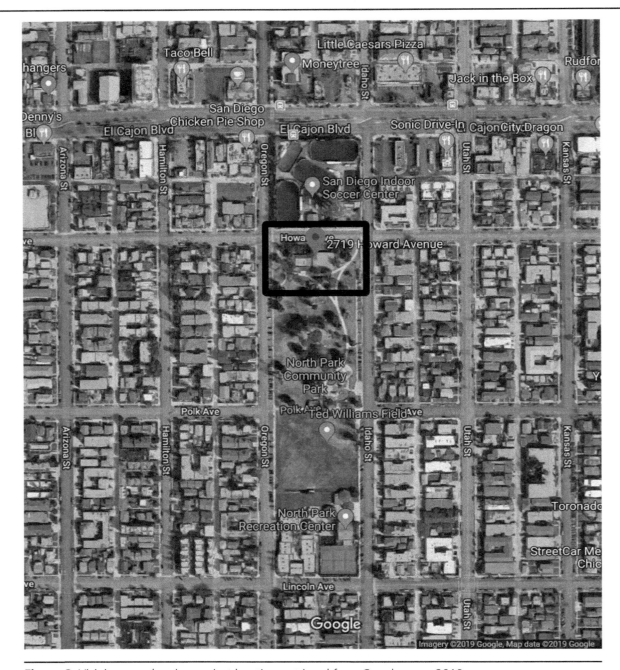

Figure 3 Vicinity map showing project location, retrieved from Google maps 2019.

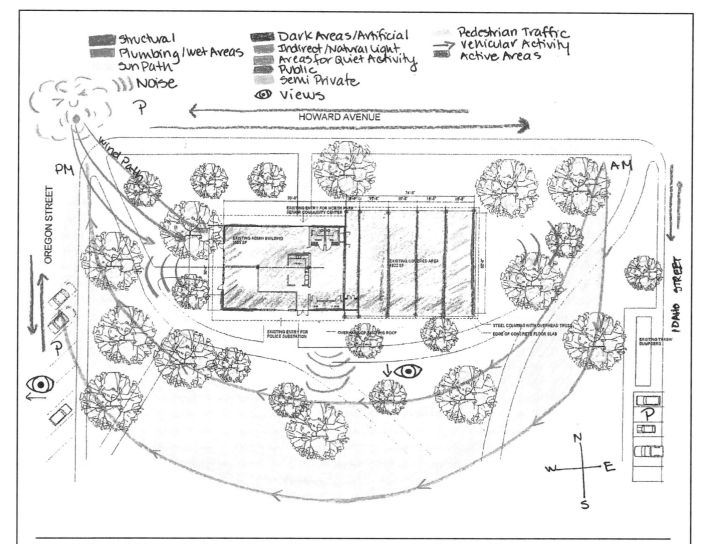

Figure 4 Composite site analysis of existing building and outdoor area within property boundaries.

- As noted on Figure 4, sun travels from the east to the west along the south side of the building. Most of the sun exposure will be on the south side, with indirect light on the north side. Sun will be on the east side in the morning and will have sun on the west side towards the end of the day. Artificial light will need to be used to supplement the indirect sunlight and on the interiors of the building.
- The existing building has two main entrances: one on the north and one on the south side.
- Prevailing breezes come from the north-west corner heading east.
- The south side of the building offers the quietest section of the site and will be the best place for private and or quiet activities. The other three sides tend to be a bit noisy either from traffic or from park activity.
- The best views are looking south toward the park. Considering re-orienting the building to have the main entrance on the west and south sides to maximize views.
- The building is a steel framed structure with wood siding and wood shingles. There are bars on the windows and entrances. Attached to the building is a covered outdoor area that was previously used as a shuffleboard court.

- Both the building and the covered outdoor area are solid in structure but neglected. It would be easy to say that it is in disrepair, but on close examination this is mostly due to the cosmetics of the building
- Electrical closet and utility room on south side of building.
- Existing dumpsters are located on south-east corner of lot.
- Fluorescent overhead lighting is currently being used—needs to be replaced.
- Interior rooms have expandable dividers to close off or open spaces.

CLIENT PROFILE

The client who will fund this project and lease the space from the City of San Diego is non-profit organization, Humanity Center for the Homeless, led by program director Debbie Krakauer. Her experience includes program management for Volunteer San Diego and Volunteer Coordinator for the San Diego Rescue Mission. She has been working with the homeless for the past 15 years with passion and dedication.

Funding and resources will come from grants through:

The Homeless Emergency Aid Program as funded through the State of California Business, Consumer Services and Housing Agency. The Homeless Emergency Aid Program was established by statute to provide localities with flexible block grant funds to address their immediate homelessness challenges.

The Homeless Emergency Aid Block Grants will provide $500 million in one-time funding to enable local governments to respond to homelessness. Allocations are as follows:

- $250 million to Continuums of Care based on 2017 homeless point in time count;
- $150 million direct allocation to a city or city that is also a county with a population of 330,000 or more as of January 1, 2018; and
- $100 million to Continuums of Care based on their percentage of the statewide 2017 homeless population.

The Grant and Per Diem (GPD) Program is offered annually (as funding permits) by the VA to fund community-based agencies providing transitional housing or service centers for homeless Veterans. Under the Capital Grant Component, VA may fund up to 65 percent of the project for the construction, acquisition, or renovation of facilities or to purchase van(s) to provide outreach and services to homeless veterans. Per Diem is available to grantees to help off-set operational expenses.

The California Department of Social Services (CDSS), Office of Child Abuse Prevention (OCAP), is committed to preventing child abuse and neglect and its lasting effects by strengthening families and the communities that surround them. The OCAP seeks to support financial literacy service programs aimed at combatting risk factors for child abuse and neglect through support of the financial empowerment of parents and reduction of financial stress on families.

Additional funding will come from private donations by local benefactors.

END-USER PROFILE(S)

Typical Visitor

50+/day homeless men, women, and children, as well as their dogs. All areas must be accessible incorporating universal design principles to accommodate a range of ages and abilities. Many potential end users will need medical care, food, rest, so safety and security are high priorities. Primary areas will be to showers and food-to-go with large outdoor, shaded waiting areas for other services. These outdoor areas need to be easily cleaned and durable materials.

- Parking for baby strollers, shopping carts, and personal storage lockers to leave belongings while bathing or using facilities.

Staff

- Program Director
- Executive Assistant
- Community Outreach Specialist
- Food Distribution Staff
- Clothing Store Staff
- Volunteers
- Janitorial/Maintenance Staff
- Receptionists
- Security

SPACE NAME, SPACE ALLOCATION AND PROGRAMMATIC REQUIREMENTS

Space Name	Sq Ft	Programmatic Requirements
Main Entry	400	Located at west and south entry doors, adjacent to reception and gathering spaces. Security is required at all entries and doors that can be locked. Security system throughout. Signage providing a map of facility and services offered. Flexible display system of services offered and event calendar.
Reception	120	Adjacent to entrance, visual access to entry for security, check in. Built-in reception desk with accessible transaction heights. Centrally located: Needs primary adjacency to gathering
Program Director	135	for private use by program director adjacent to open office area. View to east or south preferred. Should have acoustical privacy. Primary adjacency to Executive Assistant. Must have at least 120 linear feet of file storage and (1) individual 30 inch x 72 inch horizontal work desk with flexible height, dual-monitor computer. Should feel like a scholar's retreat. Reclaimed wood, open storage for books and art supplies should be visible from entry, mixed with industrial metal lockable cabinets. Must have a small table and chairs for staff meetings.

Open Office (3 @ 120 ea.) (1) Executive Assistant (1) Volunteer Coordinator (1) Community Outreach	360	All offices must have acoustical and visual privacy in 10 x 12 areas. Should contain a flexible height desk, computer and ergonomic chair for focused work, with small meeting area for six and printer, copier, lounge area.
Meeting Area	2600	For lectures/demonstrations to the public, in-house meetings and special events provide ability to block out light. Acoustical privacy from rest of building. Consult with acoustical engineer for balanced room acoustics. Flexible use space that can hold large meetings, classroom setup, overhead or screen projector, and ability to be used for self-defense or other active type classes. Storage area needed for tables and chairs as well as mats (24 inch x 30 inch) for yoga and self-defense classes. Dimmable lights for yoga, with design feature on ceiling. Integrate good task lighting for educational classes.
Clothing/Retail	3000	Should be accessible from the outdoors so that community patrons have access. "Store" needs to be flexible, with ability to have all gender/age clothing. Design should feel like a clothing boutique. Must have flexible system for exhibiting wall mounted merchandise. Lighting should have high Color Rendering Index to allow for true color distinction.
Food-To-Go Distribution Area and Storage	3600	Must include 300 SF minimum for back-of-house storage, sorting, and packaging. Open concept that feels like an upscale farmers' market. Organize areas by food type or food content. Provide for long waiting lines with clear wayfinding and note key destinations with graphics/signage/artwork to accommodate people with vision impairments or who do not read or speak English. Adjustable lighting for setting mood from daytime to evening functions. Adjacent to delivery and trash area.
Laundry	1650	Adjacent to Showers and Lockers. Provide (24) front loading washers and (24) front loading dryers. Dryers need to be located along exterior wall for venting. Accessible areas for sorting and folding clothes should be included. Use reclaimed water to provide irrigation for landscaping. Provide areas for seating and conversation throughout circulation areas. Provide positive distractions such as television monitors and music.
Showers	2000	Provide minimum of (24) 36 inch x 60 inch shower areas. Each shower shall be as universally designed and accessible as possible. Design so that gender is respected but flexible to accommodate persons of all genders. Must have acoustical and visual privacy. Safety and sanitary conditions are the highest priority. Should have adjacency to Lockers and Laundry. Must have individual stalls with room for changing, metering or timed water delivery and ability to have privacy without a lock. Provide for humidity control, natural ventilation and supplement artificial with natural light. Use reclaimed water to provide irrigation for landscaping.

Lockers	1800	Should be adjacent to Showers and Laundry. Large and tall lockers (must be at least 5 feet high), with bench seating in front of each. Slip resistant flooring. Must be able to be cleaned with products containing bleach. Supplement artificial light with natural light, preferably operable clerestory windows or louvers for natural ventilation.
Public Restrooms 10 @ 60	600	Convenient to Entry, Gathering and Meeting spaces. Must meet accessibility requirements
Storage	300	For storing tables and chairs when not in use.
Staff Breakroom	100	Remote from Entry/Reception.
Restrooms 2 @ 50	100	
Janitor's Closet	60	
Total Program Area	16,825	
+ Circulation @ 25%	+ 4206	Hallways throughout and accessibility to services.

Total Indoor   21,031 SF

Gathering	1000	Outdoor shaded area for waiting of 30 to 50 people. Should have a clean, uplifting environment promoting respect and visibility. Furnishings include options for individuals, groups with mixed levels of privacy. Outdoor features such as foliage, water features or acoustical block should be explored to reduce noise within the space and sound transfer to surroundings.

Project Total   22,031 SF

ADJACENCIES

Bubble Diagram

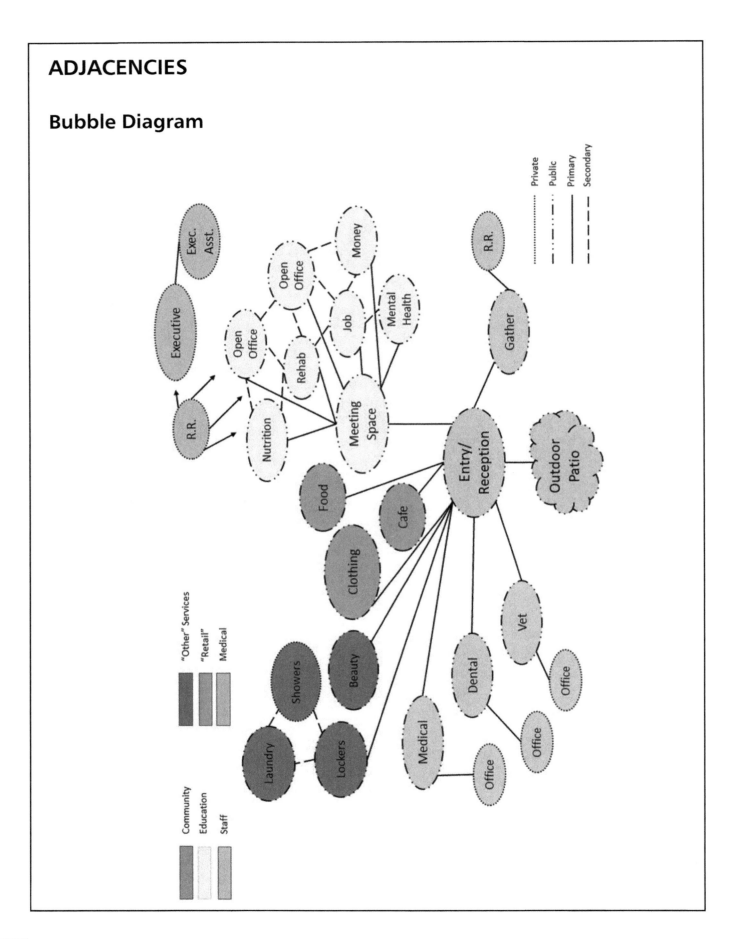

WORKS CITED

1. Bravo, C. (Jan. 25, 2019). "So Impactful": Volunteers Hear Stories of Homelessness During Annual Count. Retrieved February 2, 2019, https://www.nbcsandiego.com/news/local/So-Impactful-Volunteers-Hear-Stories-of-Homelessness-During-Annual-Count-504866692.html.
2. United States 2017 Census (https://www.census.gov/newsroom/stories/2018/homeless.html).

Appendix B
PROGRAM TEMPLATE

PROJECT NAME

Design Concept: *Tag line or summary of concept 1–5 words* (for example "A Modern Labyrinth," "Transformation," "Poetry in Motion"). *Insert text, approximately 30–100 words describing overall aesthetic, poetic metaphor, and abstract ideas for how to accomplish the project requirements.*

Figure 1 Collage of concept imagery. Add text captions here and cite copyrighted image sources as necessary.

Submitted by: _____

Date: _____

Class: _____

PROJECT PROPOSAL

SUMMARY OF PROJECT GOALS AND MISSION STATEMENT

_____(Your project name here)_____ seeks to provide _____*(list of functions)*_____ to

*(variety of end-users or target audience)*_____. Expand description to include descriptive statistics to document

evidence of need, hours of operation and expected numbers of visitors and staff.

Site Analysis Summary

Description of climate, local demographic information, neighborhood context, and other relevant site information collected from maps, online sources or site visit.

Figure 2 Insert vicinity map showing project site context, compass directions, adjacent buildings, natural features or topography, views, potential sources of noise or odors. Include work flow or behavioral map to document existing traffic patterns. Add caption or cite image source as necessary.

Figure 3 Insert your existing building shell with analytic diagrams or notes regarding existing conditions regarding structural, mechanical, electrical, plumbing considerations. What is the size of the building footprint? What alterations are possible given the noted constraints?

CLIENT PROFILE

Describe who will fund this project and review your designs. What is their philosophy and mission? What is the business model or how is the project funded? Identify key stakeholders. Who will be reviewing your designs? What is their background, area of expertise, relationship to client agency or position? Include professional headshots of key personnel. Include company or organization logo(s). Provide corporate hierarchy, organizational chart and/or work flow diagrams when needed. Cite all sources of information and graphics.

END USER PROFILE(S)

Describe who is envisioned to be using the facility including visitors and staff. Include age range, gender, abilities, preferences, and other relevant characteristics of people. Use statistics found during your literature review, photos, and quotes from surveys or interviews to provide a rich description of actual and/or potential end-users. Cite all information sources.

SPACE NAME, SPACE ALLOCATION AND REQUIREMENTS

Note: Organize list of spaces by subcategories such as patient areas, staff areas, public, private, semi-private, or by floor in a multi-story project to make it easier to space plan.

SPACE NAME	SF	PROGRAMMATIC REQUIREMENTS AND NOTES
_____	_____	Primary activities
		Secondary activities
		Number of people to accommodate
		Furnishing quantities and types
		Equipment sizes, clearances and power requirements
		Functional programmatic requirements (for example: "visual access with acoustic privacy" or "view of park")
		Aesthetic programmatic requirements (for example: "filtered natural light to limit glare" or "organic patterns and colors reminiscent of a garden"
		Other special requirements including maintenance, security, or safety issues or need for consultants such as acoustic engineer.
_____	_____	List all spaces – this could be several pages…

Program Total   _____ SF   **(<- very important that all above spaces total this #)**

+ 20–25%   **Circulation Allowance**   SF

Total Project Square Footage

_____ SF

ADJACENCY MATRIX OR BUBBLE DIAGRAM (use color and a legend)

GLOSSARY

Abstract a brief (typically 250 words) descriptive summary of a research project describing what, why, and how. It may also include an overview of the results, findings or implications.

Academy of Neuroscience for Architecture (ANFA) promotes and advances knowledge that links neuroscience research to a growing understanding of human responses to the built environment offering lectures, collaborative sessions, and conferences for students and professionals.

Action research a form of applied research conducted in a localized or practical setting (such as a classroom, workplace or facility) which mutually benefits the researcher and those being studied.

Adjacency matrix typically found in a project program to document required spatial relationships. May be expanded to a *criteria matrix* to include other needs.

Affordances coined by cognitive psychologist James J. Gibson to describe how visual perception of features in our environment enable us to understand how to use them.

American Institute of Architects (AIA) a collective voice of professional architects and policymakers working to advance quality of life in the built environment and protect the public's health, safety and welfare.

American Society for Interior Designers (ASID) professional organization dedicated to generating and disseminating applied knowledge among members and to promoting the value of interior design to the public.

Analysis diagrams drawn to document and ponder existing conditions or to represent the program requirements.

Anthropometrics the study of comparative sizes and ranges of ability in human bodies.

Applied research scientific inquiry conducted for practical purposes, to improve the quality of something or solve an identified problem.

Area take-off a construction term for cost-estimating purposes that can be applied to a case study to get estimated program net assignable floor area (NASF) or gross square floorage (GSF).

Art-based design concept an artistic theme, creative imagery or aesthetic idea applied to or imposed on a project related to design elements and principles.

Assessment the process of making a judgment about meeting an industry or professional standard. Grading is considered a component of assessment if point values or other measurements are awarded.

Authority Having Jurisdiction (AHJ) the local governing agency, offices, or individuals responsible for enforcing codes in the project's location.

Basic research scientific inquiry conducted to understand a phenomenon for general knowledge.

Behavioral mapping the act of recording participant movement and interaction with the physical environment during observation as part of Environmental-Behavior research; it can be person-centered (also known as shadowing) which follows a particular person, or place-centered in which the focus of the map is the place with people moving through it.

Benchmarks standards or points of reference against which things may be compared or assessed; evidence-based in-house standards used to inform future projects with similar project types, end-users and/or clients.

Bias a systematic mistake based on prejudice or assumption.

Biophilic design a comprehensive system which supports human's biological affinity for natural elements in the built environment.

Block diagram similar to a bubble diagram, block diagrams place program areas on to the building shell in distinct areas but are easier to translate into a schematic floor plan due to the ease of overlapping or intersecting straight edges of blocks.

Brainstorming a method for generating multiple ideas as quickly as possible emphasizing spontaneity and withholding judgment.

Branding comprehensive and cohesive marketing image strategy, related to design concept, used to help guide name of facility, motto, logo, advertising materials, menu, uniforms, and other artifacts, all designed to appeal to target end-users.

Bubble diagram diagram representing relative sizes of spaces (each drawn in its own circle) and adjacency requirements. Bold lines connecting the circles indicate direct adjacency and dashed lines often indicate convenient or indirect. No line may indicate there is no adjacency requirement between those two spaces.

Building Resource Information Knowledgebase (BRIK) comprehensive database of information related to buildings sponsored by AIA and National Institute of Building Sciences.

Building systems various operational entities consisting of assemblies of components that make up a typical facility including structural, mechanical, electrical, plumbing, security, lighting, and life safety.

Case study an in-depth examination of a previously completed, or proposed, project that has conditions related to your own project, which serves as a prototype or an example of either a successful or an unsuccessful design solution.

Certificate of Research Excellence (CORE) EDRA program showcasing award-winning design projects students can use as case studies.

Charrette a problem-based activity that involves concentrated effort to create a viable solution in a limited amount of time derived from the Beaux Arts tradition in France when students would be furiously sketching ideas in the horse-drawn cart (or French *charrette*) on their way to school.

Circulation diagram focuses on the patterns of movement of people through passageways that lead to destination spaces to inform plan arrangements.

Client the owner, organization, corporation, company, or decision-making agent who would be responsible for hiring the designer, making the key design decisions, and/or funding the project.

Client profile part of the project program which is a detailed description of the sponsoring agency or owner which typically identifies key personnel or stakeholders and their areas of expertise, background and values.

Coding partitioning qualitative responses or data into groups to transform to quantitative, or numerical data.

Cognitive ergonomics A field of engineering that seeks to design products and environments for the way our minds work.

Commercial facilities offices or factories that the public does not access which do not necessarily have to comply with ADA unless accessibility is needed to accommodate an employee.

Comparative case study the research activity of contrasting two similar projects to discern and note interesting differences.

Concept mapping a tool for brainstorming by using words to link thoughts and ideas throughout the research process.

Conference poster session a method of presenting work to an audience who is walking through a hallway or exhibit. Typically the presenter stands next to the poster allowing for passers-by to engage in one-on-one discussions with the presenter.

Construct component of a theory, mental abstractions, which can be empirically measured such as hue, intensity, age, height or intelligence, or subjectively distinguished such as comfort, motivation, anxiety, satisfaction or convenience.

Continuing Education Unit (CEU) is a unit of credit equal to 10 hours of participation in an accredited program designed for professionals with certificates or licenses to practice various professions

Contract administration fifth phase of the design process conducted during project construction and move-in in which interior designers may review shop drawings and sample submittals, respond to requests for information, generate design changes, conduct site observations, create purchase orders, receive deliveries, instruct end-users on new features, and evaluate effectiveness of built project.

Contract documents fourth phase of the design process which includes generating dimensions drawings, details and specifica-

tion to communicate design solution to builders, suppliers, and codes officials.

Corporate hierarchy diagram graphically represents the way a company or organization is configured, identifying each member and the professional relationships between them.

Council for Interior Design Accreditation (CIDA) recognized as the definitive body which generates professional standards for interior design higher education, evaluates programs, and facilitates collaboration among members to advance the interior design profession. https://accredit-id.org/about/what/

Council for Interior Design Qualification (CIDQ) the premiere certifying organization for interior design professionals which develops and administers the three-part NCIDQ Examination, which tests interior designers' knowledge of core competencies required for professional practice in the industry. https://www.cidq.org/cidq

Curtain wall non-load-bearing assemblies of the exterior or enclosure system, typically "hung" from structural elements.

Dead-end corridor a portion of a corridor that leads to an exit in only one direction. For life safety, corridors should have exit access from both directions.

Demographic data statistical, quantitative or categorical information about people in a given area, sample or population such as age, gender, income, ethnicity, education level, occupation, and so forth, used for descriptive purposes.

Demonstration a presentation technique that adds the dimension of time to show a process or interaction and add entertainment value.

Department of Environmental Health (DEH) a county agency in the United States enforcing environmental and public health laws, typically requiring special use permits for project types such as food facilities, hair and nail salons, and public swimming pools.

Design concept concise, often metaphorical or poetic, expression of the aesthetic and operational goals which communicates *how* to meet the requirements in the project program; underlying basis for all design decisions.

Design Development the third phase of the design process which fully articulates one comprehensive design solution for acceptance by the client.

Design jury a panel of professionals typically assembled by your instructor who watch your presentation and offer feedback.

District a conceptual navigation tool which represents an area someone can mentally go inside of defined by a common function, type of occupant or unifying architectural detail.

Due diligence a conscientious and concerted effort to research legal aspects of any project to limit professional liability.

Edge a non-occupiable boundary (conceptual navigational tool) used in wayfinding. Examples include walls, fences, railing, flooring transition or level change.

Embodied cognition an emerging, scientifically-grounded paradigm which links the experience of the physical environment to the development of the brain.

End-user profile outlines the target population of the project typically including the age range, abilities, and other demographic information such as special needs of the people who will be served by the project. Use statistical information from literature review and original data collection.

End-users various anticipated people who will be visiting, working or living in the designed project. Participant end-users would be current or actual user of a space who engages with the designer during the programming phase to give information. Potential end-users possess characteristics of someone who could use the space in the future.

Environment-behavior research a branch of study interested in learning how people interact with their environment.

Environmental Design Research Association (EDRA) organization promoting research-based design, social awareness and inclusiveness in the built environment.

Environmental stressors identified factors that raise the brain state of arousal through high levels of sensory input or *stimuli* such as noise (auditory), and clutter (visual), creating an unwarranted, negative side of arousal commonly known as *stress*.

Ergonomics the study of interaction of the human body with tools and furnishings while engaged in activity or work.

Evidence-based design (EBD) a process for the conscientious, explicit, and judicious use of current best evidence from research (which uses the scientific method involving experiments or quasi-experimental methods) to make and justify critical design decisions.

Feasibility study a service provided by a designer which helps client to determine if a proposed site fits a project's program requirements.

Field survey a site visit which involves measuring and visually documenting the building conditions.

Five Phases of Design a cross-disciplinary industry standard of the five billable stages of a design project for the built environment consisting of (1) Pre-Design/Programming, (2) Schematics, (3) Design Development, (4) Contract Documents, and (5) Contract Administration.

Floor plan horizontal section cut four feet above the floor showing wall thickness, relationship of architectural spaces, level changes, flooring, fixtures and built-ins and may show furnishings (furniture plan).

Focus group a method of qualitative research for social science and marketing which employs a small group of potential end-users and gathers information from their answers to questions, as well as the interactive discussions that naturally arise.

Functional analysis diagram drawn over a base plan to analyze existing conditions or qualities that tend to contrast or overlap such as public and private, light and dark, quiet and noisy, wet and dry, etc.

Functional diagram a flexible synthesis diagram which defines areas by broad or overarching functional programmatic concepts and/or spatial qualities rather than room names such as public and private, quiet and noisy, visitor and staff, and so forth. Similar to zones of use diagram but typically for larger projects.

Gantt chart a project management tool consisting of a list of tasks in a column on the left-hand side with an expanded calendar to the right used to set milestones and deadlines for individual and group projects.

Gestalt theory of perception that emphasizes the tendency to view individual things as part of a whole.

Google Scholar a user-friendly search engine providing links to peer-reviewed papers, abstracts, and technical reports.

Grade top of the ground, typically sloping away from the building for surface drainage, and usually indicated as a bold line in building sections.

Gross square feet (GSF) the total area of building or space including wall thickness.

Half-diagonal rule when two or more exits are required, at least two of the exits must be a minimum distance apart, which is at least one-half the longest diagonal distance within the building or space. That distance may be reduced to one-third if the space is equipped with automatic sprinkler fire suppression system.

Heuristic a mental shortcut that allows people to solve problems and make judgments quickly and efficiently; also referred to as rule-of-thumb strategy.

Hierarchy of needs Maslow's theory that environments affect or support human activities based on the premise that physical, emotional and social needs motivate behavior, typically illustrated in a pyramid form.

Historic precedent the first project of its kind: an archetype, an architectural icon, or a pioneer project that led the way or exemplifies a certain historic style or time period.

Human-Centered Design (HCD) an overall approach to problem-solving which starts with a concern for the well-being of people.

Human factors the study of how humans behave physically, respond psychologically, and engage sociologically in relation to environments, products, or services.

Hypothesis a tentative statement about the relationship between two or more variables. It is a specific, testable prediction about what you expect to happen in a study.

Ideation an active creative process from which multiple ideas emerge; an exhaustive search for creatively meeting project goals using diagrammatic tools while withholding judgment.

Image-based inquiry use of visuals to supplement traditional interview or surveys

Information visualization visual explanations which supports decision-making; using images, words and numbers to communicate process. Simplified versions could be called "Infographics."

InformeDesign website produced and maintained by University of Minnesota containing a database of previously published studies, abstracts and summaries gleaned from a variety of scientific sources with information related to human-centered design.

Interior design a distinct profession with specialized knowledge applied to the planning and design of interior environments that promote health, safety, and welfare while supporting and enhancing the human experience. Founded upon design and human behavior theories and research, interior designers apply evidence-based methodologies to identify, analyze, and synthesize information in generating holistic, technical, creative, and contextually-appropriate, design solutions. (NCIDQ, 2019)

Interior elevation an orthographic projection or two-dimensional drawing of a wall as viewed from the interior space.

International Interior Design Association (IIDA) commercial interior design association which supports design professionals, educators, students, firms and clients advocating for advancements in design education, legislation and leadership. http://www.iida.org

Interpretivist an approach to social science and related disciplines which align with a constructivist understanding of reality, that knowledge is constructed by relative consensus and can be generated through rich description, ethnography, and other qualitative methods.

Interior elevation orthographic project of a vertical plane ending at the intersection of perpendicular walls, or the edge of a wall, creating a two-dimensional front view.

Interview a type of personal report in which two or more people discuss personal or professional matters, in which one person asks questions of the other.

Landmark a distinct and unique external navigational tool that can be at any scale: a piece of artwork, a sign, a building, or anything else that stands out as memorable.

Likert Attitude Scale a widely used scale in which respondents are given a list of statements and asked whether they "strongly agree," "agree," are "undecided," are "neutral," "disagree," or "strongly disagree" used to measure attitudes.

Literature review a comprehensive collection and synthesis of previously published studies, articles, books, lectures and other high-quality sources that offers an overview about current knowledge relevant to a topic.

Load factor (LF) maximum floor area allowance per occupant used to calculate Occupant Load (OL). SF/LF=OL

Massing diagram a three-dimensional exploration which differentiates objects and space, or between program space and support space. It is sometimes referred to as a *mass/void diagram*, as it shows the built space in relation to open space, or positive space in relation to negative space.

Means of egress a continuous unobstructed path from any point in a building to a public way consisting of an exit access, exit and exit discharge.

Meeting minutes the detailed notes that serve as an official written record of what transpired including time, place, attendees, key points of discussion, decisions made, and further actions to be taken, often distributed to meeting members for their feedback and acceptance.

Mental map drawn by people to represent a familiar space or city and used by researchers to analyze how end-users imagine the spaces and use features to navigate.

Metaphor a poetic figure of speech that expresses an understanding of one concept in terms of another to reveal some hidden similarity or correlation between the two; used in interior design to create a mutual understanding through a combination of symbolic words and images to communicate overarching design intent.

Mission statement part of the project proposal; a summary of what the client seeks to accomplish in the project and may include a list of project goals.

Mixed methods using quantitative measures along with qualitative data collection techniques to conduct a research study.

Mock-up a crude approximation of the final product or space (at full scale), often made in foam core or cardboard often used to help understand functionality in furniture and product design.

Net square feet (NSF) the usable, assignable or occupiable or "rentable" area of a specified space (e.g. a suite, floor, or an entire building). This measurement generally excludes areas such as wall thickness, common hallways, and mechanical rooms.

Neuroplasticity a biological term for the brain's ability to alter its synaptic networks and continue to develop through reinforcing pathways or patterns of neurons (memory) and weakening or disregarding others.

Node a decision-making point (conceptual navigation tool), typically at the intersection of two paths with a directional quality of, "Here I am. Where should I go next?" An example would be an entry lobby, from which a visitor has the option of several destinations.

Observation is the use of one or more of the senses to obtain and record information on individuals, objects, or events, as a method of gathering information for interior design; can be casual, systematic, participant, simulation, or experiment.

Occupancy classification The intended use of a building, floor or space as assessed by risk factors and defined by *International Building Code (IBC)*.

Occupant load (OL) the number of people allowed to safely occupy a space by code. SF/LF=OL

Opening protective refers to a rated assembly placed in a framed opening; doors, windows and skylight are examples which operate within a framed structural opening.

Operationalize how constructs are put to use; how researchers define what they are trying to measure. For example, what components would you use to measure "happiness" in a study?

Orthographic drawing a two-dimensional view or projection of a three-dimensional object, typically using two or more additional projections to show additional views.

Paradigmatic case a project that operates as a reference point in history which functions as a change of focus or founding of a school of thought.

Parti diagram from the French verb *partir*, which means "to separate," a synthesis diagram representing the initial sketch which marks transition from informed to creative; a thoughtful first expression of a conceptual separation of parts or figural gesture that unifies; visual translation of the concept onto the floor plan.

Paths common occupiable navigational tool identifiable as traversable as in a hallway, aisle or swath of flooring material.

Pattern language a system developed by Christopher Alexander (1977) which identifies collections of time-tested qualities present in the environment which yield a meaningful or positive experience to the occupant.

Perspective view a drawing that goes to one-point or two-point vanishing points on a horizon line to give the illusion of depth.

Photo journaling a research activity which combines taking photographs and written notes to produce captions or a narrative essay to document observation.

Place-legibility coined by Kevin Lynch (1960) the system by which conceptual navigational tools such as paths, edges, districts, nodes, and landmarks in an environment work together to form a unified whole for ease of navigation by occupants. Also see Wayfinding.

Poché a French architectural term that refers to the visual weight or darkened areas indicating the thickness inside walls or between spaces.

Population all the members of a particular group of individuals that you have decided to study or to describe.

Portfolio a living archive of your work showcasing your design process and your graphic communication skills.

Positive distraction an environmental feature that elicits positive feelings and holds attention without taxing or stressing the individual including views of nature, artwork, music and so forth.

Positivist a philosophical perspective based on objective truth in which authentic knowledge or empirical evidence is that which is produced or verified through controlled experiments, systematic observation, and logical proof.

Post-occupancy evaluation (POE) a variety of research methods used to collect data on the use of a project after it is completed and is occupied; may include end-user satisfaction surveys, observation, or include sensors to measure air quality, energy efficiency and other physical aspects of the built environment.

Precedent study a project that exemplifies innovation in architecture or design in its structural, technological, or formal exploration.

Pre-Design/Programming the first phase of the design process with five main tasks: to establish goals, collect information, uncover concepts, determine needs and define the problems to solve.

Prepositions established rules or relationships between theoretical components (constructs).

Probe an interviewer's strategy using a verbal ("I see") or nonverbal (slight nod) prompt to elicit further elaboration of response by an interviewee.

Process work exploratory diagrams and preliminary sketches to show the early stages, emergence and evolution of your design ideas.

Programmatic concept a description of an abstract strategy for achieving a performance requirement or satisfying an aesthetic or functional need. Examples include: accessibility, control, hierarchy, privacy, and safety.

Project program a document that assimilates and organizes information gathered by the programmer into a form that is usable by the designer as the basis for their schematic design. Also called programming document or design brief, it varies in terms of format, length and type of detail.

Prospect and refuge theory expounded by Jay Appleton (1975) which identifies survival as the biological basis for comfort in an environment: a clear view of available resources and a feeling of security or safety.

Prototype a representation of an item at full scale as close to the look and feel of the final product as possible for client or designer feedback.

Proxemics coined by Edward T. Hall (1966) to describe the study of nonverbal, body language as social norms, or learned cultural traits, yet also having a biological basis which manifests in the distance people keep around themselves as an invisible, dynamic, personal space bubble which changes due to circumstances and relationship with the people around them.

Public accommodation businesses and facilities, such as a laundromat or a doctor's office, the public enters as a regular course of business which need to be accessible.

Public way an area open to the sky, usually a street or alley that is a minimum of 10 feet wide to allow for rescue vehicles to enter it.

Qualifiers preliminary or initial questions on a questionnaire that assess whether the respondent fits a list of certain predetermined qualifications, typically demographic information such as gender, age, education-level or regarding a person's lifestyle, habits or experiences.

Qualitative a method for data collection which is suitable for gaining an in-depth understanding for a complex social or cultural issue.

Quantitative a method of data collection or analysis which seeks to measure and compare.

Questionnaire a series of topic-related questions written to help you discover participant opinions; *standardized* would mean that an identical series of questions is distributed to the participants.

Reflected ceiling plan (RCP) a drawing that shows items located on the ceiling of a room or area as if it was reflected onto a mirror on the floor.

Request for Information (RFI) a partnering tool between contractors, vendors and designers to clarify ambiguities or resolve gaps early in the bidding, construction or contract administration phase.

Research the systematic investigation into and study of materials and sources to collect information about a particular subject, establish facts and reach new conclusions.

Research-based design concept a design concept is *derived from* analyzing the information the designer has gathered about the project or the design problem to be solved

Research-based programming using evidence produced by scientific studies supplemented with a designer's own project-specific data collection and analysis to determine the functional and aesthetic problems to solve and generate design concepts derived from this information.

Research questions an open-ended yet focused core of a study which seeks to expound on describing an existing phenomenon, relationships between phenomena or establish causation between two or more variables.

Risk factors the features or situations associated with a particular use that may be dangerous in an (fire) emergency including number of people, alertness and mobility of occupant, and spatial characteristics such as loud sound and low light levels or flammability of materials.

Room data sheets components of long project program formats that specify architectural, mechanical, electrical, plumbing requirements, security measures, and special requirements, typically used on large-scale healthcare and other specialized institutional projects. They may include sample layouts of key equipment showing sizes and clearances.

Rubric a guide or matrix used to set and communicate minimum project requirements in multiple areas of concern used for evaluative purposes.

Safety Risk Assessment (SRA) free data collection toolkit offered by The Center for Health Design for evaluating built healthcare environments. www.healthdesign.org/sra/about/toolkit.

Sample a subgroup of a population that is thought or meant to be representative of the population. The way a sample is collected determines the type of sample such as random, purposive, stratified, convenient, etc.

Scale model a simulation built at a small scale to represent the interior design solution ranging in materials, craft, detail and focus from study model (equivalent to a three-dimensional sketch) to finish model.

Schematic design the second phase of the design process which explores multiple possible design solutions.

Schematic floor plan the translation of lines in diagrams into physical design elements such as walls, counters, flooring changes and furniture layouts in space planning; used for preliminary codes review.

Section perspective an orthographic section drawn to scale, which includes a vanishing point so that all of the spaces beyond the section cut appear in perspective view.

Self-reports a type of cognitive response generated by a participant of a study including verbal, written (journal), or visual (photographs, drawings, artwork).

Shadowing person-centered behavioral observation method

Shop drawings submittals by contractors and suppliers which show their interpretation (or an alternative) in response to project specifications

Site plan a bird's eye view or top view of a project which includes some surrounding context, property boundaries, roof or building outline and compass direction, typically drawn in an engineering scale.

Sociofugal furniture arrangements that tend to discourage social interaction.

Sociopetal furniture arrangements tend to encourage social interaction

Specification describes a finish or construction material in terms of quality, method of application, assembly or installation, and other information that cannot be communicated graphically.

Stacking diagram a diagram which shows relative size and adjacency requirements between vertical elements in a multilevel project or relationships between spaces on different floors. Also called a layering diagram.

Statistic a numerical characteristic of the sample that measures relationships, such as percentages, averages, and tendencies; *descriptive* refers to a variety of methods that are used to simplify, summarize, organize, identify, and visually display such data and *inferential* are used to make to make judgments of the probability of relationship.

Storyboard a term associated with planning a sequence of shots for a television show or movie to show visuals along with notes about pace and emphasis—this technique can also be applied to the layout of a book, magazine spread, or a presentation.

Structural analysis diagram part of the site analysis when the designer is looking closely at the building shell to determine constraints (elements that are difficult or costly to move) and possibilities; highlighting loadbearing elements, vertical circulation such as stairs and elevators, and may include building systems such as mechanical, electrical and plumbing.

Structural systems include the foundation, framing and load-bearing enclosure components.

Survey to query (people) to collect data for the analysis of some aspect of a group or an area; to do a statistical study of a sample population by asking questions about knowledge, opinions, preferences, and other aspects of people's lives using a standardized questionnaire.

Synthesis gap refers to the conceptual leap between analysis (data collection, benchmarking and programming) and synthesis (defining the solutions) coined by author and architect Mark Karlen.

Synthesis diagram drawn to generate possible configurations (ideation) which meet functional and aesthetic requirements, or to simply propose something new.

Tare space the area allotted for circulation, walls, mechanical, electrical and plumbing equipment, wall thickness, and public toilets.

Theory a system of ideas intended to explain something; a way of thinking, or a set of principles used to justify an action or practice.

Third place coined by Ray Oldenburg (1991) to identify a space for relaxation and informal socializing between home (first place) and work (second place).

Thumbnail sketches tiny hand-drawn markings intended to capture initial thoughts or basic ideas. Often called a "napkin sketch" as they can be drawn anywhere and at any time you are inspired to do so.

Traffic pattern diagram represents and analyzes the variety of ways people arrive and move through a project, similar to behavioral mapping.

Transcription a documentation of questions and answers used to record an interview; typed version of audio-recorded conversation.

Universal design (UD) the design of products and environments to be usable by all people, to the greatest extent possible, and without the need for adaptation or specialized design; a design process that enables and empowers a diverse population by improving human performance, health and wellness, and social participation.

Usability test participant end-users are observed using mockups or prototypes to evaluate whether a design or space is easy to use or "user friendly;" also called *pilot tests*

Value engineering (VE) a process by which a multidisciplinary team reviews the project costs to identify ways to get the most value for the available budget while accomplishing the goals of the design intent.

Wayfinding coined by Kevin Lynch (1960) the system by which conceptual navigational tools such as paths, edges, districts, nodes, and landmarks in an environment work together to form a unified whole for ease of navigation by occupants. Also see Place-legibility.

White papers concise, authoritative reports, or problem-solving guides, proposing solutions to a complex, or current, issue. For the purpose of interior design, furniture companies issue white papers on topics such as ergonomics, privacy, co-working, collaboration, engagement, or work styles to help guide furniture.

Whole Building Design Guide (WBDG) maintains a database of exemplary residential, commercial and institutional project types that subscribe to sustainable building practices. https://www.wbdg.org.

Work flow diagram shows existing or ideal functional relationships between people or departments in a facility or organization to accomplish a task, typically falling in to categories of linear, radial, or networked.

Zones of use diagram represents different functions that may overlap in a space, typically used in kitchen design.

Zoning municipal code designations and other overlapping restrictions which regulate land use.

CREDITS

Chapter 1
1.1 Lily B. Robinson
1.2 Laura Covarrubias, Mariela Mosquera, Katie Swinburn
1.3 Sara Ford and Ahmbra Austin
1.4 Chad D. Sterud
1.5 Lily B. Robinson
1.6 Chad D. Sterud
1.7 Laura Covarrubias, Mariela Mosquera, Katie Swinburn

Chapter 2
2.1 Fairchild Books
2.2 Lily B. Robinson
2.3 Ginet Casido
2.4 Kate Daniels
2.5 and 2.6 Lily B. Robinson
2.7 Kathleen Quiroz
2.8–2.12 Lily B. Robinson
2.13 Esther Riera
2.14 Chelsea Copitas
2.15 Jordan Perata
2.16 Elena Arroyo
2.17 and 2.18 Lily B. Robinson
2.19 Mike Long
2.20 Breeann Ray

Chapter 3
3.1 Lily B. Robinson
3.2 Yuki Ito
3.3 and 3.4 Sergio Merguia
3.5-3.9 Lily B. Robinson
3.10 Sandra Gramley
3.11–3.14 Lily B. Robinson

Chapter 4
4.1 Courtesy of Knoll, Inc.
4.2 Lily B. Robinson
4.3 Ginet Casido
4.4-4.8 Lily B. Robinson
4.9–4.12 Morgan Greenseth

Chapter 5
5.1 Wellcome Library
5.2–5.8 Lily B. Robinson
5.9 Jen-Yi Chan
5.10 Norman Reyes
5.11 Tessie Bersiman
5.12 and 5.13 Lily B. Robinson
5.14 Lorraine Tinio
5.15–5.18 Yuki Endo
5.19–5.21 © 2018 Andrew Hunsaker
5.22 and 5.23 Lily B. Robinson

Chapter 6
6.1 mayrum/iStock.com
6.2 Lily B. Robinson
6.3 Carolyn Harris
6.4–6.9 Lily B. Robinson

Chapter 7
7.1a Lily B. Robinson
7.1b Design Institute of San Diego; photo by Jenny Littrell
7.2 Lily B. Robinson
7.3 Allard Jansen Architecture & Development
7.4 Andrette Crown
7.5 Lily B. Robinson
7.6 Eva Gao
7.7–7.9 Gerald W. Bouvia III
7.10 Lily B. Robinson
7.11 Leanna Duncan
7.12 Christopher Little
7.13 Lily B. Robinson
7.14 © 2019 Andrew Hunsaker
7.15 Nicole Rios
7.16a and b Norman Reyes
7.17 Megan Strombel
7.18 Gary Leivers AIA
7.19 Brie Flyge
7.20 and 7.21 Francesca Di Ventra, Rudi Haido, Jodie Nyugen, Faith Thundershield, Jesica Williams
7.22 and 7.23 Morgan Greenseth
7.24a and b Gerald Bouvia III

Chapter 8
8.1–8.4 Lily B. Robinson
8.5 and 8.6 healthdesign.org
8.7 Lily B. Robinson

INDEX